HEAVEN KNOWS WHO

CHRISTIANNA BRAND

HEAVEN KNOWS WHO

CHARLES SCRIBNER'S SONS
New York

For
HENRIETTE MEYER
τῇ φωσφόρῳ

FOREWORD

Any work on the case of Jessie M'Lachlan must owe a vast amount to the great William Roughead, who edited this, among so many others, in the Notable British Trials series. It was his favourite, 'the ideal murder'; and H. B. Irving, a great connoisseur in these matters, wrote to him that it was 'the best murder trial I ever read'.

In a humble attempt not to seem to be in my turn simply editing Mr Roughead, I scoured England and Scotland for extra scraps of information about my dear Jessie—always to find that he had been there before me. Fortunately for me, he hadn't had space to use by any means all of it and I did proudly discover a very few interesting facts which he seems to have missed, and make one—to me interesting—deduction which he didn't make. For the rest—though lots of it 'on soul and conscience' I declare I found for myself before I got access to his library and saw that he had noted it too—I gratefully acknowledge my huge indebtedness. I would like to say thank you also to Mr W. N. Roughead for his ready permission to make as much reference as ever I liked to his late father's work; he says he couldn't stop me, but it's still very pleasant to be made free of it so graciously. I should also like to thank Messrs. William Hodge Ltd, for the loan of blocks printed on pages 27 and 29 and at the end of the book. And lastly, I do thank all the people in Glasgow and Edinburgh for their wonderful helpfulness in what I rather grandly call my research; they have a heart-warming talent for making one feel not a nuisance.

Mr Roughead tells me that his father's habit of writing only M' in all surnames prefixed Mac or Mc was partly to assist the printers but largely 'just a fad.' Any fad of William Roughead's is a fad of mine.

C.B.

CHAPTER ONE

She wore a straw bonnet throughout her trial—a lilac wool gown, a little black shawl and the straw bonnet, trimmed with broad satin ribbons, its brim edged with a frilling of narrow black lace. One can't help wondering how she got it—this special bonnet to be worn during the four days of her trial for murder. Did the prison matron go out and buy it for her? Was James, her perfidious husband, commissioned to choose it, with anxious recommendations as to colour and trimming? If she had one poor, pitiful, seldom indulged little vanity, it was a fondness for pretty clothes.

This is the true story of the trial of Jessie M'Lachlan for murder—the ferocious murder of her dearest friend. It is in every possible detail authentic. If Jessie is described as having smiled or sighed, if a witness is said to have thought a thought—then there is evidence somewhere of that smile or that sigh or that thought. Where dialect is reproduced it is the reported dialect actually used by that speaker at the time. If a place or a person is described, it is from a contemporary description or picture. Background, 'plot', dialogue, character—all this, which may read like fiction, was true enough and real enough, only too true and only too real, a hundred years ago.

The murder was of a young woman named Jess M'Pherson, at 17 Sandyford Place, Glasgow, on the night of July 4, 1862. Her friend, Jessie M'Lachlan, stood her trial for four days in the Old Court, Jail Square, Glasgow—the court sitting for eleven hours of each of the first three days. At the end of this time, the jury, having deliberated for exactly fifteen minutes, returned with a unanimous verdict. It was, moreover, an unequivocal verdict. There was no question of 'not proven'.

And the trial was interesting in this, if in nothing else—that the defence was simply that the prisoner had been nowhere near the scene when the crime was committed, that it had been committed by another person, a named person, a supposedly respectable old gentleman, Mr James Fleming, of 17 Sandyford Place. Mr Fleming variously described himself as eighty-seven years of age and seventy-eight. Whether or not his word was entirely to be trusted, we shall see: but eighty-seven is obviously a more unlikely age to be embarking on murder. It may be said here that there was no question of any collusion in the murder: one person alone, in both senses of the phrase, killed poor Jess.

The crime took place, as has been said, in Glasgow, some time in the night between July 4 and July 5, not far from the scene of three other *causes celèbres*. It is interesting to note their outcomes: for of the three accused, Dr Pritchard, infamous mass murderer, was executed—the last to be publicly hanged in that same Jail Square where Jessie stood her trial; the resourceful Miss Smith was set free, and Oscar Slater, after twenty years of wrongful imprisonment was granted a free pardon. As for Jessie M'Lachlan —once again, we shall see.

She was about twenty-eight at the time of the murder: a frail, slender, rather pretty creature with a lovely figure, brown eyes in an oval face and soft straight light brown hair pulled back into a bun. Everyone seems to have liked her. Her sisters-in-law, it is true, who came of a large and cheerful family, thought she was not quite forthcoming enough and considered herself above them; and indeed she is often described as having 'a ladylike air'. But she was said to be very delicate and got easily tired: and self-contained and reserved she might be, but she was 'a very mild, gentle and kindly woman', and 'of a religious turn of mind'. Her neighbour, a lady rejoicing in the name of Mrs Clotworthy, gave testimony at the time of the trial that, 'being in great distress from a melancholy accident that happened to one of my children in falling into a sawpit' she was further discomposed by a siege of the curious flocking about her home. Mrs M'Lachlan alone refrained from joining the sensation seekers, but sent round constantly with kind enquiries. The ladies hardly knew one another, they were both people who kept themselves to themselves; but Mrs Clotworthy strongly approved of Mrs M'Lachlan. She seemed 'a feeling, kind woman and she was particularly quiet, contrasting favourably with the other neighbours who were anything but quiet'. She was especially kind to Mrs Clotworthy's children, who seem to have had a propensity for getting themselves into dangerous situations. But then she was fond of all children. She had a little boy of her own, of three years old.

She had been married four or five years and now, after several changes of address, lived at 182 Broomielaw Street—a district running along the banks of the Clyde, commonly referred to as the Broomielaw. The main industry of Glasgow, then as now, was ship-building, at that time in the process of changing over from wood to iron. It is a crowded, shabby city, with a beauty all its own—built on the foothills of a low valley but so packed with buildings that nothing of its conformation is to be seen except where the steep streets shoot up off the main highways, each ending in a skyline. It is built largely of red and yellow sandstone which weathers in its smoke and fog to a dark blue black; but, without the glitter of granite or the glow of Portland stone, it has nevertheless, its own loveliness of smokey blacks and greys, undertoned with sepia and rose. Through it all runs the reddy brown waters of the river Clyde, a tidal river up almost as far as the Broomielaw where Jessie lived. Here, as all over Glasgow, had been built tenement houses for the workers, so solid and strong that most of them stand to this day, though some are two hundred years old. They are mostly two or three storeys high, with a feature peculiar to Scotland—the 'close', presumably so called because it is on the contrary quite open, a passage at ground level running through from front to back of the building, without doors at either end. From this the stairs run up to the several flats, or houses as they are, rather confusingly, called. The opening of the passage into the street is called the 'close mouth'. (The term 'close' appears also to be given to the narrow, cobbled lanes running between the main streets, with many of these tenement houses opening on to them; these are also called vennels, or wynds. In Jessie's day, the pump would be situated in the centre of the wynd and a gutter ran down one side; they seem to have been, and indeed still are, indescribably dirty and unlovely. No traffic, of course, runs through them, and the people simply sit on the cobbles to do their gossiping, their backs against the houses, while the children play about them; above them the lines of washing hang drying on poles stuck out of the windows.)

It was in one such tenement—Clydesdale Buildings—that Jessie lived; opening out not on to a wynd, but on to Broomielaw Street itself, with only the cobbled road and the wharf-side buildings between her close-mouth and the Clyde. There was a walled-in court at the back with a door to the streets. The building is gone but many like it still stand along the Broomielaw, and the streets she walked are all the same.[1] Her 'house' was on the second floor, or 'stair' as she would call it—three rooms leading off a single passage, all on the same side of it. She had also the use of a cellar in the basement.

She was pitifully poor. Her husband, James M'Lachlan, was a sailor, and out of his pay of thirty shillings a week he must keep back twelve—ten for food, for he provided his own board when he was with his ship, which was for three or four days in each week, and a couple for himself—leaving her with only eighteen shillings for rent, heating, food, clothing and any further expenses for themselves and the child. The further expenses were heaviest of all for, it was explained at her trial, she was obliged to pay out ceaselessly for doctors and medicine and for help in the house. She suffered from a heart condition which since the birth of her baby had become very much worse—from palpitations and breathlessness, and often from a total weakness which kept her bedridden for many weeks at a time. She had been in bed four months after the birth, and the doctors had now warned them that, unless she had some sort of assistance with the work of her home, she might fall dead at any moment. So she got in a woman, a Mrs Adams, to do her washing and cleaning. 'She might be able to wash a few things for herself,' said Mrs Adams, 'but not a day's washing. She was a weakly woman and had often trouble.' She paid Mrs Adams a shilling a day and employed her twelve-year-old daughter, Sarah, to do odd chores at a further six or seven shillings a week. But how was she to pay for it all out of eighteen shillings? Her brother was very good to her, giving her constant gifts of money; all her friends were kind, even her landlords maintained a polite fiction as to the time she had to pay in. But you couldn't struggle against illness and helplessness. To try to make ends meet she let off two of her three rooms to lodgers. They can't have added

[1] Washington Street is now largely taken up by the warehouses of a whisky distillery. In wet weather there is a constant drip from the roof. The author stood under this hopefully for some time, but it was only rain water.

much to her income, for her total rent for the 'house' was five shillings a week, but anyway they were mostly sailors like her husband, and not only did they sometimes bilk her of her rent altogether but they often went off to sea leaving money owing. Her only recourse was to pawn such possessions as they left in her keeping, hastily redeeming them before the owners got back. 'They were left as a kind of pledge,' said the child, Sarah Adams, who knew all about it, 'not to pawn,' and her mother confirms, 'She was often compelled to pawn the clothes they had left with her. They were never pawned to raise money for intemperances or extravagance but to pay for medicine or the doctor, or me, or for what the house needed. In living she was very moderate. She was a very temperate woman. She did not drink unless by the doctor's orders—she would take one glass of spirits but she would take no more. She could not live more economically than she did.' She— Mrs Adams—and Sarah, were invariably employed upon these missions to the pawnshop. Jessie never went herself and she always instructed them to give false names. She evidently did not care to have too many people knowing about her business. They would not have far to go—every third shop in those days was a pawnshop (and every fourth a spirit shop).

So, all in all, she must have been thankful when a chance arose to let her rooms to a Mrs Campbell, who might be more regularly solvent or who at least wouldn't always be going off to sea. Mrs Campbell in turn sublet one room—still to a sailor—but now it was her responsibility to collect the rent. The sailor's name was John MacDonald, and Mrs Campbell had besides a young daughter who shared her room. It must have been something of a scrum—six people living in three small rooms.

On that night, then—the night of the murder—a couple of months after they had moved in, Mrs Campbell and her daughter were sleeping in what was in fact the kitchen, nearest to the front door of the apartment; her lodger was snoring away, from eleven o'clock on, in the middle room; and Mrs M'Lachlan's little boy was in the end room, ordinarily the parlour, to which he and his parents were now reduced. James M'Lachlan was away at sea. And Jessie—Jessie, alas, was not at home that night.

*   *   *

Jessie M'Lachlan's great friend was another Jessie, Jessie M'Pherson, more often called Jess. The names in this chronicle are not helpful to clear narrative. The two principals were called Jessie, there are two John Flemings, three Mr Flemings in all plus a Doctor Fleming, no relation. Two principal witnesses at the trial were called Paton, a detective was M'Laughlin—the list could go on for ever. To complicate matters—for the author at any rate —by the Scottish custom all married women are referred to by their maiden as well as their married names—'Agnes Wardrope or Christie'. To avert a major muddle, Mrs M'Lachlan is always referred to as Jessie, the murdered woman as Jess.

Jess was about thirty-eight at the time of her death—a big, brawny woman though 'of a genteel figure and generally tasteful in dress', who had once in a friendly trial put a policeman on the floor—he had asked for a kiss. She had been less on the defensive, apparently, with two other gentlemen similarly inclined, for she had suffered two 'misfortunes', one of which had resulted in a stillborn child, the other in a boy who had thrived and who at the time of her death seems to have been in Australia. She was herself an illegitimate child; her name in fact, or her mother's name, was Richardson. The mother was now married, but Jess had been brought up by foster-parents and had taken their name. They remained devoted to her, and she does seem to have been a delightful person, kind and generous and 'with a peculiar faculty for making and keeping friends'. She had been put out to service at the age of ten and had worked as a domestic servant ever since, retiring only for brief periods to allow for the 'misfortunes' and for a break of one year, when she left the family with whom she was then employed—the Flemings, of Sandyford Place—and set up a little grocery stores with a friend and ex-fellow servant, Mary Downie. But the business failed. It was run on the 'passbook system', that is to say on credit; times were hard in Glasgow, their hearts were too kind to allow them to pursue their debtors— though it was suggested when she died that she had been murdered by some enraged creditor whom she had got sent to prison —and after only a year they had to shut up shop. She went back to the Flemings and at the time of her death had, all in all, been with them—a much trusted and valued servant—for six or seven years. Jessie M'Lachlan before her marriage had worked for two years with the same family, in Sandyford Place, and it was thus that she and Jess had become such friends. The friendship had lasted ever since.

The standing joke between Jessie and Jess was 'Grandpa'. Grandpa was Mr Fleming senior, and the joke was that he wanted to marry Jess. The house belonged to his son, John Fleming, an accountant, respectable and prosperous, who lived there with his son, also John, who was about twenty, and two daughters. He was evidently a widower, for his sister, Margaret Fleming, kept house for him. His father lived with them, having a room on the ground floor and, especially when the rest of the family were away, haunting the servants' quarters in the basement and making a nuisance of himself. They were away a good deal, for they had a cottage by the sea, near Dunoon, and Miss Fleming and the girls spent most of the summer there, taking one of the two maids and leaving the other to run the house in town. John Fleming and John junior joined them at the week-ends. They appear not to have loved Grandpa so dearly that they often took him with them. More commonly he was left at home in Sandyford Place with Jess.

Jessie, of course, knew the old gentleman well. She called him 'Grandpa', and after she was married he now and again dropped in to see her in her own home and have a cup or 'a dram'. They seemed quite intimate and friendly, said a witness who was once present when he called, 'like familiar acquaintances'. He was affable to her husband also, and on two occasions at least there are accounts of James M'Lachlan going round with his wife to Sandyford Place and having a drink with the old man—though of course in the basement, with Jess. The Fleming family were at this time on the way up socially; and it may well be that the grandfather, who had started life as a hand-loom weaver, was more easy in the company of these humble people than his son and his grandson would have been. On the other hand, he was considered a little eccentric, and one of his oddities may have lain in this disposition to be friendly with their domestic staff.

On Friday night, July 4, 1862, Jessie had arranged to go round to Sandyford Place and see her friend. They met very frequently: they were as affectionate and easily intimate as two devoted sisters. Jess M'Pherson earned about fourteen pounds a year, but she had her keep above that, and she was always kind and generous to poor ailing and harassed Jessie. She was always giving her things

17

that 'she would require to buy for herself straight after'; and once when a friend suggested that she should summon Jessie for money still owing for goods from her grocery shop she said 'never to heed, for Jessie had been to great expense on account of her illness and she'd pay when she got better.' Jess had stayed three weeks with the M'Lachlans at the time she opened her shop with no question of payment between them; and on one occasion —it would doubtless be while she was working on her own— when she couldn't pay her baker's bill, Jessie had pawned some clothes and her husband's watch to help her; it can't have been much of a watch, the whole bill was four shillings. Jess spent much of her meagre off time at the Broomielaw, and Jessie was always in and out of the basement at Sandyford Place. She knew it well, of course; she had lived there herself for two years, and many an evening, especially when the family were away and Jess therefore not so busy, she would go round and spend an hour talking over old times, confiding her own troubles and listening to Jess's complaints about the old gentleman.

For the joke about Grandpa courting Jess was now growing exceedingly thin. Jess herself had never for one instant entertained the idea, the whole thing had at first amused and now disgusted her; but James Fleming was apparently quite serious, and had been for a long time, and was becoming worse than a nuisance. He half lived in the kitchen and, in her own word, 'tormented' her with his attentions. Only a week before she died, when she was walking in the street, a friend, a Mrs Smith, had met her and thought her looking ill and depressed. She confessed that she was both. 'You don't know how I'm situated; I have a miserable life of it.' She couldn't get rid of the old man, she said, he made excuses to come down to the basement with the newspapers or 'to make up the sugar and tea', and she couldn't be bothered with him any longer; it was making her ill. It wasn't so bad when the family was at home, but as soon as they left her alone with him it was misery. He wouldn't let her out of his sight, no one else was allowed into the house, and sooner than let her run round and buy so much as a cabbage he'd go out and get it himself. And she burst out suddenly and violently that he was an old wretch and an old devil. . . . 'Why, what has he done to you?' asked Mrs Smith, horrified and curious. But Jess wouldn't tell. That there was something to tell she did not conceal, but she couldn't speak of it

18

in front of Mrs Smith's husband. She promised to come round the following Sunday and confide it all to her, over a cup of tea.

Several people testified later to the same sort of thing. Though half a dozen ex-servants were found to say they had never seen any signs in the old gentleman of 'indecency', most of them agreed that he was interfering and inquisitive and not seldom 'tipsy'. One young lady who refrained from coming forward could have gone even further; for in the spring of 1852, he being then rising eighty by his present reckoning, he had been suddenly smitten by his conscience and made a voluntary confession to the Moderator and elders of his kirk that he had been guilty of the sin of fornication and had an illegitimate child by one Janet Dunsmore, a domestic servant. He was rebuked and admonished and then all was forgiven; for never had the witnesses seen so striking and edifying a display of remorse.

Miss Dunsmore did not come forward at Jessie's trial or at the subsequent enquiry, but Mary M'Kinnon, foster-sister of Jess, said again that Jess was tormented by the old man, that he was an old devil; the doorbell couldn't ring without his poking his head out of his bedroom window, or coming downstairs, to find out what it was about and he was for ever hanging about her kitchen; her heart was broken with him, and when she'd completed this six months' service she'd give in her notice. And to Elizabeth Halliday, at that time a fellow-servant with her at the house in Dunoon, she had said—as much as three years ago—that he was 'a nasty body or a dirty body'; she had been left alone with him recently at Dunoon, and Elizabeth got the impression, though it was not openly stated, that he had been behaving indecently. She was surprised when Jess, having left to open her shop and the venture having failed, went back into the service of the Fleming family.

By the summer of 1862, however, Jess had had enough of it. She was seriously thinking—perhaps because her child was there? —of emigrating to Australia.

Jessie had not been round to Sandyford Place for a couple of weeks. The fact of the matter was that she had pawned her cloak. She was, as ever, weighed down by money troubles, and £4 19s in arrears with her rent. She paid 5s a week, quarterly, for her 'house' and had to be constantly dunned for it—though dunned may be too hard a word, for the agents obviously liked her and were sorry for her and made things as easy as they could: a kindly fabrication had even been built up allowing her to believe that she had still two months' grace before she must settle. But the rent was not all; and now even her cloak was in pawn and, though the weather was fine, it was still early in July and, delicate as she was, she could not go out at night without it. She wanted to leave her visit till late: if she went too early the old man would still be up and they couldn't talk freely before him—last time she and her husband had gone there together, though Jess had taken them into her own room, he followed them there and resolutely sat them out. She would leave it till ten, by which time he should have gone off to bed. But it meant that she must have her cloak. She got hold of Mary Adams, who was in the house that morning doing some washing for the lodger, Mrs Campbell, and asked her to go to the pawn for her. She gave her a dressing glass and told her to ask for six shillings on it, 'lift' the cloak out of pawn and come back with the change. So off went Mrs Adams and returned triumphantly with the cloak and one and fourpence ha'penny left over.

Mrs M'Lachlan, thanking her, explained that she wanted the cloak to go round and see Jess, by whom Mary Adams understood Jess M'Pherson, whom she herself knew very well. Nor was she surprised when Mrs M'Lachlan explained that she was going late to try to avoid the old man. And by the way, she added, would Mary Adams drop in on her way home at the locksmith's at the foot of Carrick Street and ask him to call round for the check key to the front door—it would have to be repaired, the door wouldn't open from the outside without it, and she didn't like troubling Mrs Campbell all the time to open it to her. Oh, and could Mrs Adams come in and sit with the child while she was out that evening?—she would only be an hour or so.

Mary Adams agreed, but by half-past nine she had not turned up, nor had the smith arrived. (Mrs Adams had in fact forgotten all about him). Mrs M'Lachlan was not unduly worried by her non-arrival. Mrs Campbell was easy and good-natured and would let her in when she got back from Jess's, which shouldn't be later than eleven; and if the boy woke and cried while she was out, would go along and hush him to sleep again. She tucked him up in bed and put on her cloak and began to tie the strings of her bonnet. . . .

It was a 'drab-coloured' velvet bonnet, a sort of rather dull light brown; and the cloak was light grey. Beneath it she wore a dark brown coberg gown—a fine wool or wool-and-cotton mixture, rather like cashmere—with a trimmed bodice and, round its crinolined skirt, two flounces. It was only her well-worn everyday going-out gown; but within a few days it was to become one of the two most talked about dresses in all England and Scotland. The other was cinnamon coloured trimmed with blue velvet and had no flounces.

As she stood there tying up her bonnet someone knocked at the front door. Mrs Campbell, who was getting ready for bed, went and answered it; her preparations apparently did not include undressing, so no doubt she did not keep the visitors waiting. She probably thought it was her own lodger, the sailor, John Mac-Donald; but it wasn't, it was a Mrs Fraser, a friend of Jessie's, with her two children. Mrs Campbell showed them down to the room at the end of the corridor and went and got back into bed.

Jessie was happy enough to see Christina Fraser, but she was already rather pressed for time. A friend's child was ill and she had been remiss in not enquiring after it and had intended calling in on her way to Sandyford Place. She was rather late already; and besides she had meant to beg a small favour. Her sister Ann was, like Jess, contemplating emigrating to Australia and the sick child's father, James M'Gregor, was in a position to write her a certificate of good character. However, so was Mrs Fraser, who had known them all from their childhood, and that would do instead. Mrs Fraser was happy to oblige and sat down with pen and paper. But Jessie had no envelopes and she went along to Mrs Campbell's room and asked if Mrs Campbell's daughter would mind running round to the post office for her and getting some. (They seem to have kept late hours in the Broomielaw. It was after half-past nine, but a three-year-old child had only just been put to bed, Mrs Fraser with her children was out visiting, far from home, Jessie herself had not yet even started out; and the local post office was still open for the sale of envelopes).

Mrs Campbell was, as we have seen already—fully dressed—in bed. The girl went off for the envelopes and duly came back with them; and meanwhile Mrs M'Lachlan went across to what in fact was the kitchen cupboard and took out an empty glass bottle which belonged to Mrs Campbell. She said nothing to its owner about it, but it was, after all, only an empty bottle and she probably gave no thought as to whose it was. With this in her hand and carrying a little black basket, borrowed from Mrs Campbell, she called to Tommy Fraser and together they went round the corner to a shop in Argyle Street for 'a dram' to offer to her guest. A gill and a half of rum was measured out into the bottle, at a cost of sevenpence ha'penny; she would give Mrs Fraser a glass and have a drop with her and then take the rest round to Jess. She bought a few biscuits to go with the rum and, having been out only a few minutes, she and Tommy went back to the house. Mrs Fraser was waiting for them and let them in, not troubling Mrs Campbell again.

Mrs Fraser had meanwhile been struggling with the certificate; but she 'could not please herself with it', and indeed we all know the difficulties of writing recommendations of our friends. She suggested at last that she should take it home and think it over, and that Jessie should call the following evening for the finished result. This was agreed to and they drank their rum and had a little gossip, and then it really was time to be going—though the certificate was no longer required of him, Jessie still intended to call in on Mr M'Gregor and ask after his child. So off they went, the four of them together, Jessie carrying the little black basket with the rest of the rum and the biscuits. Mrs Campbell, hearing them go, wondered, no doubt a little ruefully, what time her landlady would be back—Mrs M'Lachlan was always talking about having the check key attended to but it never seemed to get done, and Mrs Campbell would have to get up when she did return and open the door for her. Moreover, her own lodger, MacDonald, wasn't in yet, and he too would have to be admitted. Perhaps Mrs Campbell had some reason after all for keeping her clothes on when she went to bed.

But as it happened, she was not very much disturbed that night. MacDonald came in at about eleven and went to his room; and from then on Mrs Campbell lay fast asleep.

When she did wake it was to hear Mrs M'Lachlan's little boy crying. As he did not stop she got up and went along to the end room to find out if anything was wrong. The child was alone. She picked him up and comforted him, gave him 'a piece'—i.e. something to eat—and put him back to sleep in his mother's bed: being

Mrs Campbell, she first fully dressed him. He went off at once and she returned to her room, but as she went she examined the front door to see that it was still safely locked. It was just as she had left it after admitting her lodger, MacDonald, at eleven.

She glanced out of the window. A bonny clear morning; and the hands of the big clock in the Broomielaw standing at half-past five.

Three and a half hours later Jessie M'Lachlan came home, and now she was wearing, not her own dark brown coberg dress but a cinnamon-coloured merino—which had belonged to Jess.

CHAPTER TWO

Friday, July 4, 1862, and 'a bonny clear night'.

Jessie went off up the Broomielaw with her friends: turned right up Washington Street to the point where Stobcross Street, running at an angle into Argyle Street, forms a 'gushet'. It would take them ten minutes, perhaps, with a further ten minutes to go on past the Gushet House (this no longer stands), up North Street to Sauchiehall Street and Sandyford Place. She had evidently changed her mind about calling in on the M'Gregors, for they did not see her that night. At the corner of Stobcross Street she said good night to Mrs Fraser and the children, and here, crossing the street towards the Gushet House, she fades away into the evening and out of our sight—the slight, frail figure in the brown bonnet and light grey cloak over the dark brown crinolined dress, one hand holding the little black basket with the rum and the biscuits for Jess: walking away in the twilight of a summer's evening from home and friends and such happiness as she knew into a blackness of horror and mystery as deep and dark as the night was bright and fair.

It was ten minutes past ten.

No. 17 Sandyford Place is one of twenty-eight houses that form part of Sauchiehall Street—the road has been uphill all the way from the Broomielaw and now we are well above the Clyde. Numbers twenty-eight to sixteen have gardens running down to the street, but at No. 18 a driveway sweeps in, railed off from the street, emerging again at the end of the 'place'. No. 17 is therefore second last of this row, with no front garden, and only the pavement, the drive, a little patch of grass and the railings between it and Sauchiehall Street[1]. It is nowadays a medical research centre, its back garden built over, and painted a sombre grey—a solid two-storeyed house with a basement, not by any means too large for the seven or eight people who in 1862 inhabited it—especially as the mistress of the house was John Fleming's sister, who would presumably occupy a room to herself. The servants' bedroom and

[1] See p. 31

24

the kitchen offices were in the basement, the dining-room, a small parlour and one bedroom at ground level, and the drawing-room and probably three smallish bedrooms on the top floor. Jess M'Pherson slept in the basement, the unfortunate John junior was obliged to share his grandfather's room—and, indeed, bed—on the ground floor; the rest sorted themselves out upstairs.

Half a dozen steps ran up to the front door, forming an arch over an area. The door led into a wide vestibule; the dining-room door was to your right as you entered, its two large windows looking out on to Sandyford Place. Ahead of you on the left were the stairs leading up to the top floor; where they started, the vestibule narrowed into a passage. Off this, behind the dining-room, there was a small parlour, its door facing the top of the stairs leading down to the basement. At the end of the passage directly opposite the front door was old Mr Fleming's bedroom, which he shared with young John. The windows of this room and of the parlour were therefore in the back wall of the house: they looked over a walled garden, long and narrow, with a wash-house and coal shed at the end, and a door—kept locked—leading out into a lane. This door had no knocker or bell.

Going down to the basement, the stairs took a turn to the left at the bottom and landed you in a wide-ish passage, between two doors, facing you. The one to your right led into Jess M'Pherson's bedroom, under the dining-room; the one to your left into the kitchen, beneath the back parlour. Under old Fleming's bedroom there was a smaller room where he kept his possessions, presumably leaving the upstairs wardrobe accommodation to John. The windows of this room and of the kitchen looked on to the walled garden behind the house, and between them a narrow passage ran down to the back door.

The windows of Jess M'Pherson's room looked out on to Sandyford Place—or rather into the area. Next to this room, under the arched bridge formed by the front doorsteps across the area was the pantry. It had a window with iron bars, forming a sort of small gate into the area, into which was let a smaller window. This gate was the only way you could get into the area, and there was no way up out of the area—which of course was railed—into Sandyford Place.

This, then, was the house which Jessie set out to visit on the

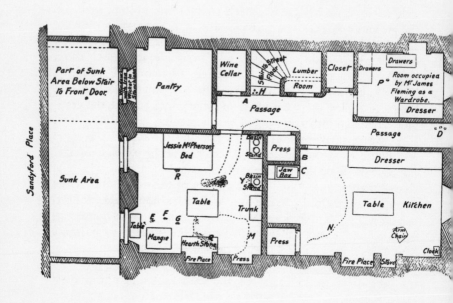

Part of Sunk Area Below Stair to Front Door.

Sandyford Place

Sunk Area

Pantry

Wine Cellar

Stair to Street Floor

H

A Passage

Lumber Room

Closet

Drawers

Drawers

P^m Room occupied by Mr James Fleming as a Wardrobe.

Dresser

Passage

D

Jessie McPherson Bed

R

Press

B

Dresser

Basin Stand

Jaw Box

C

Y

Basin Stand

Table

Trunk

Table

Kitchen

E F G

Table

N

Arm Chair

Mangle

M

Clock

Hearth Stone

Press

Fire Place

Press

Fire Place

Stove

Scale of Feet For Plan

10 9 8 7 6 5 4 3 2 1 0   10   20   30 FEET

Ground plan of sunk floor of 17 Sandyford Place

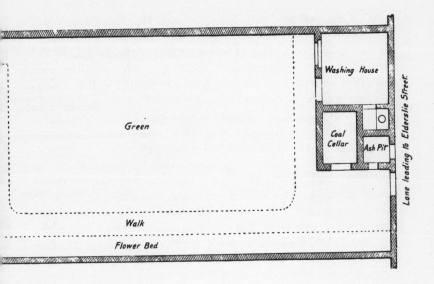

A—*Finger marks on corner of wall.*
B—*Blood marks behind kitchen door.*
C—*Blood marks on jaw-box.*
D—*Spots of blood at back door.*
E F G —*Foot marks.*
H—*Drops of blood.*
L—*Where the body was found.*
M—*Dotted line showing margin of washed part of floor.*
N—*Dotted line showing margin of washed part of floor.*
P—*Spot of blood.*
Q—*Spurts of blood on hearthstone.*
R—*Droppings of blood.*
Y—*Blood on basin-stand and floor.*

Friday night. It was a house she knew well, having lived there herself as a servant. She had left the Broomielaw at a little before ten; she would arrive, if she ever arrived there at all, at about twenty minutes past.

P.C. Campbell was patrolling his beat. He passed Sandyford Place perhaps once in an hour or so, but his orders were to concentrate mainly on a patch of waste ground where the drunks and prostitutes were 'bothersome'. If there were comings and goings that night in Sandyford Place and the lane behind it, P.C. Campbell saw nothing of them at all.

At eleven o'clock, Mr Littlejohn, who kept a liquor shop at the top of North Street, four or five minutes' walk from 17 Sandyford Place, closed his door and went off upstairs to bed.

A few minutes before that—there was a little dispute about the time here, but from the evidence it would appear that it was just before eleven—a Mrs Walker went out into Elderslie Street to take a breath of fresh air. Mrs Walker was in the family way and feeling not too well. She was expecting her husband home at any moment and thought she would wait at their 'close-mouth' till he arrived; or it may well be that she simply thought she might have a gossip with a neighbour—Mrs Walker was to show herself adept at inventing little excuses of this kind. She suggests, for example, that as she was innocently passing the house of the neighbour, Miss Dykes, Miss Dykes popped out and opened a conversation with her and then came out on to the pavement and stood gossiping with her; Miss Dykes, however, says simply 'It was at her request that I came out of my house and stood talking.'

Both Mrs Walker and Miss Dykes were proprietresses of shops in Elderslie Street and they both knew Jess M'Pherson. Miss Dykes had seen her that very evening, when she came in between six and seven for some washing powder. Jess had never said anything to her against old Mr Fleming, and Miss Dykes thought she had no appearance of being unhappy at No. 17: she had spoken with respect of John Fleming, his son. But one evening about a month ago she had come into the shop just as someone was leaving it after—unsuccessfully—trying to borrow money from Miss Dykes; and Miss Dykes had passed the remark to Miss M'Pherson that some people seemed to think one was made of money. Jess doubtless said the equivalent of 'are you telling *me*?'

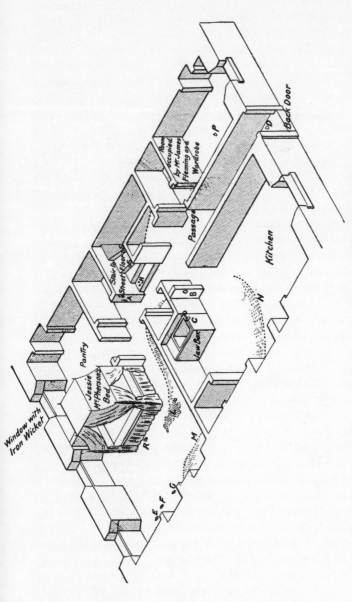

Isometrical view of sunk floor of 17 Sandyford Place

A—Finger marks B—Blood marks behind kitchen door C—Blood marks on jaw-box. D—Spots of blood at back door E F G —Foot marks H—Drops of blood L—Where the body was found M—Dotted line showing margin of washed part of floor N—Dotted line showing margin of washed part of floor P—Spot of blood R—Droppings of blood S—Blood on breasts of steps

She said it was a bad thing to lend money, she herself had money owing from two different people and she couldn't get it back. Miss Dykes suggested it was a funny thing if Mr Fleming, who was a 'writer'—an accountant—couldn't fix that for her, and Jess said she didn't dare tell Mr Fleming. Once before she had confided in him, and he had reproved her for lending money to fellow-servants and had kept back the money from the other woman's wages till it was repaid. She said that she was now owed four pounds by a former servant who had been married out of the house, and when she had asked it back she got the height of abuse, but she was going to ask again, come what would. . . .

Miss Dykes, by the way, said it was half-past ten when she joined Mrs Walker and that they stood gossiping not a quarter but three-quarters of an hour. This Mrs Walker ever after stoutly denied; and, as has been said, in this case it was probably Miss Dykes who was mistaken.

At any rate, it was as Miss Dykes emerged from her house that Mrs Walker casually observed—though she was seldom casual about observing her neighbours' business—that a woman had come out of the lane which ran along behind the houses of Sandyford Place—the back doors of their gardens opening into it—and went off across Elderslie Street in the direction of North Street. The ladies remained chatting for ten minutes or so till, at about a quarter past eleven, Miss Dykes heard a 'skliffling' of feet behind her (from which she judges that the walker had bad shoes on, or very light ones) and they both saw a woman come down Elderslie Street from Sauchiehall Street towards the entry to the lane behind Sandyford Place. Mrs Walker described her as pretty tall and square shouldered: she could not be sure that it was the woman she had seen before. Both agreed that she wore a dark bonnet and a brown dress: Mrs Walker said she had a grey cloak, Miss Dykes couldn't be sure; they both thought she was carrying something.

The ladies were ready to be scandalised. 'Whose servant is that going into the lane at this time of night?' asked Miss Dykes indignantly. (A Miss M'Intyre who was passing caught the words and hoped they would not be so censorious of *her*). But the married woman was more worldly wise than Miss Dykes. 'You see that man that's just passed her? He looked right into her face. She'll meet him on the waste-ground.' But the man passed on, so the ladies were disappointed.

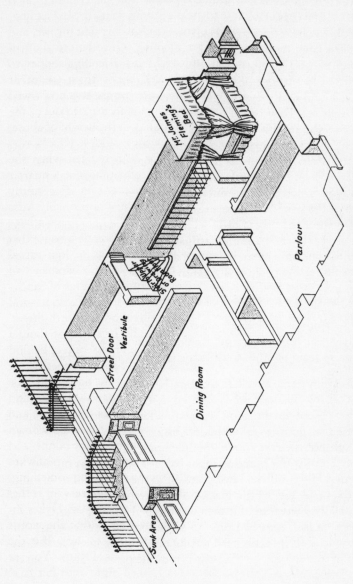

Isometrical view of street flat of 17 Sandyford Place

Sunk Area

Dining Room

Parlour

Street Door

Vestibule

Servant's Room Lobby

Mr James Fleming's Bed

Miss M'Intyre was innocently on the way home to Sandyford Place from a visit to her brother; she was spending a few nights at No. 80. She passed by Mrs Walker and Miss Dykes; and she, also, saw the woman (in a grey cloak or grey shawl) as she turned off into the lane. At the corner of Sandyford Place there was a little group of people, apparently discussing something that had just occurred to surprise or alarm them; something they 'had heard', some sound that they thought had 'come from that house where the light is'. They broke up as she approached; and then as she passed No. 17 she too heard a sound that made her stop and listen: a low, wailing noise, like the moaning of a person in very great distress. 'There was no wind that night, a calm night. The sound was quite distinctly audible to me, a moaning, doleful kind of sound which rather frightened me.' There was a light in one or both of the windows in the area.

She stood still for a little while listening, wondering whether she ought not to go and investigate; but she was frightened, and after the one long moan the sound did not come again. She walked on as fast as she could along Sandyford Place.

A quarter past eleven.

P.C. Campbell plodded on round his beat, plagued by those bothersome prostitutes and drunks on the waste ground, hearing nothing, seeing nothing, while the skirts of fame whisked by him.

Mr Stewart, a jeweller, lived at No. 16. The house adjoined No. 17, to the west of it, the lay-outs being similar; and Mr Stewart slept in the room corresponding to old Mr Fleming's on the first floor: overlooking the back garden, that is, and above, though not directly above, the Flemings' kitchen.

Mr Stewart got home at about half-past ten on the night of the murder. His family had just gone off to the country, but he called up the maid and a little girl who was keeping her company and they all 'had worship'. He then went to bed and fell asleep at once, before he had even had time to settle himself comfortably—still sitting half upright, his head resting on the head-board, and there-fore separated only by the board from the party wall between the two houses.

He 'wakened in a fright'. He couldn't be sure what had waked him, but he thought it was a scream, and his first impression was

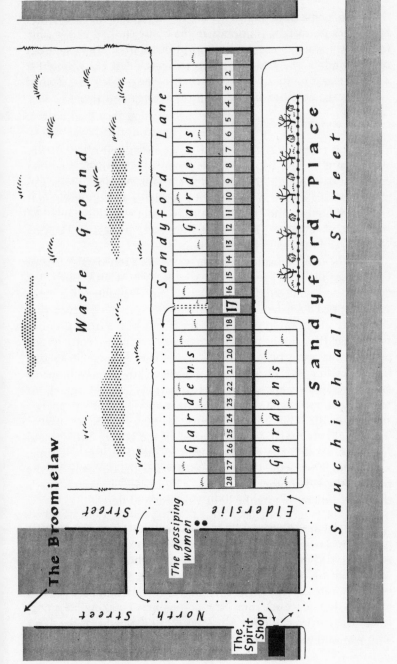

Sandyford Place, showing Jessie M'Lachlan's route to and from the spirit shop

that it had come from within the room—his second that it couldn't have, because there was nobody in the house (he had presumably forgotten the maid and the little girl downstairs). He looked out of the window and saw that it was still pitch dark: he thought it must be about midnight or not later than one o'clock. He listened but he heard no more and he went off to sleep again.

P.C. Campbell trudged on.

The sun rose at 3.41 that morning. At about four o'clock three sisters came rolling happily home from their brother's wedding celebrations—though one hastens to say that Peterina at least had had 'only half a glass of wine at the marriage and no spirits nor any other liquor', and there is no suggestion that the others had been less abstemious. They were Margaret, Jessie and Peterina M'Lean, and the eldest was twenty-four.

It was 'a lovely morning, still and calm'. In a tree outside one of the houses in Sandyford Place a whole flock of little birds had gathered and were singing their hearts out. Delighted, the three girls stopped to listen. As they stood there they observed that there was a light on in the house: the blinds of the front ground-floor room (the dining-room) were down, but in the centre of one several slats were open, and through these they could all distinctly see the gasolier hanging from the ceiling, in which one or two of the lights were burning. 'How curious,' said Margaret, 'to have a light burning at this time of the morning!' 'Perhaps there's sickness in the house,' said Peterina, 'or they have a late party.' They could all clearly see the number of the house, No. 17; and Margaret, though she didn't happen to mention it at the time, knew who lived there. On the Tuesday after the discovery of the murder she led another sister past it and pointed it out. 'That's the house where we saw the light after the wedding.'

A little later—between four and five that morning—yet another reveller was said to have been passing Sandyford Place and to have seen 'an old man resembling Mr Fleming' at the door of No. 17. A Mr Sheridan Knowles, butcher, had been told so by a Mr Ritchie; or at any rate Mr Knowles thought it was Mr Ritchie who had told him, but he wasn't sure. Nor, at the time of making his report to the authorities could Mr Knowles recall the name of the party who was said to have seen the old man, though he knew it was a short name. Mr Knowles had said to Mr Ritchie—if it was Mr Ritchie—that the party ought to inform the authorities, and Mr Ritchie—if it was Mr Ritchie—had replied that the party didn't want to get mixed up in the case. Later, said Mr Knowles, Mrs M'Lachlan's life being in danger, he had again spoken to Mr Ritchie, and Mr. Ritchie now denied ever having mentioned such an incident. Mr Knowles, however, had found Mr Ritchie 'only middling truthful in matters generally'.

Mr Ritchie, questioned, forthrightly repudiated all knowledge of the affair. He had known Jess M'Pherson when she had lived in Falkirk and used to come to his shop, but he had no recollection of ever conversing with Mr Knowles about the murder at all. 'In point of fact, I don't know any party who saw an old man resembling Mr Fleming at said door; nor did I ever hear of such a thing until now.'

So that was the end of a beautiful friendship no doubt, but at any rate the end of any sort of proof that the old man had been seen up and about that night.

At six o'clock P.C. Campbell was relieved and retired home to bed, having missed his chance of more than a very small share in the notoriety that was soon to surround everyone connected with Sandyford Place.

P.C. Cameron succeeded him. One half of the day beat came on at six and the other half at eight, whereupon the first half had time off for breakfast, so that between eight and nine only half the day beat were operating and Cameron was the only man on duty—with his station at the head of North Street, where he stayed until nine. Between eight and nine, therefore, there was no eye of the law to remark any comings and goings round Sandyford Place.

There was, however, one very sharp-eyed observer.

Donald M'Quarrie, 'the historic milkboy', was thirteen years of age and was employed with three other boys in distributing the milk which was taken round by horse and cart under the supervision of George Paton, a young man of twenty-five. Paton had been on this round for nearly a year, calling 'twice every lawful day and once on Sunday'. M'Quarrie had been with him almost all that time and they were both well familiar with the habits of tenants at Sandyford Place, where they served sixteen houses.

Many houses took no milk in the summer months or at week-ends, their occupants being out of town, but he had never known No. 17 to take none. A maidservant always answered the door and took in the milk, except occasionally on a Friday, when old Mr Fleming would appear, and on Monday afternoons, when he paid the account. Donald M'Quarrie knew Mr Fleming well from seeing him on these occasions. He would usually be wearing a black coat.

On the Friday morning before the murder it was Jess M'Pherson as usual who opened the door. She handed M'Quarrie the jug and asked for two penn'orth. That afternoon Mr Fleming appeared and said they didn't want any more.

Next morning, Saturday, at their usual time—between half-past seven and a quarter to eight—the cart drew up almost exactly opposite No. 17, the last house but one in the row. M'Quarrie ran up the front steps with his can and rang the bell.

After only a small delay he heard the rattle of the chain coming off the inside of the door, and the door opened and old Mr Fleming appeared. He was fully dressed, Donald was to say later—in black coat and trousers: better dressed than M'Quarrie had ever seen him before (the inference would be that he usually wore up his old black suit in the house). He said briefly that 'he was for nae milk' and shut the door again.

M'Quarrie was surprised and so was George Paton. No. 17 never took 'nae milk'. Paton had been serving other customers but keeping an eye on his boys, and he had observed that the door of No. 17 was opened with very little delay, though only a 'small bit', so that he had not seen who was inside it. (A milkman's 'very little delay' would allow for a minute or two—the customer would not commonly be crouching in the hall ready to spring out for milk: most of the maids on his round would have to make their way up from the basement). He asked M'Quarrie who it was that had answered the door and refused milk. M'Quarrie said it was old Mr Fleming.

They had now finished in Sandyford Place and were ready to move on. George Paton looked at his watch and saw that it was just twenty to eight.

And at 182 Broomielaw Street, Mrs. Campbell also was taking in the milk. The mistress of the house had not yet come home.

CHAPTER THREE

At nine o'clock, Mrs M'Lachlan knocked at the door of her 'house' in the Broomielaw. Mrs Campbell opened to her and, with only a murmured greeting she passed straight on down the corridor to her own room. She was wearing her brown bonnet and the grey cloak; and under the cloak she carried a very large bundle.

She reappeared shortly afterwards, carrying a clothes basket, and went downstairs to the cellar where she was in the habit of keeping some of her things—no doubt those displaced when she let her two rooms; and now Mrs Campbell saw that she was wearing a dress she had not been seen wearing before, a dress of reddish merino, trimmed with blue velvet, pleated at the back. She returned to her own room and later called out to Mrs Campbell asking her to kindle a fire in her room for her. She then went out, taking her little boy. It was hardly an hour since she had come home.

She was back some time between one and two and Mrs Campbell followed her down to her room and asked for the return of the little black basket she had borrowed the night before. She was now wearing a dress of her own which Mrs Campbell recognised; a dress of blue and black shaded poplin.

Poor Jessie had had a very active morning. She had been first to an ironmonger's and there asked to see a bonnet-box, with a lock to it. She was shown several and chose one of them, a black japanned box, of a popular model. She was carrying a bundle and she put the bundle into the box and locked the padlock and kept the key. The assistant serving her was a young man named Nish who at the time of the trial was in Antigua; but the proprietor recognised their private mark on the bottom of the box and his son had overheard the whole transaction. She asked Nish to put an Edinburgh address on the box: the witness understood her to say that she would be taking it to Edinburgh or at any rate taking it to the Edinburgh station. Meantime, she said, she would

37

leave it and come back for it later: before four o'clock—they closed at four on Saturdays. But she did not, in fact, come back for it that day.

Mary Adams lodged with a Mrs Rainny. Mrs Adams was the woman who did Mrs M'Lachlan's washing, who had pawned the looking-glass for her the evening before, and who had forgotten to give the message to the locksmith. She had been too unwell to keep her promise to go round and sit with the baby, but this morning by six o'clock she had duly got herself up and gone off out to work. She was still out when Jessie called at the house some time after eleven.

A small child opened the door.

Mary Adams being out Jessie asked Mrs Rainny 'if she had a wee boy to go a message for her.' No suitable wee boy being available she asked if Mrs Rainny would go herself (she seems—perhaps because her constant ill-health had accustomed her to relying upon assistance, perhaps because she herself was always kind and obliging and she took it for granted in others—to have been very ready to ask such favours of people).

Mrs Rainny agreed, and was given a pawn ticket and a 'paper note'—a pound, or ten shillings—and instructed to go round to Hutchinson's pawn in Argyle Street and 'lift' a bundle.

It seems probable that it was while Mrs Rainny was away on this errand, or before she left, that Jessie went out again. Some time in the morning she bought herself a new bonnet—paying four and tenpence for it, which seems not expensive considering that 'it was to be sent home to her'. She had on no bonnet while she was at Mrs Rainny's; and it may be said here that the pale brown velvet she had worn when she set out the evening before, and still wore when she came home the next morning, was from that hour never seen again.

According to Mrs Rainny it was between eleven and half past that Mrs M'Lachlan came to her house. It was after eleven but certainly before twelve—they banked their takings at twelve that day—that the accountants collecting the rents for the Broomielaw estate received a surprise visit from their habitually errant tenant, with four pounds to pay off on her arrears. She was at this time almost five pounds in their debt, but had been given till the end of August to settle.

From their office in West Nile Street it was a fifteen minutes' walk to Lundie's pawnshop in Great Clyde Street—up through Mitchell Street and across the Cowcaddens. Jessie arrived there some time after twelve. She had at that time no child with her: she had perhaps left it at Mrs Rainny's?—she had told her she was wearied with carrying the boy about the streets. She went into one of the booths and the pawnbroker's son, Robert Lundie, attended her. She gave her name as Mary M'Donald of 5 St Vincent Street and said that her mistress was behind in her rent and had sent her to pawn some silver. She produced it—six silver tablespoons, six plated dessert spoons, six silver toddy ladles, a silver fish slice, a silver soup divider—whatever that may have been—and two silver teaspoons, a plated sauce spoon and six plated forks. She asked six pounds ten shillings for them but was offered and accepted six pounds fifteen.

All the silver was marked with an 'F'.

Mrs Rainny, meanwhile, had been to the pawn and redeemed the bundle and brought it home unexamined. Mrs M'Lachlan opened it out in front of her. It contained a 'black and blue shaded poplin gown'—this explains why it was later described by some witnesses as blue and by some as black—and she asked leave to change into it there: she was 'going down the water wi' her man' and wanted to wear it, and besides she was taking the one she had on, to the dyer's. Mrs Rainny thought this was a pity: it was a nice dress, a cinnamon brown merino—but Jessie said no, she would prefer it black. She gave Mrs Rainny a penny for her two elder children and a shilling for the youngest: presumably the small boy who had opened the door for her but was too young to be sent to the pawnshop.

A glance at Jessie's curious finances may at this time be profitable. She had the night before sent out to pawn a mirror for six shillings to raise money to redeem her cloak; because she couldn't go out without the cloak. Of this she had paid out four shillings and sevenpence ha'penny to lift the cloak, sevenpence ha'penny for rum, and whatever was the cost of the biscuits. Since ten o'clock this morning, however, she had paid for the black japanned box (from later events one may deduce this to have cost four and six or five shillings) and four pounds off her arrears in rent. She had handed Mrs Rainny 'a paper note' to redeem the poplin dress from Hutchinson's pawn; and she had probably bought her four-and-tenpenny bonnet, though this may have been done later. But all this had come *before* she went to the pawn-shop with the silver; she herself in a statement made later agreed that it had happened before she pawned the silver. It was after-wards that she was able to be so liberal to the youngest Rainny; but in any event Mrs Rainny had had change to give her back from the paper note out of which she had paid the three shillings and a penny ha'penny on the poplin dress.

She left a message for Mary Adams with Mrs Rainny and went on.

Miss M'Crone in the dyer's shop in Argyle Street was surprised when the client—the same 'Mrs M'Donald', that had gone to the pawnshop—wanted her nice cinnamon-coloured merino dyed black. But the woman insisted, and she further drew her attention to the grey cloak she wore and said she wanted it cleaned; she was going out to buy a plaid and would bring the cloak back. She was away about half an hour and came back in a black plaid, carrying the cloak (a plaid is a big, heavy, woollen shawl, as much like an ordinary carriage rug as anything else, worn folded into a triangle over the shoulders, which was common in Scotland and is still worn in out of the way parts). Miss M'Crone remarked that the tassels on the cloak were 'no use' and suggested that she should cut them off. She did so and gave the tassels to the cus-tomer who took them away with her. Miss Crone fixed the letters 'M'D' on a corner of the dress and sent it off to the dyers. The dress had no flounces.

Whatever time Jessie may have got home for her lunch, at two o'clock, according to Mrs Campbell's evidence, taking the little boy with her, she was off out again. She was back very soon and left again at some time about three or four o'clock, taking a black leather trunk with her. But Mrs Campbell's memory does seem to have become a little confused, as well it might with all this to-ing and fro-ing; for someone else had in fact dealt with this famous black trunk. (Mrs Campbell further says that when Jessie again went out, later that night, she was wearing her cus-tomary grey cloak; but we know that this cloak had been left that afternoon at the cleaner's).

Miss Sarah Adams was a highly experienced young woman. At twelve years old, she had already quite a record of servitude to her credit: she had been with Mrs M'Lachlan at her three past addresses. Moreover, she had been mixed up in a court case before this, having two years ago been called to give evidence on behalf of the pursuer, a Miss Mackay. This grateful lady had presented her with a dress and a bonnet in gratitude—as previously promised; whereupon Sarah's evidence was discovered by her mother to have been a prearranged tarraddiddle. That a child of ten could be bribed to tell a false story may be sad but seems, perhaps, not so very heinous; her mother, however, thrashed her and very rightly 'put her back to tell the truth'. Her mother was the Mary Adams of the washing, the pawned mirror and the forgotten message to the locksmith.

Sarah Adams is the only witness to have found an unkind word to say about Jessie M'Lachlan. 'Was she a good tempered woman?'

'Yes.'

'Was she kind to you?'

'Yes.' She qualifies, 'She never struck me; but she has flyted on me; she flyted on me more than anybody else in the house. When I went a message and did not come back quick, I used to get a flyting.'

'But she was not a cross, ill-tempered woman, was she?'

'No,' says Sarah. But she again qualifies. 'Sometimes she was.'

'But she never lifted her hand?'

'No, not to me.' And now she flat out contradicts herself. 'I cannot say that she was very good tempered.'

Poor little, pitiful veteran slavey of only twelve years old: and poor, harassed, ailing, exasperated Jessie—who after all was only twenty-eight herself.

Sarah had left the Broomielaw some weeks before the murder and gone into service elsewhere; but on that famous Saturday, the day after the murder, it being her day off, she called in at about half past three in the afternoon to see Mrs M'Lachlan—whether by arrangement to do some work, or merely as a visitor, is not apparent. Mrs M'Lachlan, at any rate, immediately requested another of her favours. She was writing in her room when Sarah arrived—writing an address which, however, Sarah did not understand for though she could read print she 'couldna read writing.' She asked if Sarah would go a message for her—would she carry a trunk to the Hamilton station? This was agreed, and, picking up the written label and a little hammer, she told the child to come down to the cellar with her; and to bring

41

the baby. By the time twelve years old had struggled down three flights of stairs humping three years old, she was already fixing the label to the trunk, presumably with the aid of the little hammer. She told Sarah to 'pass by the cellar' but later called to her to come and see if the trunk were not too heavy for her. It was a small black leather trunk of her own which Sarah had often seen before, now tied up with a thin twine. Sarah found that she was able to carry it.

She was given a shilling and told to take the trunk by way of the Broomielaw Bridge to the station of the Hamilton railway. She was not to open it, and she was to say nothing about it to her mother—Mrs M'Lachlan thought for some unspecified reason that her mother might be angry. In fact she had better not tell anyone at all about it.

So Sarah staggered off with her burden which the clerk at the station, David Barclay, found to weigh twenty-one pounds. It was labelled: 'Mrs Bain, Hamilton station: to lie till called for.' He charged her fourpence on it and it was duly sent off and on the same day duly arrived at Hamilton. Sarah went back to the Broomielaw and was rewarded with threepence.

No sooner can Sarah have left, than her mother Mary Adams arrived, having received the message left with Mrs Rainny. She noted, somewhat to her surprise, for she knew it to have been in pawn, that Mrs M'Lachlan was wearing her black and blue shaded poplin. She made no comment but merely said she had heard Mrs M'Lachlan had been asking for her, adding, 'Had you to go on your own errand?' This she said because she knew that Mrs M'Lachlan never went herself to the pawnshop. Since she presumably can have known nothing of the adventure with the silver, she must have been referring to the poplin dress, not yet having heard that Mrs Rainny had gone to lift it. Jessie made no direct answer; but now asked her to go to Clark's and redeem whatever was in pawn there. She handed over the three tickets, and two pounds in money.

Mrs Adams, who only last night had raised six urgently needed shillings on the looking-glass, was naturally somewhat puzzled. She said, joking: 'Who have you been robbing?' Jessie said it was money that her husband had left for the tailor. Mrs Adams went off and redeemed a silver watch, a dress coat and two shirts of James M'Lachlan's, and a ring of Jessie's, and was rewarded with the crinoline wires of a petticoat which, Jessie suggested, she might be able to cut down for Sarah: the little boy had pushed them against the fire and damaged them.

Mrs Adams ran no more errands that day, 'unless for the house'; but Mrs M'Lachlan asked her to come again on Monday—she wanted some more parcels out of pawn.

She went out only once again, according to Mrs Campbell, taking her baby with her. When she returned, she showed Mrs Campbell a little bonnet that she had bought for him.

Poor Jessie!

That evening, P.C. Campbell, all unaware of the tragedy so near at hand, was once again patrolling his beat. In the post box of the Receiving House at Sandyford Toll was a letter to his father, a ploughman, which he had recently posted. It was by the date of this letter that he later confirmed this particular evening, Saturday, July 5, as being the one on which he observed an apparently trivial incident at Sandyford Place, though whether or not this calculation was correct remains extremely doubtful.

He had been trying the door of No. 16—in the course of his ordinary duties, to see that it was safely locked—and he noticed that the door of No. 17 had opened and two women had come out on the steps, neither of whom, he was certain, was Jessie M'Lachlan. One woman appeared to be seeing the other woman off: a rather tall, dark, thin woman, 'a respectable servant type,' in a light gown and a white apron with a white 'mutch' with long white ties over her shoulders—in other words, a servant's cap. The other was a girl of about twenty-two as to whom P.C. Campbell is not very gallant—'a low-set, stout woman with a red, fat face' but 'of a decent servant-like appearance and seemed quite sober.' She wore a white straw bonnet with blue ribbons and a dark grey cloak. They remained on the doorstep talking for five minutes or so, in low voices, then the younger went off towards Sauchiehall Street and the other went in and closed the door. He was not aware of having ever seen either before; he certainly never saw them again.

CHAPTER FOUR

Meanwhile on that Saturday, at 17 Sandyford Place, things had not been standing still. Mary Brown, aged sixteen, used now and again to go there and do a bit of the rough work for Jess. She was one of a family of six, her mother a widow and 'lying in a decline.' Mary had had instructions to come along on the Saturday morning and she was seen off by four of her family and the declining mother at twenty minutes past eight, which if she walked pretty quick would bring her to Sandyford Place at a quarter to nine. She did walk pretty quick, for she had another job to go on to afterwards; so it must have been about a quarter to when she went up to the front door steps and rang the bell.

There was a little delay, 'longer than a servant would have taken to answer because a servant comes quickly to the door' and then the door was opened as far as the chain would allow and the old gentleman peered out. (We know that the chain had been released at twenty to eight, for Donald M'Quarrie, the milk-boy, had heard the rattle; so evidently the door had been re-fastened afterwards).

Mr Fleming said, 'Well?'

'I'm the girl who does the steps for Jessie,' said Mary Brown. He opened the door, let her in, and replaced the chain.

He had on a black coat and black trousers. The coat looked as if it had been noo ta'en oot of a kist, said Mary, not like a coat he had had on the night before: it had creases in it. It was the sort of a long-tailed coat that she had seen gentlemen wear at funerals and at church on Sundays. It was buttoned up across the front, tight up to the neck and he seemed to have on no waist-coat for his shirt showed between the bottom of the coat in front and the top of his trousers. All in all, Mary thought, he was not like a man dressed for the day, but like one who had hurriedly put on a coat; and indeed it was true that the old gentleman usually pottered about the house in his shirtsleeves most of the morning, when he was at home.

She did not ask for Jess M'Pherson, and he did not mention her. He appeared perfectly calm and normal, and it never entered her head for a moment that anything might be wrong.

She was starting off down to the basement but he stopped her. He indicated a part of the lobby and asked her if she would wash it. It was the part where she was now standing at the head of the basement stairs—where the hall narrowed down to a passage about three feet wide and six feet long, passing the stairs and leading to his bedroom at the rear of the house. The patch was considerably marked—at first sight it looked as though people had been 'trampling' between the top of the basement stairs and the old man's bedroom and the back parlour, with soot on their feet. She agreed to wash the patch and would have gone down for water and cleaning materials but he went himself to a cupboard on the ground floor and got a pail and filled it with water and got a piece of cloth—a strip of clean flannel that looked as though it had been torn off a flannel vest—and stood over her while she got down on her hands and knees to it. On closer examination—so Mary later said, but this may be doubtful—it seemed to her that there had been some stain there and someone had taken a sooty cloth and rubbed over it, to hide it; the soot was dry by now but she could recognise the smell as she washed it. The door of Mr Fleming's bedroom was open and she washed inside it as far as the 'waxcloth' extended. She thought that the mark which the soot had been intended to conceal was a bloody footprint; she couldn't be sure, but it might be that of a woman. It was close to the bedroom door, leading in from the top of the basement stairs. The stain that the soot had been put over was liker blood than anything else, said Mary; but if any redness came off on the cloth, it was not visible— because of the soot. It took ten minutes of hard rubbing to get it off.

She stood up and lifted the pail to take it down to the basement and empty out the dirty water, but the old man again stopped her. He told her to leave it where it was. Then he fished in his pocket and gave her sixpence. 'Is that all?' she said, surprised— referring to the work, not the sixpence: she could not see ahead a hundred years, when the rate of three-and-six an hour would be commonplace. He said yes, that was all, and showed her off the premises. But before she left he 'catched a grip of her by the hand

and put his other hand on her waist and said she was a nice girl.' Whatever his extremity, old Mr Fleming was apparently still up to his tricks.

Mary, however, had her sixpence and must have gone her way rejoicing—her next assignment was with a Mrs Napier and she worked four hours there for a penny ha'penny.

She did not, however, particularly mention Sandyford Place to her mother when, that afternoon, she handed over her earnings, and it was not till after she heard of the murder that she thought of telling anyone about it: and then it was 'the lady next door.' Mrs Brown, overhearing her, administered what Sarah Adams would have called a flyting and told her never to open her mouth about it again, for fear she might get into some hobble. 'Mary,' she said, 'it was strange in you to go in when you didna' see the girl.' 'Mother,' said Mary, 'it was all one to me when the man asked me to come in.' She proceeded to describe the lobby fornent the bedroom door—there was something like stains on it and it was like rubbed over with black soot, and the water was quite black as if something had been spilled on it and something black rubbed over it. She had had a great rubbing, said Mary, to rub it off; and the old man had given her a piece of white flannel like as if it had been torn off a semmet and also a bucket with an iron handle, full of water and he had said, 'Scrub it well, my girl.' It was old Mr Fleming, she knew him well, for many a time she had seen him and run off to hide from him when she was going to see Jessie; she was feared to let him see her go in, in case he might object to it. Having satisfied her own curiosity, Mrs Brown told her in future to hold her tongue and not be blethering about things she had no right to. Mary, however, could not resist confiding in a girl called Bella Beveridge, and faithless Bella told a policeman and Mary was hauled up to tell it all again, before the Sheriff. So that's what comes of blethering when your mother tells you not to.

Old Fleming had spent much of his life in Anderston, a ward or district of Glasgow, first as a hand-loom weaver and later as a small manufacturer, making damask cloth and shawls. In his old age, his son, the prosperous accountant, had arranged a little job for him—presumably largely to keep him out of mischief, in which case he was not entirely successful—pottering about, collecting small weekly rents. (The properties were old and decayed, John Fleming cheerfully admitted—they were not his properties. They were generally high houses with common stairs and the tenants did not stay long—not so much from dissatisfaction with their surroundings, however, as from an inability to keep up with the rent. They were mostly in the lower part of the town, about the Old Wynd—a very good name for Fleming, senior; one at least was in the Broomielaw, where poor Jessie˙M'Lachlan also had her dwelling). For this work he was paid forty pounds a year and at the time of the murder he had 150 pounds in one bank which he had not touched for some considerable time, and thirty pounds in another, to which he was gradually adding. Those who did business with him had no complaint to make as to his mental faculties.

As we know, Mr Fleming was up on the Saturday betimes, to announce that he 'was for nae milk.' Some time later that day he turned up at John Fleming's office, or counting-house, in St Vincent Place and remained about half an hour there. He said nothing about Jess to anyone in the office.

Elizabeth Brownlie was servant to Mr Stewart, the jeweller who lived next door at No. 16 and had heard the scream in the night. The family having gone off that day to their summer residence, she had had in a friend to keep her company that evening—like Sarah Adams, a little girl of twelve years old—who had finally stayed overnight. It seems likely that they slept in the small back room, corresponding to the room where old Mr Fleming kept his wardrobe—the lay-out of the houses was the same. The room where Jess slept was in fact the laundry; the back room was probably intended for the servant's bedroom but owing to young John's having to share a bedroom with him, Grandpa's possessions overflowed from the ground floor to the basement and poor Jess was crowded out. (There was a shed at the back of the garden known as the 'wash-house'—but there was still a mangle in Jessie's room and one doctor at least recognised it as really a laundry and referred to it as such throughout). If we suppose that at No. 16 Elizabeth retained her rights, she would be using the back room, therefore, overlooking the garden; and would have only the party wall between herself and the Flemings' kitchen. Through this wall you could hear, for example, a coal being broken in the kitchen—the hearth was up against this wall. But that night Elizabeth and the child heard nothing.

Elizabeth knew Jess to speak to and was acquainted with Mr Fleming—the tiresome old man was always snooping on the servant girls next door and Jess had confirmed that he knew everything that went on there. This watch he could maintain without the use of spectacles; indeed Jess had told her that he could see perfectly, even to read the newspapers.

On the morning after the murder, however, Elizabeth in her turn unwittingly did a little spying. At about half-past ten, she saw the old man come out into the back garden looking round surreptitiously as though to see that he was not observed and then go down to the shed at the end for some coals. Her curiosity perhaps was piqued by this. At any rate she popped round that afternoon to borrow a spade.

The old man answered the door. He told her to come with him and they went down through the basement to the back door and out into the garden, where the tools were kept in a shed at the further end. But halfway down the garden he stopped and turned back; he said that the door was locked so he couldn't get the spade after all, and 'the girl was out.'

Elizabeth suggested that the key might be in the kitchen, but he said no it wasn't, because he had looked. She glanced in at the kitchen as she passed the door; screens of linen were airing before the fire, but she did not particularly notice anything else. She went off saying she'd come another time for the spade, and he said, yes, to come some other time.

That evening at about six, Andrew Darnley turned up. He was a pattern-maker from Falkirk and had known Jess when she worked in his father's house—the family had kept up with her since, though the reason of her leaving their service had been one of her two 'misfortunes.' He rang the front door bell and an old gentleman answered.

Andrew asked 'if this was whaur Mr Fleming stopped.' The old man said yes. He then asked if there was one, Jess M'Pherson, here. The old man said yes. He appeared to be a little deaf. Andrew, persisting, said well, was she in the house? The old man said no.

'Do you no ken whaur she is?' said Andrew, and when he said again no, 'Well, has she been gone long?'

The old gentleman said she had been out a good while. ('That's what he said,' repeated Andrew Darnley firmly, at the trial). He left his name and said he would be going home to Falkirk that night; and went away.

The next day was Sunday. If Jessie M'Lachlan left her house that day, we have no record of it. Mr Fleming, however, was up and dressed by the time the milk boy called: once again he was for nae milk. At ten to eleven a friend met him trotting off to Mr Aikman's, the Presbyterian church in Anderston—a 'ward' or district of Glasgow where he had had his manufacturing business, no distance from Sandyford Place.

He made some remark about the weather and Mr M'Allister asked, 'Are you still going down to the old church, Mr Fleming?'

'Yes,' said the old gentleman, 'it's no use changing now.'

This was the church where, ten years ago, he had made his confession of fornication. No doubt he considered that the devil who knew might be better than the devil who didn't: no offence intended to the Reverend Aikman.

That evening at about seven Andrew Darnley presented himself again at the front door of No. 17. He had not after all gone home to Falkirk, as he had told Mr Fleming he would the evening before, but had stayed the night with a friend. Mr Fleming answered the bell and he asked if Jess was in tonight.

Mr Fleming said, 'No.' Andrew, who probably knew all about his being fashious if Jess had visitors, remarked that she was surely often oot the noo? The old man made no reply and Andrew said he had a friend waiting for him, and took his departure.

On Monday morning Mr Fleming was up and dressed as before to receive the milk boy; and as before took nae milk. George Paton and Donald M'Quarrie thought it all very strange. No. 17 which had, for the past year at any rate, regularly taken milk morning and afternoon, had now had none since the two penn'-orth on Friday morning.

By nine the exemplary old gentleman was at the counting-house ready for work. John Fleming and his son, John junior, were due back from Dunoon that morning—the trip took from two to three hours. He did not wait to see them but conducted his business and started off on his rounds, rent collecting. His business was to hand over two pounds, six shillings and eightpence in small rents: it was all in silver. (It seems odd that he had not paid it in during the half hour he spent in the office on the Saturday, but perhaps he had something else on his mind at the moment). He said nothing to anyone about anything being unusual at Sandyford Place.

His grandson got to the counting-house at about eleven: his son John two or three hours later.

Mr Fleming's first call was upon Mr Daniel Paton, who, like Jessie, lived in the Broomielaw. Mr Paton was a dealer in second-hand clothes and furniture and often did a bit of business with old Mr Fleming; he would go round to Sandyford Place and had bought clothes from him that had belonged to any of the three gentlemen residing there—grandfather, father and son. He had been offered nothing, however, since a fortnight ago, when he had bought a pair of trousers and a brownish-grey coat which he thought must have belonged to John junior, for it was too large for the old man. Today, however, Mr Fleming was here only to collect the month's rent. (Unlike poor Jessie, Mr Paton was able to pay). Mr Fleming was wearing a black coat, or at any rate a darkish coat; there seemed nothing remarkable about it—Mr Paton, with his intimate knowledge of and interest in the Fleming wardrobes, thought he would have noticed if it had been new. But he wasn't too sure, altogether; he thought it was the long-tailed black coat that Mr Fleming often wore on his rounds but it might have been the blue beaver, rather longer than a shooting jacket, with big pockets at the side. He could not say whether Mr Fleming had on his black trousers or the steel grey. Mr Fleming seemed quite calm and—appropriately enough for the work he was employed upon—collected.

But Miss Elizabeth Mitchell of Albion Street, where he paid his next call, was another observant sixteen-year-old and more positive than Mr Paton. Mr Fleming had had on his good black clothes, not the clothes he wore for ordinary—his usual clothes were black but very brown from the wear, his long-tailed coat glazed, and greasy looking about the sleeves. He had seemed to her to be very much 'raised', very flushed, more flushed than was ordinary and though he sometimes had a staring eye, today it was more staring than ever, not restless but fixed and staring. He did not sit down but stood with his back to the dresser, quite agitated-like. After he had gone Mrs Mitchell remarked on it,

'Mary,' she said, 'Mr Fleming is very raised like today and has on his best clothes.' Mr Fleming had just walked into the house, said Mrs Mitchell, and stood with both his hands stretched out and his hat raised a little from his forehead—whether by some astral force or by some hitherto unsuspected third hand is not apparent. He did not appear drunk; there was nothing drunk-like about him. She said to Mary that she wondered, could something be wrong? Mary said she was sure she couldn't say.

He seemed very anxious, said Mary, to get the money, but this was perhaps because it was already overdue. Mrs Mitchell had taken the house through him but he had turned her out for non-payment of rent, and apparently allowed her to keep the tenancy only on condition of her sub-letting. Her tenants had let her down and she still couldn't pay so he had told her she would have to give up altogether. Nevertheless, Mary insisted, if he was raised, it was nothing to do with them; there was no bad feeling.

While Mr Fleming was toddling about among his tenants, Mrs Adams had, according to her promise made on the Saturday afternoon, gone round to the Broomielaw. She arrived at mid-day and did some washing but she could not recollect whether it was before or after the washing that she was sent on yet another of her missions, to the pawnshop. This time it was to Mr Clark's. Mrs M'Lachlan gave her sixteen shillings and sixpence and the two tickets, and she redeemed a pair of trousers and a waist-coat and jacket of James M'Lachlan's, paying out fifteen shillings and ninepence and giving back the change to Jessie. There is no more news of Mrs M'Lachlan on that Monday.

Mr Fleming was back at the house by half-past two, for at that hour Paton, the milkman, called with the milk bill. The old man appeared on the doorstep. He seemed perfectly calm. He said nothing to explain their having taken no milk since the Friday and did not mention Jess M'Pherson; George Paton assumed that he was to go on calling. The milk bill was one and fivepence ha'penny which seems reasonable enough: John Fleming and his son would have been there during the previous week and the bill would cover milk for four, from Monday afternoon to Friday morning.

At half-past four that afternoon, young John Fleming came home.

CHAPTER FIVE

The two Flemings, father and son, left the counting house together at four o'clock and took the omnibus for North Street. They had not been home since early on Friday, for they had gone straight from the office to Dunoon that night, and this morning had come straight from Dunoon to the office. At North Street they parted, the son going on ahead and the father stopping off to do some shopping. He went first to the flesher's and ordered some collops which the flesher's boy was to deliver—and did indeed deliver with such despatch that they arrived on the doorstep at the same time as John junior. Mr Fleming then went on to the grocer's.

Young John went bounding up the steps. To his surprise his grandfather was there, taking in the parcel from the butcher's. He said as they went into the house, 'Where's Jess?'

Mr Fleming put down the parcel of meat at the head of the basement stairs. He said, 'She's awa'. She's cut. I havna' seen her since Friday.' And, he added, her door was locked.

John thought it extraordinary. He went with his grandfather into the parlour at the back of the house and began, with growing concern, to question him. Indeed, he was 'rather strong with him', he later confessed; he was 'blowing him up', for he felt sure something must be wrong. Hadn't Grandpa thought of getting the door forced open?

No, he hadn't, said Grandpa. He'd just thought she must be awa' seeing friends.

Young John knew jolly well that Jess was not just away seeing friends; she had been with them far too long to do that sort of thing. He began to feel very 'queer'. From the moment he'd heard about that locked door he'd thought something must be up. He said: 'Didn't it occur to you that she might be dead?'

The old man did not answer; he just stood and stared at his grandson. But after a little while he repeated: 'I havna' seen her since Friday,' and added 'Dead or not dead, she's awa'.'

The bell rang again and John ran to open it and admitted his father. He was concerned but perhaps a bit excited also at the odd bit of news he had to communicate, and anxious to get in with it before Grandpa. He threw out a hand towards the parcel of meat at the top of the kitchen stairs. He said: 'There's no use sending anything for dinner here; there's no one to cook it.' He indicated the old man. 'He says he hasn't seen her since Friday and her room door's locked.' He added: 'She may be lying there dead for all he knows.'

Mr John Fleming also was concerned and astonished. Jess M'Pherson was very steady and reliable; he trusted her implicitly. He threw his hat on to the hall table and said to the others to come away downstairs with him, and he led the way down to the basement.

He glanced first into the kitchen, but the maid wasn't there and he hardly really looked about him; he did observe that the fire in the grate was low. He went on to Jess's room. The door was locked and there was no key at any rate on the outside—he had no idea whether or not there should be a key to that door.

His first thought was to go into the adjoining pantry and get out into the area through the little barred 'wicket gate' and to look in through the bedroom windows, or even to climb through into the room—he had forgotten for the moment that they too were barred. But as he was getting the little gate open it occurred to him that the key to the pantry might fit the bedroom lock. The key was in its lock and he took it out and went to the bedroom door.

Young John had meanwhile gone off down the passage to the back door. The door was locked on the inside. The basement seemed very close—there was no actual smell but it was close and stuffy—and he opened the door to let in some air and, leaving it open, returned to his father and grandfather. Mr Fleming was just going back to the bedroom with the pantry key.

The key turned in the lock, the door opened and they all three crowded in.

The room was very dark, the blinds drawn and the shutters half closed. Mr Fleming started across to let in some light.

She was lying face down on the floor beside the bed: poor Jess. Her body was naked from the small of the back downwards, a piece of carpet had been thrown over her head and shoulders.

The bedclothes were heaped, blood-stained, upon the bed, the furniture was in confusion. All about the room were splotches of blood.

Into the babel of horrified exclamation, old Mr Fleming's voice piped out clearly. He threw up his hands. 'She's been lying there all this time,' he cried, 'and me in the house!'

Down through the ages echo the words of Lady Macbeth, wringing the little hands that all the perfumes of Arabia would not make sweet again: 'What—in our house?'

Mr Fleming took one look, rushed his father and son upstairs and ran on out into the street to look for help. He knocked at one door after another in vain: everyone was either out or away. At last he met a man at the end of the row and, gasping out his story, begged the gentleman to come back with him. 'No, no,' said this excellent citizen, 'you've told me enough already to put me off my dinner,' and, like the Levite, he went his way. Mr Fleming hurried on. He came to the butcher's shop where fifteen minutes ago he had been buying collops for dinner, and rushed in and begged the butcher, Mr Train, to run to the police office, for something dreadful had happened in his house and his servant was lying dead in her bedroom. Mr Train dashed off and Mr Fleming went on up the road in the direction of North Street.

What must have been his relief when he ran full tilt into a doctor!

This was Dr Ebenezer Watson, who was on the steps of his house, probably, like Mr Fleming, going home to his dinner. He turned at once, however, and started back with him to Sandyford Place. On the way Mr Fleming collected Mr Chrystal, the grocer, in whose shop also he had so recently made purchases.

Mr Fleming was by now in a state of very natural excitement, bordering on panic. The herd instinct was evidently strong upon him: for of what use after all were all these strangers likely to have been to him? The poor woman was clearly dead. The police were all that was necessary—even Dr Watson was expendable, for they would bring their own police surgeon. Perhaps there was something to be said after all for the staunch citizen; he would have been put off his dinner to no real purpose.

Mr Fleming, Dr Watson and the grocer hurried along, and as they went Mr Fleming once again poured out his story. And part of his story was that, as he had put the pantry key into the lock of

54

the bedroom door, this had forced out another key which was on the inside of the lock and which had fallen to the floor inside the room. Later Dr Watson thought he heard him repeat the same thing to a policeman.

There was nothing Dr Watson could do. He took one look at the body, stooped down and touched it briefly and, straightening himself, said: 'Quite cold. Been dead for some time.' It was obviously not a case of suicide. Had they sent for the police?

Mr Train the butcher had got hold of P.C. Cameron. P.C. Cameron was told by Mr Fleming what had happened, and to him also—as Dr Watson could confirm—Mr Fleming repeated the story about the key on the inside of the bedroom door: only Cameron understood that Mr Fleming had actually peered through the keyhole, seen the key and used the pantry key to push it out, and had heard the key fall on the bedroom floor inside. When the constable came to realise that this was not suicide but murder, he got a candle and searched about for the key. He could not find it. He said so to Mr Fleming, who said well, he'd thought he heard a key fall but he was rather confused.

All this had not gone unobserved by the neighbours. At about five o'clock Mrs Walker—she who had gossiped with Miss Dykes on the pavement on the Friday night and seen the woman in the grey cloak turn into the lane—happened to be looking out of the window, and she saw a policeman running into her husband's shop, which was three doors down Elderslie Street. Mrs Walker leapt to the convenient assumption that some of her children had been about some mischief and hurried down to the shop to find out what was happening. By the time she got there the policeman had left, but she learned from the shopman that he had been there wanting a candle, as Fleming's servant had been got dead in a cellar or some other place, the door of which was locked. Mrs Walker was stricken at having missed him, but she wasn't a woman to be at a loss for long. She asked if the shopman had given the constable any matches and, on hearing the joyful tidings that he hadn't, felt impelled to snatch up a box of lucifers and hurry with it to Sandyford Place.

Mr Fleming was in the act of closing the front door on admitting the returning policeman, but true to his craving for company at this time, he opened it again and welcomed her in. To her joy she found quite a little crowd there—old Mr Fleming, young Mr

John Fleming, Chrystal the grocer and a gentleman she did not know—all standing in the lobby. Mr Fleming said that this was a fearful thing and she asked the particulars. He told her, adding that, strange to say, when he put the pantry key into the lock of the room door the key of the room door had fallen out inside the room. Her impression at this time was that Jess had committed suicide. She heard old Mr Fleming say that the last time he had seen her had been on the Friday night, about half-past nine, and that he had found her door locked on the Saturday morning. She asked him, seeing that Jess had stopped so long away, if he had never thought of looking for the girl. He said no. She said but hadn't he thought of getting the door opened and looking whether her trunk was away or whether the house had been robbed? The old man did not answer. Mr Fleming said, 'Mrs Walker is asking you——' and repeated the question. 'No,' said the old man, 'I never thought.' 'Did you hear no noise?' persisted Mrs Walker. 'Oh, ay,' said the old gentleman, 'I heard some moans.'

What must have been the feelings of Mrs Walker and all the company? He had never thought of harm having come to Jess, and yet he had 'heard some moans'. He had heard them in the early hours of the morning, he further explained. 'I rose on ma elbow and looked at ma watch and it was just four.'

Astonishment upon astonishment. 'When you were upon your elbow,' cried Mrs Walker, 'could you no have got up and cried down what was the matter?'

Once again the old man remained silent and once again Mr Fleming repeated the question. Grandpa then replied that no, he hadna' thought of it. 'Are you sure of the time—Saturday morning at four o'clock?' said Mr Fleming. 'It would not be the Sabbath morning,' protested Mrs Walker, who evidently thought that to be committing suicide or murder on a Sunday would really be going too far. 'No, no,' said the old man, 'I was twice at the kirk on the Sabbath.' So perhaps she was just checking the day.

Mrs Walker thought about it. Surely she had seen Jess M'Pherson in her shop on the Saturday?—about six o'clock, or seven. 'Na,' said old Fleming, 'it would be the Friday night, Mrs Walker; it couldna be the Saturday—for I did not see her that day.' But it certainly hadn't been the Friday, for Mrs Walker had been at the coast (it must have been a lovely summer; no one seems to have been able to keep away from the seaside). However, she agreed, it might have been the Thursday. . . .

Mrs Walker was later in trouble with the Press, and went before the Fiscal to deny that she had ever said to anyone that, when she had suggested she'd seen Jess on the Saturday, the old man had said, 'Na, Mrs Walker, it must have been Friday afternoon,' and when she asked him 'Why Friday?' had made no reply but 'given a look which flashed conviction on my mind that he knew too well that neither I nor anyone else had seen Jess alive on Saturday; a feeling which every succeeding day had served to strengthen.' Nor had she said that when she went down to the basement the floors were quite damp and bore evident signs of washing, though she had learned that two hours later they were quite dry. In fact she had noticed no signs of blood nor of dampness: the stone floors were so dark that you couldn't have told without touching them whether they were damp or not. The kitchen had appeared quite tidy and there was a good fire in it.

Jess M'Pherson had never said anything to her about old Mr Fleming. 'I make it a point never to speak to servants concerning what takes place in their masters' houses,' said Mrs Walker righteously. The shop doubtless served many families in and about Sandyford Place, and she had their future custom still to consider.

After this testimony Mrs Walker, alas, is heard of no more. She retired to bed and hoped she would be troubled no further, for she 'was not able to rise from her bed let alone go into any court.' Another little Walker had in fact arrived to create an excuse for enquiry any time a policeman might be seen hurrying about his sensational business.

At about half-past five Dr Fleming (no relation), the police surgeon, turned up (he said in court that it was half-past four, and this seems to have gone through unchallenged even by the keen eye of Mr Roughead; but this would have brought him to the house before the Flemings, *père et fils*, got home, and he is obviously mistaken). After him came a detective officer, Donald Campbell, and at about half-past nine Alexander M'Call, Assistant Superintendent in the Glasgow Police. Robert Jeffrey, a third police officer, arrived to assist in examining the scene and searching the house generally, and at eleven o'clock yet another doctor was sent for to pronounce upon the body. This was George

Macleod, who the following day was to make the post-mortem and, with Dr Fleming, compile the official report.

A detailed account of their findings will be given later. Suffice to say for the moment that poor Jess had quite obviously been murdered. She lay on her face near the foot of the bed, which was to the right as you came through the door. Her body was half clad in a semmet, a shift and a woollen polka—a sort of knitted vest, a chemise or short petticoat and a short woollen dressing-gown—but these had been pulled up over her head and shoulders, leaving the lower half of her body bare. A piece of carpet had been thrown down over the upper part. About her head, face and hands there were forty wounds.

An iron cleaver was found in a drawer of the kitchen dresser.

The bedroom was in confusion. The bed appeared to have been slept in; the bedclothes were stained with blood and had been pulled down into a heap at the foot of the bed. A blood-stained sheet which looked as though it had been taken off the bed was rolled up under the washstand; it was rather damp. Under one of the tables near the body was rolled the silver cruet stand from the dining-room upstairs, minus its bottles. There was blood all about the room, and close to the window wall three bloody prints of a naked left foot. And a chest that had held Jess M'Pherson's clothes stood open—the few remaining contents thrown back, all stained with blood, as though, said Dr Fleming at the trial, some bloody hand had been at work among them. . . .

All Jess's best clothes had disappeared, and her everyday dress was gone from its hook—a cinnamon-coloured dress trimmed with blue velvet, but with no flounces.

In the lobby between the bedroom and the kitchen there were smears of blood. There was blood on the kitchen sink, and in a chest of drawers in old Fleming's wardrobe-room across the passage were two shirts, newly dressed, spotted with blood.

But more fantastic still, the floors of the kitchen and the bedroom and the stone flags of the lobby had recently been washed. The kitchen floor was the drier, but it still looked damp. The lobby flagstones were absolutely moist. On the wooden floor of the bedroom, outside the part that had been washed, there were three bloody imprints of a small naked foot.

And most fantastic of all—the face, neck and chest of the corpse appeared to have been washed.

This is not fiction; this all happened—on a Monday evening, July 7, 1862.

Later that evening the police asked Mr Fleming if anything more was missing than the clothes from the chest downstairs. He had not thought of looking and would hardly know, for he was not sure what had been taken to the summer residence at Dunoon. They went into the dining-room—that room where, at four o'clock on the Saturday morning, the three merry wedding guests had seen the gasolier alight—and there found the sideboard standing open. The day-to-day silver spoons and forks were gone: all that remained was a single silver teaspoon which was found in a cup on a shelf in the kitchen. The silver teapot and stand and the silver cream jug were still in the sideboard (there were two other silver tea services in the house), and so were the glass bottles from the cruet which lay tumbled under the table in the murdered woman's room below. Mr Fleming indicated the tea-set. 'They might have gotten away with that,' he said, 'if they had been wanting plunder,' and the detectives agreed that 'an old thief, an accustomed thief, would have taken away more than was taken. One not practised in thieving might leave something behind.' On the other hand, to have left a plated thing like the empty cruet-stand seemed to Police Officer Jeffrey like the trick of an old thief, and altogether the whole thing was a mystery that they could not see the bottom of. He had not, he candidly admitted at the trial, seen the bottom of it even yet.

However, certain articles, both silver and silver plated, were missing after all: six silver toddy ladles, a silver fish slice, a silver soup divider, a plated sauce spoon. . . .

Etcetera, etcetera; the full list lay already in the keeping of Mr Lundie's pawn. Two days earlier 'Mrs M'Donald' had raised six pounds fifteen on it.

So the night dragged on. Under the yellow-blue light of the gas lamps or holding their candles close, the doctors and policemen crouched over the dead body or padded with probing fingers and eager eyes about the house. Police Officer Campbell had got hold of a little bit of stick and was measuring the bloody footprints on the bedroom floor. He compared their length by putting his bit of stick against the soles of the dead woman's feet. The stick was quite appreciably shorter. So the footprints had not been made by Jess M'Pherson, but he thought they were those of a woman.

In the early hours of the morning Mr Fleming took his father and son with him and sought refuge elsewhere, turning over his home to the authorities. One by one the doctors and policemen packed away their instruments and snapped shut their notebooks and crawled home to take a few hours' rest before it all began again next day. A uniformed man or two left in charge of the closed and shuttered house, dawn breaking and the birds beginning to sing in the trees along Sauchiehall Street.

And alone in her bedroom, lying there half naked, with her secrets still held close in her wounded hands, poor Jess M'Pherson lay as she had lain for three full days and three full nights, and would lie at least two days more till they had done with her.

CHAPTER SIX

Tuesday, July 8. A great day in the lives of the newspaper editors of Glasgow had they but known it, and indeed of all Scotland and England too. All they needed was one Jessie M'Lachlan a month, one of them was to say a few weeks later, to make them all millionaires.

But today there was time for only a very brief notice. 'Suspected Murder'—and a few lines about the discoveries at Sandyford Place. It sounded not very promising—a mere servant maid done to death by some horrid burglar, or perhaps by a 'follower' clandestinely introduced to the bedroom—and interesting only in its having occurred in the home of the gentry in the West End. There was much to report of more interest. A monster pineapple was on exhibition in a Glasgow shop window, weighing ten pounds, twelve inches long and twenty-two in girth. The introduction of iron vessels into the royal and mercantile navies was causing strikes among the Lower Strata of Society, led by the iron boiler-makers and the wooden shipbuilders. The High Sheriff of Leicestershire had mysteriously disappeared. There had been an amusing Deception in the Canadian courts of the International Exhibition in Hyde Park—a man had stood so still that he was thought to be a waxwork and was praised as a very masterpiece of the art of Madame Tussaud; every trick was tried in endeavours to discover the truth until some bold spirit thought of moving the wheel against which the figure negligently leaned, when the man fell over and all was discovered. The *Glasgow Herald* opined that he would not lack for hospitality for many a day to come. You could visit the Exhibition and see for yourself for only twenty-five shillings, cabin class, and six shillings steerage; servants in cabins, however, Full Fees.

And a Minister of the Gospel, working in Northumberland, had preached a fine sermon, here reproduced in full, against the seduction of virgins, a misdemeanour 'carried on chiefly among the poor.' In America, though New Orleans and the whole line of the Mississippi had fallen and the great naval station at Norfolk had passed into Northern hands, though Tennessee was overrun and the Northern powers had never yet been pushed back from any point once attained, yet the *Glasgow Herald* was still confident of a Southern victory (it must have greatly comforted General Lee could he have known). And a lady living in a Salubrious Part would welcome a Small Boy as Companion to her own. All parties having claims against the Argyle Gunpowder Co. should lodge them within eleven days; a quantity of old Hair Bagging was advertised for, also a cast-iron water tank. Alexander Friedlander has always a supply of FINE HEALTHY LEECHES on hand; James Fullerton of Argyle Street has fine Japanned tin Travelling Boxes. . . .

And the beautiful, very fast sailing clipper ship *Edouard et Julie*, newly coppered, is now actively loading and will soon say when she will sail.

Meanwhile—'Suspected Murder'. We learn that yesterday afternoon a horrid discovery took place at the residence of Mr John Fleming, No. 17 Sandyford Place. . . .

That morning Sarah Adams went round again to the Broomie-law. How she got the time off we don't know—she was nowadays employed elsewhere and her free day was Saturday; and she had no time due to her, for she had been to see Jessie on the previous Saturday. Nor do we know why she came; but by now 'the murder had been heard about' and she and her mother both knew of Mrs M'Lachlan's close friendship with the dead woman—and knew, moreover, that on the very night of the murder she had been planning a visit to Sandyford Place. So maybe Miss Adams just sneaked a few minutes off and popped round out of curiosity. Or maybe her mother, or even her employer, sent her.

All she got out of the visit, however, was that she observed on the table a straw bonnet 'trimmed with a blue or other ribbon' and a black plaid, neither of which she had ever seen before.

The dates of Jessie's movements for the rest of the week are confused and confusing, most of the witnesses being satisfied with 'it was the Tuesday or the Wednesday or the Thursday, but I can't be certain.' But certain it is that on one of those days she took a little trip to Hamilton; and since all agree that it *may* have been the Tuesday and she herself says that it *was* the Tuesday, we may assume that it probably was so. And from that the rest follows. In any case the dates are of no importance. Without wearisome ifs and ans, therefore, we will assume that they happened in the following sequence. . . .

On the Tuesday—that we do know—David Barclay, the clerk at the station who on Saturday had received the trunk from the little girl, Sarah Adams, and sent it on to Hamilton, noticed a woman walking up and down past his office. She came in at last and asked him if the box had been despatched. He told her it had been. So Jessie went to Hamilton.

A Mrs Chassels, wife of a carter, lived in Almada Street, Hamilton, close by to the station. On the Tuesday afternoon at half-past two a strange woman presented herself at the door and asked if they had a boy to go over to the station and carry a box for her; it wasn't a heavy one. (It weighed, as we know, twenty-one pounds: Sarah Adams, twelve years old, had staggered with it up the cellar stairs and to the station in Glasgow.) So Master James Chassels, the same age as Sarah, went with the lady to the station and she sent him in to ask for a box addressed to Mrs Bain. The lady came in later and signed for the box, 'Mrs M'Lachlan'. She asked the child to carry it back to his mother's house, and she went with him.

Jessie had presumably gone to the house because the people there were carters, but she was soon, as usual, throwing herself upon the kindness of strangers. Could she come in for a while? And might she have a cup of tea? And could the boy next take the box to a saddler's shop and get it mended? Oh, and did they know of a tailor of the name of Fraser?

Mrs Chassels knew no tailor called Fraser but she knew of one called Shaw. She said that James should take the trunk to Mr Cherry's, and meanwhile to come away in and she would make a pot of tea. While she was out of the room—all unsuspecting that her visitor might have a motive other than tea in wishing her absent a few minutes—the lady must have opened the box and taken out a bundle, for she had one when Mrs Chassels returned which she hadn't had when she arrived. It was tied up in a printed cotton kerchief and, as it was 'a pretty large bundle', it is perhaps not surprising that some of its contents were escaping—Mrs Chassels especially noted part of a dress and the bottom of a flounce bound with its own material. The lady explained that it was a merino wrapper. Mrs Chassels had brought half a glass of spirits with the tea—realising, no doubt, that though she showed no agitation, this frail-looking creature was nervously and physically exhausted—and the woman drank both and paid for them and for James's services and departed, taking the bundle with her. James walked along with her a little and she asked him the way to Mr Shaw, the tailor's, but she did not say whether or not she was going there.

An hour later a woman entered a public-house in the small village of Low Waters, a mile out of Hamilton, and asked for half a glass of whisky. She looked so exhausted that the proprietress, Mrs Gibson, brought her a whole glass. She was not precisely appropriately dressed for a long country walk, for she wore a black watered silk dress, a black shawl and a bonnet with blue and black ribbons, and she was carrying a large bundle under her arm. She paid a penny for her drink and started off again.

Was this the bonnet spotted by Miss Sarah Adams on the table during her exploratory visit to the Broomielaw? It must surely have been; and yet it is curious that Jessie, who subsequently admitted so much, steadily denied this harmless visit to the pub at Low Waters.

It was a hot, dry, dusty day. She dragged herself wearily on through the straggling village street, out into the country again with hardly any buildings in sight and only long fields of grazing land, divided off by hedges from the road, and came at about half-past four to a fork where a road, branching off, led to Meikle Earnock and the Tommy Linn Park. Here she met some children, two small girls of eleven, Marion Farley and her friend Margaret Gibson. She stopped and questioned them. 'Could you tell us a burn where to get a drink of water? For all the lang road that I've travelled I havna' seen a burn or a sheugh [a stream or an irrigational canal] whaur a person might wat their lips.'

The children pointed out the Tommy Linn burn further up the Meikle Earnock road and watched her till she passed the first oak tree, and then lost sight of her.

When, creeping back to the station that evening, she ran into a Master Mirrilees, a big boy of 'nine past', she was carrying no bundle. But she gave him a big square of cotton, saying, 'Here, boy, I found this handkerchief. Take it home and hem it.' Mirrilees, not being too handy with his needle, took it home and got his mother to hem it instead; and so the printed cotton kerchief she had noted earlier found its way straight back to Mrs Chassels.

That evening Robert Lundie, the pawnbroker, returned to Glasgow, having been absent since the Saturday, and, for the first time learning of the murder and of the plate missing from the house, looked at the silver that had been pawned on the Saturday; and, finding it all marked with an 'F', took it straight away to the police.

And the following day, Wednesday, July 9, old James Fleming was arrested as being concerned with the murder of Jess M'Pherson, questioned for four hours and committed to prison. In Scotland, unlike England, there is no public inquest—the preliminary investigation into a criminal case is conducted by the Procurator-Fiscal, as Crown Prosecutor, and the result kept secret.

All this time the black japanned bonnet box, locked and with the key in Mrs M'Lachlan's possession, had remained at the ironmonger's where she had bought it—an hour after getting home on the Saturday morning. But on the Wednesday she appeared and asked for it. She explained that she had changed her mind about collecting it on the Saturday afternoon as she hadn't had to go away after all; and she now asked the assistant, Nish (he who at the time of the trial was in Antigua), to alter the address he had written on the label (which the other assistants later remembered as having had something to do with Edinburgh) and to put instead: 'Mrs Darnley, Ayr; lie till called for'. The box was to be sent to the station, and off trotted someone upon yet another of Jessie's errands, though afterwards no one could remember who it was that went.

So the box was despatched to Ayr station, to lie to be called for, and *was* called for in due course—not at Ayr but back at Glasgow, and not by any Mrs Darnley but by Jessie's husband, James M'Lachlan.

M'Lachlan had got home from his ship in the early hours of Thursday morning. What must have been his wife's feelings as she waited for him to arrive? And what must have been his feelings when he came? His ship had been in Ireland, he can have heard nothing of the murder; she docked at midnight and he had come straight home.

Exactly what was the character of James M'Lachlan it is difficult, from his brief appearances in his wife's story, to fathom. He was a nice-looking fellow, aged about thirty, and looked a typical sailor, bred to the sea and having been as far abroad as Australia. His employers thought highly of him. He came of a large and respectable family from round about Greenock and three of his sisters were married and living there. He does seem to have been very fond of his wife. Their friend, Mrs Fraser, gave evidence that they 'lived together very comfortably', and he himself said that he had 'the utmost confidence in her' and that he 'never saw anything to give him reason to doubt her.' She seems to have had less than the utmost confidence in *him*, however (and, as it would seem from later events, with perhaps some reason), for it is pretty certain that she did not tell him all the truth about her present troubles. On seeing in the newspapers a description of a woman wanted in connection with the murder, he remarked to Jessie, 'That's unco' like you.'

'It's ower like me,' said poor Jessie.

It must have been with some trumped-up explanation, therefore, that she persuaded him to get back the black japanned box from Ayr and somehow dispose of it: he had a sister in Greenock with whom he was on particularly good terms—couldn't he take it and leave it in her safe keeping? She told him, possibly, the story she later told the legal authorities: that Jess had sent her some clothes, asking her to get them dyed and altered, and now the police were seeking them and she was afraid of their being found in her possession. She had bought a box and sent them off to Ayr to be out of the way, but after all the box would remain at the station and might at any time be opened and examined, and things would look worse than ever. He begged her to tell the police the whole truth and be done with it; and she was to say later that they agreed that she would wait till the Monday and tell them then. He was due to sail again with his ship on Saturday but he arranged to stay at home. Meanwhile, at her anxious desire, he went off to the railway station and there bribed or cajoled a porter into sending a private note by the guard of the next train to the clerk at Ayr station. The clerk got the note and sent back the box by the morning train to Glasgow, still addressed to Mrs Darnley. James

M'Lachlan collected it and took it back to his sister's house in Greenock.

Next morning the box was unpacked and the contents spread out on the bed. James M'Lachlan appears to have told his sister the whole story—or as much as he knew. Jessie would confess to pawning the silver, he said, but these clothes had nothing to do with it—she had told him that Jess had sent them, asking her to get them cleaned and altered. So they put them away in a drawer. ('You did not put them into the bed?' enquired Lord Deas at the trial: a new low, one might think, in judicial irony), where they remained till the Wednesday. On that day they were packed back into the box and sent off, addressed this time to 'Mr Thomson, County Buildings: to lie till called for.'

County Buildings is the Sheriffs' Court of the City of Glasgow, and Mr Thomson was Sub-Inspector Audley Thompson of the Glasgow Police.

CHAPTER SEVEN

We must now consider in more detail the state of the body and the scene where it was found. It was not, alas, a sight for the chicken-hearted.

The bedroom was in fact, as has been said, the laundry of the house. It measured fourteen feet by fourteen, with a four-foot square table in the centre. The door was towards one end of the east wall—to your right as you came in; the windows, looking out on to Sandyford Place were in the north wall. The bed was placed rather oddly, sideways against the wall, midway between the door and the window wall, its head not up against anything: it was a large fourposter, probably five or six feet wide. Opposite was the hearth and the mangle, and along the south wall, to your left as you entered, and facing the windows, were two wash-stands and the trunk or chest which held the dead woman's best clothes. In the corner opposite the door was a built-in cupboard. (See plan, p. 27 and ground plan at end of book.)

The body was found lying face downwards in the entrance to the narrow space—about two feet wide—between the bed and the central table: its feet towards the windows, its head towards the door—its position was afterwards to be significant. It was naked up as far as the waist. The clothes (the knitted jacket-vest, the chemise and the woollen dressing gown) were rucked up from the waist round the shoulders and head, the head enveloped in them, and they were damp when the body was found, and much stained with blood. A small mat or piece of carpet covered the upper part of the body as though it had been thrown down care-lessly on top of it.

The full and official description of the injuries is so dreadful as to make nightmarish reading for the layman. We will confine ourselves therefore to such details as may be necessary to any solution of the mystery.

There was little cadaveric rigidity—rigor mortis—a state which sets in (and also passes off) after a space of time varying with the conditions under which the corpse remains. There were no signs whatsoever of decomposition.

There were forty wounds about the head, neck, face, hands and arms.

First, there were three deep, incised wounds, one across the middle of the forehead, two across the bridge of the nose; and these, alone among the wounds, ran transversely, straight across the face. Any of these three wounds would probably have caused stupor; but, except possibly eventually from loss of blood, even together they would not have caused death. The lethal injuries were to the right side of the head. There were three major cuts, midway between the ear and the top of the head, cleaving right into the skull, and three other severe scalp wounds a little further back. On the left side of the head there were ten more wounds, less severe in character; and there were a few shallow cuts on the back of the neck.

With the exception of the three cuts across the forehead and the bridge of the nose, all the wounds sloped from above downwards, and from behind forwards. Of the deep cuts, several grew more shallow towards the back of the head.

On the right temple was a further small wound which had not injured the bone beneath.

There was a large bruise on the top of the right shoulder and another on the back of the right upper arm. Dr Watson, who was first to examine the body, noted one 'remarkable' bruise in the small of the back; but none of the other doctors observed, or at any rate could later recollect it.

There were flesh wounds of greater or less extent on both arms, both wrists and both hands; the right hand being 'dreadfully mutilated'.

And finally there were some small abrasions of the knees and shins, which were also soiled. The feet and legs were extended to their uttermost.

There was an accumulation of blood beneath the head but not, said Dr Watson who first examined it, a pool of blood. The face was lying upon the rucked-up, blood-stained clothes. And, strange to relate, as has been said, the face, neck and chest of the corpse appeared to have been washed; not just wiped, but washed with water. Yet there was coagulated blood upon the face, which had come there since the face had been washed.

In other words—someone, after some *but not all* of the injuries, had been inflicted, had bathed the face and throat.

The room was in a horrid confusion. There is no official mention of scattered clothes but they were certainly there; on the other hand it was not true as one report avers, that poor Jess's clothes had been 'evidently torn off by a person not much skilled in doffing female habiliments.' The bed looked as though it might have been slept in but it was now in complete upheaval. The bedclothes were heaped at the foot, not tucked in at all. There had been blood on the blankets but it had been washed out. A sheet had been torn off and lay under one of the washstands, that nearest the door. It showed no blood until it was unrolled; it was then found to be damp all over as though it had been washed, but it was smeared with blood from one end to the other and in some parts saturated. There was blood upon the mattress; a good deal of it, 'about half the breadth of the crown of my hat,' said Police Office Jeffrey, 'on the edge of the bed; and there was a piece more, over where the bolsters had been lying; it was like where a person's shoulder would lie, a small bit down from the pillow.' The pillows, both patched with blood, had been thrown down—'scattered'—upon the bed.

There was a good deal of blood where the body lay, and three large drops nearer the head of the bed. Against the wall facing the windows were the chest and the two washstands. Under the first of these was the rolled-up sheet; the second was smeared with blood, there was blood on the white basin, and blood on the floor all about it. The chest—a common type used by servants to keep their clothes in—was closed, but its lock had apparently been broken long ago. It proved to be almost empty: such 'trimmings and ribbons and bits of gowns' as it still contained had been raked through with a bloody hand, and a band-box inside it had had its lock forced by the same hand.

But strangest of all, in the corner opposite the door, on the other side of the central table from where the body lay, there was a large area of the floor, part wood, part 'waxcloth', which though it was now dry had all the appearance of having been washed. It formed an irregular circle and though it was cleaner than the rest of the floor, it had a reddish colour as though there had been blood split there, and the edges seemed still bloody; at one side, half on the wood, half on the hearthstone, there were big, elongated splashes of blood, as though blood had spurted out in the general direction of the window, and the wall.

There was a small table under the window furthest from the door. Between this table and the hearth, skirting round the mangle, were the three bloody imprints of a naked foot.

The kitchen was a longer room than the bedroom, though rather narrower. The hearth was on the same side as the hearth in the bedroom, the opposite side from the door. There was a large central table. The floor was of stone of a very dark blue colour; a type of stone, said an architect, O'Neill, in evidence, that would dry quickly.

And here also, there were signs of blood. There was a stain on the jaw-box—the sink—as though a bloody hand had clutched at it. The mat in the doorway was so steeped in blood that it actually stuck to the floor; and halfway up the doorposts and across the inside of the door were streaks 'as though a brush had been dipped in blood and drawn across it'; or, said the same witness, as though a woman's skirts, stained with blood, had swept through the door.

These marks, in the clear light of a July evening at five o'clock were perfectly obvious; 'if your eye had been turned in that direction, they might have been seen at once'.

Between the fireplace and the sink, there was a large patch which looked as though it had been washed; there was no actual sign of blood but the floor had a greasy appearance, with a reddish tinge. There was a fire burning in the kitchen and by the evening the floor was dry; but when first observed an hour after the discovery of the body, it had the appearance of being still quite moist. It was hard to tell, for the stone was dark; but still it looked very recently done.

And all about this area, between the kitchen hearth and the sink, at the perimeter of the washed space, were the marks of shuffling feet—small scratches, confused footmarks, the turn of a heel, the twist of the ball of a naked foot on the polished stone.

The stones of the lobby between the kitchen and the bedroom were of the same dark blue as the kitchen. Here also—blood. Blood at the end of the passage, by the back door into the walled garden. Blood on the stairs, and particularly on the lowest step;

blood on the wall at the foot of the stairs. Blood on the built-in pantry cupboard between the kitchen and bedroom doors—inside the cupboard, high up at the top of the door: two patches, three or four inches square. (The door opened outwards into the lobby.)

And once again the floor had been washed. But this time it remained, three days and two nights after the murder—absolutely damp.

Nor had it been so well washed but that a trail remained clearly to be seen between the kitchen and the bedroom door: a 'bloody track about the breadth of a body, part of it blood, the rest just marks of streaking'; as though the victim had been dragged through the passage while the arterial blood still flowed: or at any rate, so soon after death that it was still fluid enough to leave its trail.

At the end of the passage, near the back door, was the small room where old Mr Fleming kept his clothes. Here there were some spots of blood in the centre of the floor. Of all the drawers and cupboards, only one drawer was locked. The old gentleman on request had handed over a bunch of keys; one key unlocked this drawer. In it was a pile of laundered and folded shirts. The sleeves of the two topmost shirts were spotted with small spots of blood.

No positive signs of blood were found on any cloths with which the floors could have been washed; but thrown into a cellar were several, still damp, which might well have been used.

In a drawer in the kitchen was found a cleaver, which could have been the instrument which caused the wounds—one doctor thought those on the wrists had been caused by a finer blade, but this theory never came to anything. There was no blood on the blade of the cleaver but it was extensively marked with fresh rust on both sides—suggestive of its having been recently washed. There was a considerable quantity of blood, however, dried into the join between the blade and the wooden handle, though the methods of those days could not establish for certain that it was human blood. (The cleaver is preserved in the museum at the police head-quarters in Glasgow: a smooth wooden handle and a broad blade, perhaps five inches at its widest point. It looks very innocent hanging meekly there.)

On the Saturday following the discovery of the murder, the

house having been in police hands since the Monday, Bernard M'Laughlin, a Sheriff's officer, was introduced there to make yet further examination of the scene of the death. He found 'on the kitchen dresser' an iron hammer with marks of blood on one side of the head. This little item had apparently escaped the attention of the police investigators, satisfied, as they no doubt were with their blood-stained cleaver. He discovered further and made much of, a pair of man's socks, old and much worn, which lay in Jess's bedroom between the head of the bed and the window; but as, despite the most eager scrutiny, they proved innocent of blood or any other guilty sign, this treasure amounted to little. In the kitchen grate he found and sifted a great quantity of ashes, looking for signs of any clothing having been burnt there. He did find a button, which he treated with the utmost reverence, but that too came to nothing; and anyway, his colleagues had kept the fire burning away merrily all the time they had been in occupation.

Upstairs, Mary Brown had evidently done her work well, for no sign was remarked of the bloody footstep covered with soot which she had, on the Saturday morning, been employed to wash away. But in the old gentleman's bedroom, Police Officer Jeffrey—Mr Fleming being by then in custody—had a good rootle round. He discovered a grey canvas bag, apparently a dirty-linen bag, which had been washed but still showed blood-stains—variously described as a patch the size of a shilling on one side, and as a stain extending all over the bottom of the bag. And 'under a chair', or, as he later explained, 'under the chair cover', he found a long narrow strip of cotton cloth with small spots of blood on it. The blood, when he saw it, 'seemed to be old'; and it does sound a little like a bandage from some old, trifling injury, which had somehow got stuffed away there and been forgotten. Little was made of it at the trial, and had it been incriminating, it would surely have been too easy for the old man to have thrown it on the kitchen fire and so got rid of it?

From all these signs and symptoms, Joseph Fleming, surgeon of police, assisted by Dr George Husband Baird Macleod, M.D., F.R.C.S., came to the following conclusions:

1. That this woman was murdered and that with extreme ferocity.
2. That her death had taken place within three days.

3. That a severe struggle had taken place before death.
4. That such an instrument as a cleaver for cutting meat or a similar weapon was that most likely to have caused the fatal injuries found.
5. That the injuries had been inflicted before or immediately after death.
6. That all the wounds on the neck and head with the exception of those on the nose and forehead had apparently been inflicted by a person standing over the deceased as she lay on her face on the ground.
7. That the comparatively slight degree of strength shown in the blows would point to a female or a weak man as having inflicted them; and,
8. Lastly, that the body had been drawn by the head, with the face downwards, along the lobby from the kitchen to the front room.

This is the truth on soul and conscience.

Geo. H. B. Macleod, M.D., F.R.C.S.
Joseph Fleming, Surgeon.

Of these, their number three seems based on very slight evidence: and their 'lastly' to be, if the evidence is examined, not the least extraordinary proposition to be put forward in this most extraordinary case.

CHAPTER EIGHT

Upon what information the police first suspected Jessie M'Lachlan of being concerned in the murder, is not certainly known. Old Fleming himself is suspected of having put forward her name or it may have been someone nearer home. From the small size of the naked footprints and from the marks on the stairs and kitchen door of the swish of a blood-stained skirt, they had early made up their minds that a woman might well be implicated. As early as Monday, the day of the discovery, they were asking Miss Dykes whether she had seen a woman enter the lane behind Sandyford Place that night. How they can have got on to this, one can't imagine: if Mrs Walker had told them of the woman in grey who turned into the lane while they two stood gossiping, Miss Dykes would surely have been reminded of this episode, but in fact it was not until much later that she recalled it. It may simply be that the police were asking all persons living thereabouts after any woman who might have come to the house—with no reference to the woman Miss Dykes and Mrs Walker saw.

On July 9, at any rate—the Wednesday—Lundie, the pawnbroker had laid information as to the missing silver having been left with him; and a description of the woman who had pledged it was given in the newspapers—a fair or sandy-haired woman with an oval face, whose hands and arms were too white to be those of a working woman. This description was later altered for no apparent reason: the woman, on the contrary, had been very dark with a hard, hatchet face, short, and 'ordinarily stout'. But long before she read either description, Mrs Campbell must surely have been growing suspicious. She would hear of the murder on the Monday night or Tuesday morning, would learn that the woman had already been dead some days. Her first question would surely have been to Jessie, 'Didn't you go to see her on Saturday evening?' Jessie would say, no doubt, that she had changed her mind; but now a new and terrible idea would strike Mrs Campbell. She had let Mrs M'Lachlan in at nine the next morning. She probably thought at the time, if she thought about it at all, that her landlady had been out already and was coming in again. But in the light of the murder giving it closer attention—that couldn't be: for how could she have come in when she returned from her visit that night, since she had no key? And now she would recall the bundle carried under the cloak, the change of dress, the sudden acquisition of money. . . . And, with much inward shrinking, no doubt, for she seems from the way she gave her evidence to have been an honest, good-hearted woman, she would confide her shocking fears to first one friend, then another, and wonder what she ought to do. Mrs Adams would hear of it, almost certainly, and Sarah would soon get to know and so the match would be set to the first small kindlings of the bonfire of gossip, conjecture and 'information to the police'. The pawnbroker's (first) description would be added confirmation and Jessie was known to frequent such places, albeit by proxy. It may well have been the deciding factor. At any rate that day, the day the description was published—it was also the day of old Fleming's apprehension, however, which does rather point to him as the informant—the police became interested for the first time in Mrs M'Lachlan. They set a watch on the house, three times came and questioned her, and at four o'clock on the Sunday made their spring. The child was hastily handed over into Mrs Campbell's care, and Jessie and her husband were bundled into a cab and driven off, both under arrest, on charges of murder and theft.

Now the hunt was up. With Jessie out of the way, the bonfire of scandal really got going.

The police within the next few days were very active indeed around the Broomielaw. There was a good deal of juggling over keys—which amounted to this, that there proved to be no existing 'check key' to the front door of her 'house', and that no other key in the place could be found to fit it. Mary Adams must have told about the allegedly burnt crinoline, for a detective went off round to their house and there took possession of the wires that had been given her to cut down for Sarah. On part of these wires he 'considered there had been blood'. And Mrs Adams nosed round and finally dug up a sleeve torn out of a dress and handed that also over to the police—a sleeve from Mrs M'Lachlan's familiar brown coburg dress with the flounces. Mrs Adams had last seen her wearing it on that fatal Friday, before she went out to see Jess. And Mrs Campbell explained about the bottle which Jessie had borrowed to go out for her sevenpence ha'porth of rum, to stand treat to her visitor, Mrs Fraser, and later to Jess; and lo!—there in the cupboard in the basement at Sandyford Place was a bottle with no cork in it, smelling of rum.

In her room at the Broomielaw, despite her extravagance in 'lifting' pawned articles on the Monday following the murder, there were still to be found forty-one pawn-tickets, old and new: all in the name of Fraser, with various Christian names.

And away up in Hamilton, while the lady who had asked about the sheugh or burn to quench her thirst was undergoing such tribulations, Margaret Gibson, one of the two little girls, was making a horrid discovery. Wandering that Sunday near the Tommy Linn park, towards which she and Marion Fairley had directed the lady, she noticed some pieces of flannel thrust in under the roots of a hedge. She pulled out a piece and saw that it was 'all blood'.

The child was scared and ran off. But she told her friend Marion and next day they returned to the spot and found the flannel still lying there. They had another fascinated look and then went off and left it. Further on, however, in Templeton Park, they came across another prize: bundled under a hedge was a brown coburg dress, torn but entire—except for one sleeve.

Meanwhile, Jessie languished in the Glasgow prison. She had been examined upon entry, and the exciting discovery was made that on her left hand were the marks of a cut and also of a bite or bites. Any hopes that these might have held out, however, were deflated by the decided opinion given by the police surgeon at the trial, that the incisions were too small and close together to have been caused by human teeth, and were probably exactly what she said they were—the scars of a bite from her own small dog.

The footprints, however, were a different matter.

There had been three footprints, all of a naked left foot, marked in blood in one corner of Jess M'Pherson's room. The board containing two of these had been cut away—the third was indistinct and not thought worthy of much notice. As we know, Assistant

77

Superintendent Alexander M'Call had got busy with a small piece of stick, 'a thin spale', with which he measured the length of the footprints and which he then applied to the sole of the dead woman's foot. Such considerations as the difference between a foot supporting nothing and a foot with the full weight of the body on it, seem to have been of no importance to him. Jess M'Pherson's foot was longer—half an inch longer, and there was no sign in the footprint of her bunion. It was all so convincing that he thought it not worth while to bother with a footrule. He had measured with the stick, 'keeping my finger and thumb at the place'—what more could you want? Detective Officer Donald Campbell was of the same opinion. He too had dispensed with a footrule. Still, he cut his piece of spale exactly to the length of the mark on the floor, before applying it to the dead woman's foot which was something, and he measured length *and* breadth. He too was satisfied that 'the foot of the deceased was rather longer'.

Dr Macleod seems to have been much more exact. He compared the prints with the dead woman's foot, 'contour, size and everything' and found her feet longer, broader—larger in every way (though quite in what other way they could have shown larger it is difficult to see. Moreover, under examination at the trial, when asked, 'Each foot?' he answered readily, 'Each foot', though the prints were only of the left foot). It fell to him also to compare the prints with James Fleming's foot; but the old man had flat feet whereas the print showed a high instep, and the two were so perfectly different that he did not think it necessary to compare them minutely. His impression was—before any suspicion attached to the prisoner, he hastened to add—that the prints had been made by a female foot, a well-formed female foot with a high instep; and what had been his impression then, had by the time he came into court become his opinion.

By this time also, it was his opinion that the footprints could have been made by the left foot of the prisoner, Jessie M'Lachlan.

Here—all honour to him—he had been to even more pains to make no mistake. After several experiments with his own foot, soaked in various agents, he decided that nothing but blood would given an accurate effect and he accordingly got hold of a small phial of bullock's blood. From his experiments it would appear that the bedroom had a wooden floor, partly covered with 'waxcloth', a kind of linoleum, the footprints having been found on the wooden part. He therefore smeared some blood on a piece of waxcloth and, Mrs M'Lachlan then being in custody, invited her to put her left foot in the blood and then step on to a plank of wood. The prisoner showed no objection, indeed, said the witness, she seemed quite to court the test; though, bullock's blood and all, and especially in the distressing circumstances, it can hardly have been agreeable. But it was all no good: the prints on the plank were quite useless. It then proved that the plank had previously been oiled 'for some other purpose'; and one can almost hear Dr Macleod saying testily that if you wanted a thing done you had to do it yourself and wasn't it possible, for heaven's sake, to produce an ordinary piece of dry wood? One was found at last resembling in age and condition the flooring at Sandyford Place, and this was put on one side, a piece of waxcloth next to it and beyond the waxcloth a fresh pool of blood. Poor Jessie again paddled in the blood and stepped on to the plank. This time all went splendidly, and Dr Macleod was able to report: 'two impressions were got which corresponded with a degree of accuracy which was quite marvellous with the marks taken from the house. In the minutest detail of measurement and outline did they tally with the original, and, in fact, each of them was, if possible, closer to the Sandyford footmark than they were to one another.'

It was but a short step from Dr Macleod's 'could have been made by the prisoner' to 'were made'. From this time on, Jessie's presence at Sandyford Place that night was held to be conclusively established.

(There is in the Police Museum in Glasgow, a piece of board with an impression of a woman's foot, said to be that cut from the floor in Sandyford Place. It is extraordinarily clear, a small foot with a narrow heel, high arch, and every toe distinct. From the fact that it appears to be outlined in some agent other than the original blood which forms the impression—as though a thick paint brush had been drawn around it—the author can't help wondering whether it is not more likely to be the footprint in bullock's blood made by the prisoner for Dr Macleod—it is so remarkably clear. Either way, it is a strangely poignant relic of that long-ago, terrible night.)

CHAPTER NINE

The evidence for the prosecution at her trial opened with two declarations of the prisoner, dated Monday, July 14—the day after her apprehension: Wednesday, the 16th, and Monday week, the 21st. These, declared Alexander Strathern, the Sheriff-Substitute of Lanarkshire, 'were emitted by her in his presence, freely and voluntary, in her sound and sober senses, and after receiving the usual warning.'

Her first examination lasted four hours—so though in her sound and sober senses, a woman of her physique must also have been somewhat at the end of her nervous tether by the time she was done. At the end of that time, she made a very long first statement. Before that, however, her husband had been questioned and she was in ignorance of the information he had given. James M'Lachlan had been arrested with her, and thus made liable to questioning—at a time when the authorities were perfectly aware that he had in all probability been far away with his ship when the crime was committed and was therefore beyond suspicion. The newspapers on that day, the Tuesday, were proclaiming their entire conviction of his innocence, since he had clearly been absent with his ship: and since these articles will have been written on the previous day, one would think the police might have arrived by Tuesday at the same—quite correct—conclusion. The fact is that it suited their book a lot better to close their eyes to these inconvenient facts, get his statement out of him and then suddenly see the light and let him go.

This decision—to haul James M'Lachlan in quickly and get in their questions before the probability of his innocence should be absolutely proven—was widely held at the time to have been a disingenuous and deliberately unfair proceeding. 'The object of the examinations (of the prisoner, Jessie M'Lachlan)' says the *Journal of Jurisprudence*, 1862, Vol. VI, p. 513, 'appear to have been two. Lord Deas (the judge at the trial) explains one of them, which is common to all such examinations. "One great object," said his Lordship, "is to allow the prisoner an opportunity, if the prisoner thinks proper, to make some explanation of the circumstances which seem to weigh against her." This,' continues the journal, 'we had hitherto understood to be the only object of such examinations; but in this case at least there would appear to have been another great object. What this was, Lord Deas failed to explain, but it may be easily gathered from the circumstances. We regret to say that it appears to have been nothing else but to lead the prisoner into falsehoods with the effect, if not for the purpose, of destroying her credit on every point. . . .' A vicious practice in a matter of criminal investigation, it goes on, was certainly a fair subject for criticism by the superior wisdom of the principal Court of the Judicature.

In this case the superior wisdom failed.

The declarations were made in the presence of Alexander Strathern, Esq., Sheriff-Substitute of Lanarkshire—Glasgow is in the county of Lanarkshire—the Procurator-Fiscal, signing himself Jno. Gemmel, the curious current abbreviation of John: Peter Morton, clerk in the Sheriff-Substitute's office and Bernard M'Laughlin, Sheriff-officer in Glasgow. Jno. Gemmel was to rise to great heights in his profession—a round-faced man with a great fringe of curly fair whiskers ringing his face from his ears down under his chin, like a fiery halo worn in the wrong place; with thick lips and pale, prominent eyes. It was said of him that no criminal great or small ever escaped punishment with his goodwill. It was further said of him at the time of the trial that he was a close personal friend of the Flemings.

Before this formidable galaxy, weary and frightened, unaware of much that the police already knew and tormented by four hours of questioning which revealed terrifying glimpses of how much they did know—Jessie embarked upon the first of her statements. It began with a flat denial that she had seen Jess M'Pherson at all on the Friday night.

Taken straight through, in a series of (rather jerky) declarations, these statements by suspects make misleading reading. We find ourselves confronted with a close-woven web of lies, truths and evasions, apparently thought out in advance and deliberately put forward; the mind boggles at the guile which could prepare and carry through so complicated a manœuvre, countering every foreseen exigency with unlovely cunning. To understand their

81

true import, one must abandon this notion of a preconceived explanation put forward in one piece; and visualise instead the slow, harrowing, mounting tension of question and answer, question and answer—a covering lie or two thought up in advance perhaps, a frantic effort to mix lies in with the provable truth—but on the whole an impromptu effort to meet each question as it comes with an answer which will not cancel out other answers, which in itself is not open to be disproved. No terror so dreadful to witness as the turning, twisting terror of the hunted hare; no ordeal more harrowing than the turning and twisting under these first revealing questionings, of the suspect who has something to hide.

Jessie M'Lachlan had a great deal to hide.

She admitted, of course, that she had known Jess M'Pherson well; they had been close friends for the past six or seven years. But, she said, she had not seen her since the Saturday evening six days before the murder: June 28. She, Jessie, had been at Sandyford Place the night before that, going round by the back garden gate, and had talked over Jess M'Pherson's plan for emigrating—to New Zealand, Jessie said in her statement; elsewhere, Australia is mentioned. Jessie had promised to get a schedule from the emigration society in Jamaica Street and next evening Jess came round to see if she had got it—which, in fact, she hadn't.

This was plain enough sailing (though not to the Antipodes); and Elizabeth Brownlie next door could confirm having seen Jess admit a woman at the back door of Sandyford Place one night some time before the murder—she thought it was more like a fortnight before and that she had a man with her, but it is not of importance. Jess had remarked to Elizabeth that that auld deevil was jist awa' tae his bed. ('Did you understand the "old devil" to refer to old Mr Fleming?' asked Jessie's counsel at the trial. 'I suppose we all understand that,' remarked the judge, sourly. His Lordship was notably 'for' old Mr Fleming.)

Anyway, Jess had come round to the Broomielaw on that Saturday, June 28; and that was the last time Jessie had seen her.

'Were you in or near Mr Fleming's house on the evening of Friday, the fourth of this month, July?'

'No,' said Jessie.

'Or on the morning of the next day, Saturday?'

82

'No,' said Jessie.

'Did you see Jess M'Pherson on that night, or that morning? Were you concerned in assaulting or murdering her? Were you concerned in stealing silver plate from M'Pherson's house on said night or said morning. . . .?'

No, no, no, said Jessie.

What was she doing then on said Friday night; what were her movements. . . :?

On said Friday, said Jessie, she was at home all day until seven in the evening, when she went out on some business about her rent; but the factor was not home. And then at ten o'clock— here she would begin to walk warily—she went out with her friend Mrs Fraser and saw her home as far as the Gushet House in Anderston. . . .

'And then?'

Well, and then she had intended to call in at the house of James M'Gregor, a friend of her husband's (to enquire after the sick child). . . .

'Did you go there?'

No, she had changed her mind. One can imagine the inward shiver of terror as she veered away from the major danger point. 'I returned home.'

'By which streets?'

'By way of Argyle Street, James Watt Street and Broomielaw.'

'What time did you get home?'

Even this simple story, which she probably *had* decided upon in advance, showed her as a poor liar. 'A quarter-past eleven,' she said; but from the Gushet House to the Broomielaw was a ten-minutes' walk and even allowing for her farewells to Mrs Fraser and the children, she should have been home by at any rate half-past ten.

The police by now had talked to Mrs Campbell: they knew all about the key. They knew that Mrs Campbell had not admitted Jessie at a quarter-past eleven that night. 'How did you let your-self in?'

There could be no rational answer. She simply lied blindly. 'By means of a check lock key.'

'Where did you get the key?'

'I had it with me. It's one of the keys from the cupboard in the passage; there are two keys to the cupboard. . . .'

'Did you see anyone that evening?'

John M'Donald, said Jessie, had been going up the stairs ahead of her. He had stayed in only a minute and then gone off out again. (John M'Donald was Mrs Campbell's lodger; by the time this fib came before the Court, most conveniently absent, in a place described by Mrs Campbell as Karashae; but at any rate in the East Indies, and out of contradiction's way.)

And she had gone straight to bed, without seeing Mrs Campbell, and half an hour later had heard Mrs Campbell open the door to John M'Donald (but that would have been nearly midnight, and Mrs Campbell's evidence was that M'Donald came in and went to bed at eleven). And she, Jessie, had remained in bed all night, with her little boy; and sometime before eight next morning had got up and dressed and popped round the corner to get some coals from the house of an old woman in West College Street; and, said Jessie, now feverishly elaborating, had come back with a large basket containing the coals over which she had draped a piece of old carpet which she had taken out with her. Mrs Campbell had not seen her go out, but she was up and let her in when she got back.

'Why—if you had a check key?'

'I had forgotten to take the check key with me,' said poor Jessie.

At five o'clock that morning, Mrs Campbell had told them, she had been wakened by the child's crying and gone in and dressed him and put him to bed again. But no, said Jessie; this must have happened during the quarter of an hour—at about eight—while she had been out for the coals.

Very well. And then?

She had given him breakfast and stayed in her room with him till about noon.

And then?

Well, and then—and then she had gone round to the pawn office of Mr Lundie in East Clyde Street. . . .

What for?

'To pawn something,' said Jessie, wretchedly. 'To pawn some silver plate.'

How their hearts must have leapt!—Andrew Strathern, Sheriff-Substitute, and all his merry men. 'What silver plate?'

She was coming to a part of her story now that definitely had been prepared. She said: 'I received it from old Mr James

84

Fleming.' Mr James Fleming was at this time in the custody of the police.

Under what circumstances?

She recited her piece. She had received the plate from him on the evening before the murder, Friday. 'He came to my house about a quarter-past eight that evening and I let him in and took him into our parlour. He carried a parcel wrapped tightly up in a white cloth, and laid it down on the table. He asked me if I would go a message for him, and he would pay me well for it. I asked him what it was and he said he wanted me to pawn some silver plate which was in the parcel. I said the pawnbroker would know the plate did not belong to me. He said I was to say it was rent I had to pay. I asked what name I would give as a pledger and if I would give Mr John Fleming's name and he said no, not to put down Mr Fleming's name, as it would be in the directory. I then said, "What name will I give?" and he said I was to give the name of Mary M'Kay or M'Donald, No. 5 or No. 35 St Vincent Street, and that I was to seek three pounds ten upon the plate, or as much as I could get. He said he was short of money and had to go to the Highlands, and did not like to lift money out of the bank.' She had agreed to pawn the plate and he had gone off, saying he would see her again the next afternoon.

Very well. Now, had anyone else been present at this conversation? Had anyone seen Mr Fleming at the house?

No, they had been alone together, said Jessie. Mrs Campbell had been at home, but might well not have seen him.

'So you went to the pawn?'

She had gone to the pawn. 'It was then between twelve and one o'clock on the Saturday. I laid down the parcel, rolled up, as old Mr Fleming had given it to me. The pawnbroker's young man who attended me opened down the parcel and then it was I saw for the first time what it contained.' The young man had offered her more than the three pounds ten, and she had said she would take as much as he could give her, 'as the articles would not lie long in pawn.' She had said the money was for rent; and gave the name of Mary M'Kay or Mary M'Donald 'as old Fleming had told me.' 'I got the money and a pawn ticket and left the silver plate in the same cover which old Fleming had brought the articles in. . . .'

And so on. She had recognised the articles, she said, having known them when she worked in the Fleming household. They were shown her and she identified them. She returned straight home from the pawn office and was there at about a quarter-past one.

And then what?

The interlude at the pawnbroker's had been a little respite when she could stick to facts uncomplicated by part untruths. Now poor Jessie must start fabricating again. She even threw in a little embellishing detail. 'I remained in the house and at about a quarter to three old Fleming came there. I was at the moment cleaning the brasses of the door and he and I turned into the parlour.' She had explained that she had got more for the silver than he had expected; and she handed over the money—six pounds, fifteen shillings—and the pawn ticket. 'He thereupon offered me five pounds for having done the message and not to mention it to any person. I told him that five pounds was too much for me and I took four pounds from him. He repeated that I was to tell no one of what I had done for him in case it would come to his son's ears; and that a pound or two would do him when he was away in the Highlands. On this Fleming left the house.'

He must have reflected rather ruefully as he went that he had been to a great deal of trouble and put himself in a very awkward position—all for thirty-five shillings; and even that was a lot more than he had been prepared to retain.

So Jessie had gone off to Mr Caldwell, the factor, arriving there about four o'clock; and paid over the whole of the money Mr Fleming had given her.

'I am shown a man,' the declaration adds at this point, with apparent insouciance, 'who calls himself James Fleming, and I declare and identify that man as the person who gave me said silver plate on said Friday, and to whom I gave the money and pawn ticket on the Saturday.'

With what fearful eyes must they have gazed upon one another, those two: suddenly confronted in that bleak and menacing place, both under the threat of a penalty of death, both fighting for safety through the webs of their falsehoods, each at the other's expense . . . *Ecce homo*! 'I am shown the man. . . .'

Perhaps after this encounter Jessie felt that she could not use old Fleming's ill-gotten money for her rent, even in fancy; for she amended and said she had had money enough of her own to have paid the rent anyway: if she had seen the factor on the Friday, she could have paid it then, she had five pounds ten of her own in the house which she had got from her brother 'in the end of May last'. She went off into details of money her brother had given her in the past. . . .

'On the Friday night, when you went out to convey Mrs Fraser as far as the Gushet House—what were you wearing?'

'I was dressed in a brown merino dress with three large flounces, a large light-grey cloth cloak and a brown velvet bonnet.'

'Where are they now?'

She had taken them next day to Mr Murray, the dryer's shop, said Jessie, to have the cloak cleaned; and had left the dress to be .dyed black. She had given her own name. 'I took the velvet off the frame of the said bonnet because it was old and I gave it to a salt and whiting girl at the door of my house on Tuesday last.'

This alas, is all we ever hear of the salt and whiting girl; and said bonnet vanishes as completely from our sight.

'Have you a brown merino dress without flounces?'

She must have searched her mind for what this question foreboded. She said at last that she had had one but she had given the skirt of it to her washerwoman, last summer.

'Did you open down the merino dress you left to be dyed?'

Whatever this may have meant, Jessie said that she had not.

'Is the washerwoman referred to, Mary Adams? And has she been in the habit of washing for you for the past three years? And did she call at your house on the afternoon or evening of Friday, July the fourth. . . ?'

'No,' said Jessie.

'You didn't see her on July the fourth——?'

'No,' said Jessie.

'—and ask her to come in and take care of your little boy, James, while you went and saw the late Jess M'Pherson on that Friday night?'

'No,' said Jessie.

'Does Mary Adams stay with a Mrs Rainny in Holm Street? And did you call at Mrs Rainny's house on Saturday, July the fifth. . . .?'

'Yes, that I did do,' said Jessie.

'Did you call there twice?'

'I called there once. I wanted Mrs Adams to go a message but she wasn't in and Mrs Rainny said that she would go the message. The message was to redeem a black and blue check poplin dress, which I have on now, as an under-dress. Mrs Rainny went and got it for me from the pawn.'

'What dress were you wearing at that time?'

'The brown dress,' said Jessie.

'But hadn't you taken the brown dress to be dyed?'

'Not at that time,' said Jessie; and indeed it was true that it was not till after the poplin had been redeemed that she had taken the brown dress to be dyed—only it hadn't been a dark brown dress with big flounces.

'Did you leave word for Mary Adams to call at your house?'

There's nothing they don't know, Jessie must have thought, wearily starting off on this new tack. Who could have dreamed that anyone would track down Mrs Rainny—who, after all, was only one's washerwoman's landlady—and winkle out all these details? She said that yes, she had left word; and Mrs Adams had come and she had given her two pounds to redeem some things from the pawn for her. And had come again next day and been given eleven shillings to redeem some further articles. 'I gave her no more money.'

'Have you two crinolines?'

'No, I haven't. I've got one.'

'At that time—Friday and Saturday—had you two crinolines?'

'Yes, but one was burnt on the Saturday, in an accident.'

'Where are the wires of that crinoline?'

'I gave them to Mary Adams.'

'Have you a black bonnet?—a new black bonnet?'

Yes, she had a new bonnet. She had bought a new bonnet on Wednesday last, the ninth, and paid four and six for it. 'I now see and identify the said bonnet,' acknowledged Jessie, confronted with her one poor little self-indulgence out of all this spending spree. It was 'in the same state as I purchased it'. (It must be admitted that in this respect it was somewhat remarkable; so many of the clothes which had passed through Jessie's hands since that Saturday had suffered considerable changes.)

'Has Mary Adams a young daughter named Sarah?'

She must have known what was coming; she must have known that Sarah had broken her undertaking 'to tell no person that she had been to the station.' She admitted that Mrs Adams had a daughter, Sarah.

'And did you on that Saturday send her with a trunk to the Hamilton railway?'

Jessie, who had blankly denied other undeniable facts, admitted this one.

'How was it addressed?'

'I addressed it with the name, "Mrs Bain, Hamilton; to lie till called for".'

'What was in it?'

Ah, that they couldn't know! And in fact they didn't. It was not till the following Thursday that P.C.s Stewart and Cooper collected the blood-stained clothes from the Tommy Linn park. The trunk had been empty, she said. She had intended to go up to Hamilton on the Saturday and stay for a day or two with a Mrs Shaw there, 'but who I, through mistake, understood was called Mrs Bain.' (Only Jessie, with her disposition to make use of kindly strangers, would have contemplated a day or two's visit to someone whose name she did not even know; and anyway, Mrs Shaw or Bain, by whatever name would have awaited her in vain, for she did not turn up on the Saturday as arranged, but went on the Tuesday instead 'and called at Mrs Shaw's house but found she was not within': enquiring the way, if we remember, of Master James Chassels; after having learnt from his mother—no doubt for the first time—of the existence of a Mrs Shaw.)

What then of said empty trunk?

She had got said trunk from Hamilton station on said day and returned home with it, reaching Glasgow about six o'clock that evening. Said trunk was now in her house—a leather trunk with a glazed cover (how did Jessie propose to produce said trunk?— we know that it was with Mr Cherry, the saddler, having its straps and hinges attended to. In fact Superintendent M'Call collected it from him the following day. It was certainly empty by then).

But why send an empty trunk to Hamilton, anyway?

'I meant the empty trunk to lie at the Glasgow station; but through some mistake of Sarah's——'

'That is the little girl, Adams?'

'The little girl, Adams—through some mistake of the little girl Adams, it had been sent on to Hamilton.'

'What was the use to you of an empty trunk?'

'I meant to have put my clothes in the trunk at the station,' said Jessie, 'because the little girl couldn't have carried the trunk and the clothes together.' That was a neat one!

'How then were you going to get your clothes to the trunk?'

'I carried them to the Glasgow station in a bag: a black leather bag. . . .'

'But the trunk had gone on to Hamilton?'

'Yes, so I took them in the black bag to Hamilton.'

The police at this time, as we have noted, did not know what had happened to the contents of the trunk. They dropped that line of enquiry for the moment and for some reason confronted her with two sheets: 'I am shown and identify as my property two sheets to which a sealed label is attached and which is docquetted and subscribed as relative hereto. My attention is called to the mark or impression of a key appearing on one of said sheets. I declare that the impression was made upwards of a twelvemonth ago, and while I resided in a house in Stobcross Street. . . .' If anything be needed to contradict an impression of a sustained narrative statement on the prisoner's part, it is these rolling sentences, so obviously police reported and compressed. They conclude rather touchingly: 'The impression is of the check key of the outer door of that house and was made by my child making water on it as it lay on the sheet, which left an impression of iron-mould on the sheet.' (The princess who had a pea put under her seven mattresses never thought of this form of reprisal.) Jessie's sister, Ann M'Intosh, could testify to the occurrence, she added. It seems unlikely that she was called on to do so, however, for the iron-mould impression played no part in the trial after all.

After this diversion, they returned to the empty trunk and to Mrs Shaw in Hamilton. The trunk, Jessie said, she had taken downstairs from her 'house' on the second floor to the cellar door at the foot of the stair, intending to send a boy with it to the station; but at that moment 'the girl Adams' had turned up and she had sent it with her. The trunk had not been in the cellar that day (whether it had or not seems of little significance). As to Mrs Shaw, her husband was cutter to a tailor in Hamilton and lived, Jessie thought, in Castle Street (unfortunately Mrs Chassels, when innocently supplying her with the name, had not added an address).

Confronted with the chemise and flannel petticoat she had been wearing on admission to prison, she identified them as her own and made the following rather muddling statement: 'I put on said chemise and petticoat on the evening of July the third. I had two chemises, but one of which I have since put on; that now shown me I have torn up, having been destroyed by my child. I had no flannel petticoat except that now shown me. I washed it on Wednesday, the day before I put it on. All which,' she adds abruptly, 'I declare to be the truth.' It may have been the truth, but it is difficult to follow. She presumably meant that she had washed her chemise and petticoat and put them on clean on the Thursday, and worn the same until now, the following Monday week (from the amount of time Mary Adams spent at the Broomielaw washing, however, Jessie was particular about cleanliness). How the chemise 'now shown me' can have been 'the one I have torn up, having been destroyed by my child', one doesn't quite see. Master M'Lachlan seems to have been a destructive small boy in the matter of his mother's clothing. But perhaps it all happened in the one apocryphal holocaust where the crinolined petticoat was also destroyed.

She adds, further, that she had still owed Jess M'Pherson the sum of twenty-five shillings for groceries, a debt hanging over from the time two years ago when Jess had had her shop; but Jess had said not to return it, because she had always meant to give a present to the baby—so to buy something for him with it instead. (Had Jessie remembered this when she bought the little bonnet for him that Mrs Campbell had seen the day after Jess died?)

And now the confrontations came thick and fast. 'On being shown a black shawl or plaid—that shawl or plaid is not my property and I never had it in my possession and I did not leave it at Murray's (the dyer) before mentioned, to be dipped in black dye, on Monday last, the seventh July current, nor did I send it.' Well, that seems true enough; in court Miss M'Crone of Murray's testified only to a grey cloak for cleaning and a brown dress to

91

be dyed—Jessie had gone away after arranging for the cloak to be dyed, and returned wearing a black plaid and handed over the cloak; and that evening showed a black plaid to Mrs Campbell and told her she had bought it for three or four shillings. Was there some confusion here? The grey cloak, now cleaned, she acknowledged, though it had not been in two pieces when she left it at Murray's—this also was true, for she had gone there wearing it. And she admitted the brown dress, now dyed black, but 'its flounces were wanting'. She denied giving a false name—M'Donald—to the dyer. She had received a ticket for the garments which she supposed was somewhere about the house. And finally, 'I dyed said dress black to get further use out of it as, in its brown state, it was a good deal soiled and faded. And this I also declare to be truth.'

CHAPTER TEN

So the first long, frightening day was over. She had heard, very likely, of her husband having been set free; but with what an anxious heart for the safety of her delicate boy, with what terrors for her own predicament, must she have dragged herself wearily to her prison cell. It was a new cell to her: she arrived there—it was almost seven o'clock—to find herself sharing it with two women, thieves, who were to be her companions day and night for the next eight weeks. These were Agnes Christie (or Wardrope) and Catherine Fairley, and they seem to have liked Jessie, as everyone always did—very different in character and station though she doubtless was. She looked very sad, Agnes Christie said, and very depressed. 'According to custom among the prisoners', they asked her what she had been committed for. 'You've heard about the murder in Sandyford Place?' she said, 'about the old man killing his servant? It's on the same matter.' 'Are you in for that?' asked Agnes Christie, astonished. Jessie doubtless looked to her, as she must have looked to anyone, an unlikely person to have literally hacked another woman to death. 'Oh no, Mr Fleming's in for that,' said Jessie. She had been a servant in the house for two years, she explained, and went on to tell the story of the old man having come round with the silver for her to pawn—adding, however, that he had kept the whole of the six pounds fifteen and given her nothing to recompense her for her trouble—a departure from the story she had earlier that day told the Sheriff Substitute, which perhaps in retrospect seemed to her to have sounded pretty fishy. But now, she said, old Fleming was denying having given her the plate or, indeed, ever having known her at all; he had set a trap for her and so she had been sent to prison. She declared herself innocent of the murder; she had been nowhere near Sandyford Place that night. She neither suggested nor denied in these conversations that old Fleming had killed poor Jess; she said only that she herself had not. 'She was not very communicative,' added Miss Christie; but there doesn't really seem much to complain of in that respect, at any rate at this stage.

To all this information the ladies Christie and Fairley appended 'their mark'.

James M'Lachlan, while his sad wife slept uneasily in her close prison cell, was thinking things over. Their joint apprehension had doubtless been a fearful shock to him; he could not know that the authorities had every intention of immediately releasing him again. That he must eventually be safe, of course, was certain —he could produce any amount of proof that he had been far away across the seas at the time of the murder—and indeed upon this proof he had now been set free. But as we know, Jessie had certainly been less than frank with him, and he must have been staggered to find her—let alone himself—so deeply involved. And there remained the matter of the black japanned box. He had, as we also know, got back the box from Ayr station, where she had sent it 'to lie till called for', and taken it to his sister, Mrs Reid, in Greenock. He said later and Jessie also said that she had told him that Jess had sent her some things to get cleaned and altered for her, and she was afraid of these being found in her possession, but we can't know just how clear she had really made it all, and it may well be that, when he opened the box and spread the contents on his sister's bed, this was the first he knew of all it really contained. He must at any rate have been bewildered by the whole menacing business and very much frightened—for Jessie, no doubt, but for himself as well and for his child and for all concerned with them. He had got his sister to pack the stuff away in a drawer, and there it remained till he was released from prison, having so far said nothing about it. He arrived at Mrs Reid's that night in a state of 'dreadful agitation' and they talked it all over—she said afterwards, and it isn't hard to believe, that her own advice was that he should give the things up to the police. He had three other sisters living in Greenock, all of whom must by now have known about Jessie, and they probably didn't sit back either in companionable silence. At any rate, he spent 'a night of agonising suspense', torn, he said, between love and pity for his wife and his sense of duty—he said nothing about his sense of personal preservation. Next morning he arose with his mind decided: he would give the box up, he said to his sister, and give himself up too. The

94

clothes were packed back, a porter named Donald Laurie was summoned, and the box went off on its travels again. It was addressed this time to 'Mr Thomson, County Buildings, Glasgow'. But before it ever got to County Buildings it was collected—there was fourpence to pay on it—from Bridge Street Station.

It was collected, as we know, by Superintendent M'Call; for James M'Lachlan had decided to put duty first.

The box contained—not at all to the astonishment of the authorities—a black watered silk gown, a black silk polka, a 'changing-coloured' silk dress, a black silk velvet cloak and a broadcloth cloak. Counsel at the trial got a little tied up with the changing-coloured dress; it just looked brown to him. But Superintendent M'Call said firmly that it had been described as changing-coloured to him; and anyway, that was the dress. Counsel, however, continued to refer to it bleakly as brown.

All the dresses in the box had belonged to Jess M'Pherson. A former fellow-servant who, just to complicate matters, was also called Mrs M'Lachlan, recognised them; and another, Mary Downie, who had been a close friend of Jess for nine years, the same friend who had opened the grocery shop with her, knew them all well. She had been with Jess when she bought the black watered silk, she knew when and where the others had been purchased. (Sad little echo of those happy shopping expeditions with the savings from £25 a year to be spent!) Jess M'Pherson, we know, had been 'tasteful in dress'.

All the clothes had been kept in the chest in the dead woman's room: the chest that had been found almost empty, 'raked through with a bloody hand.'

The Fiscal had Jessie up for questioning again.

She was brought from the prison to the County Buildings by cab, and a struggling mob jostled to peer in at the pale face, suddenly grown so careworn and thin. It was said that when these crowds gathered James M'Lachlan wandered among them to catch a glimpse of his wife and to hear the arguments for and against her: he would be on the spot, he had just come out of County Buildings himself, having informed against her. What must his feelings have been, watching the slender figure hustled in to be questioned for hours over those stolen clothes which he himself had delivered into the hands of her accusers? It is impossible to believe that there was not some anxiety for his own safety in whatever mixture of emotions impelled him to this act. Yet— who can judge the human heart? We can't know what pressure was brought to bear on him by that large, rather oppressive family of his. The family conclaves must have been pretty formidable.

Jessie knew nothing of the discovery of the black japanned box. She thought it was still the trunk they were asking about, and she now filled in a few details of yesterday's story. When she got to Hamilton on that Tuesday, the day after the murder was discovered, she elaborated, she had gone to a shop to enquire for Mrs Bain, with whom she was to stay, and had asked the woman in the shop for some tea and ham and eggs, and at the same time had arranged for a boy to go to the station with her and carry her trunk. She had found that the hinges of the trunk were broken, which must have happened on the journey for it hadn't been like that when she sent it off. On the way back the boy had stopped by the roadside, and she opened the trunk and put in the black bag in which she had carried her clothes from Glasgow—the trunk having been sent on to Hamilton through Sarah's error. But back at the shop, while she waited for her tea, she had taken the bag out of the trunk again as the trunk had to go to the menders, and, the bag being rather small, transferred the clothes to a kerchief and tied them up in that.

Why had she asked for her friend as Mrs Bain if the name was really Mrs Shaw?

Well, her friend had recently married, said Jessie, and she must have got the name wrong; when Mrs Chassels at the shop told her of a tailor's cutter called Shaw, she had decided to call on Mrs Shaw and see if she was her friend. The boy was to show her the way, which he did. . . .

'Did you go to Shaw's house?'

'Yes, but I found the door locked.'

'What time was this?'

'Between four and five o'clock.' She had told the boy to ask the saddler to return the mended trunk to his mother's shop, and she would collect it at the beginning of the following week: she would be up then to look for a room in Hamilton (Mrs Bain—Shaw having failed her) as she wanted to come there for her child's health and her own.

Alas, the air of Hamilton was to prove not very beneficial to Jessie after all.

'What was in the bundle wrapped up in the handkerchief?'

What was in the bundle? 'Some shirts of my husband's,' said Jessie desperately, 'and some baby clothes and my blue and black checked poplin dress. . . .'

'What happened to these things?'

'I brought them back with me to Glasgow.'

'In what?'

'In the black bag and the kerchief.'

'Where is the kerchief now?'

'This is it—the one I'm wearing round my neck,' said Jessie. But they knew very well that it was not, that it had been given to Mirrilees Chassels with instructions to get it hemmed. We can imagine the ironic triumph with which they made her take the kerchief from her neck and hand it over, then and there. '. . . the handkerchief I have round my neck, and now give up, is that in which I tied the clothes, and a sealed label is attached thereto, which is docquetted and subscribed as relative thereto.'

And so they sprang their trap. 'Is it not true that in fact you gave the handkerchief to a boy in Hamilton . . .?'

What was there to do—but to deny it blankly?

And now the questions followed thick and fast, some relevant, some not, so that you must answer them quickly, not appearing to have to think out your answers, never knowing, because you had not time to reflect, whether what you said would do harm or not: whether you had best tell the truth or lie. Had you two crinolines? I had two, as I said before, but one of them was burned. How long had you had the flannel petticoat you wore when you were apprehended? I had had it four years. Has it not been recently hemmed? I re-hemmed it after I washed it—both parts, top and bottom—a fortnight ago. How long had you had the shift you wore when you were apprehended? I've had it for six months. Ann gave it to me, my sister in Edinburgh. The coals you say you got on that Saturday morning—where did you get them? I got them from a woman. What woman? I think she's the wife of the man who keeps the coal depot. How much coal did you buy? Well—a quarter of a hundredweight. How much did you pay? I think it was three-halfpence farthing. Did you

97

borrow a pair of stockings from Mrs Campbell who lives in your house? Yes, I did; about two months ago. What became of them? I only wore them once, the day I borrowed them; then they got mixed up by mistake with my husband's socks. Where are they now? I suppose they're at home, or with his things aboard his ship. What boots have you? Have you none older than the ones you were wearing when you came here?' 'I had an old pair, the only pair I had for wearing. Where are they? I threw them out. When? On—on that Friday, July the fourth. Why? I was cleaning out my room: I threw them out with a lot of other rubbish. And bought a new pair? Yes; yes I bought a new pair (which I now see and identify, and a sealed label attached thereto is docquetted and subscribed as relative thereto).

On that evening, the Friday evening when Mrs Fraser came to your house, did you take a bottle out of Mrs Campbell's cupboard? Yes, I did, and went to the public-house and wanted a gill and a half of whisky, but the bottle was too small and one of the shopmen gave me a pint bottle to contain the whisky, and I left Mrs Campbell's bottle instead. The pint bottle was in our house when I was apprehended. . . .

(Ah yes, Jessie; but Mrs Fraser says it was rum you brought back in the bottle!)

Did the late Jess M'Pherson have a black watered silk dress?

Yes. Yes, she had.

And another dress of silk, a changing colour with flounces and with cotton cloth beneath?

Yes, she had.

And a velvet cloak, the front lined with blue silk? And a drab-coloured cloth cloak? And a black dyed harness plaid? And a black silk polka?

I don't know that she had a black silk polka.

Do you not know perfectly well that she had a black silk polka?

I think she told me she had a black silk polka.

But you never saw it?

No, I never saw it.

The other things, however, you did see?

Yes, the other things I did see.

How recently? When did you see them last?

I haven't seen them recently.

What none of them? None of these articles?

None of these articles; not recently.

Not in her possession?

No, not in her possession——

Or anywhere else?

—not in her possession or anywhere else.

Then what are these two silk dresses (having a sealed label attached), and what are these two cloaks (having a sealed label attached), and what is this piece of twilled cloth? And are they not Jessie M'Pherson's? And what is this black japanned box, with sealed label attached, and did you not despatch to Ayr on Tuesday or Wednesday, the eighth or ninth of this month, the said tin box, containing the said dresses, cloaks and plaid, wrapped in the said cotton cloth and addressed to Mrs Darnley, Ayr, to lie till called for . . .?

Did it flash through her mind then that James, her own husband, had betrayed her?

The answers that read so slick and coherently in fact were wild impromptu explanations, meeting each crisis as it came: had she had a prepared reply, she would not have denied recent knowledge of the clothes. Tricked into that falsehood and then confronted with police omniscience, she sought frantically to recover. The things had been sent to her by Jess, she said. On the Friday (little knowing she would have no further use for them!) Jess had given them to a little girl to take round to the Broomielaw—Jessie didn't know the name of the little girl, but it was the one who cleaned the knives at Sandyford Place. There was a message with them. . . .

What message? What about?

Well, about the clothes. 'Jess asked me to take the watered silk to Anderson's in Buchanan Street and get it dressed; and the changing-coloured silk to be opened down and dyed brown. And the cloth cloak to be dyed black——'

'Why?'

'She'd spoilt it by washing it.' She embarked on another of her rather pathetic embellishments, harking back, perhaps, to some past discussion. 'The black velvet cloak was to have a puffing of silk round the bottom to lengthen it, and which puffing Jess was afterwards to send down to me. . . .'

'And the black plaid?'

'The black plaid was to be re-dyed because it was not well done.'

'And you got said things—when?'

'On the Friday, about five o'clock, wrapped up in said cotton twilled cloth.'

'Did you take said things to the dyer in Buchanan Street?'

'No, I meant to take them on the Saturday, but I wasn't well enough.'

'On the Monday, then, or the Tuesday?'

'No; I couldn't, I had to stay at home with my child; I wasn't out at all on Monday or Tuesday. . . .''

But she had already admitted to being out on the Saturday, paying her rent, pawning the silver, going to Mrs Rainny's house with the errand about the blue and black poplin dress; had already admitted to the long day at Hamilton on the Tuesday—when, she now said, she hadn't been out of the house.

'*But these clothes have been found in the black japanned box, and your husband has given information about this box. . . .*'

So now she knew. 'Yes, I put them in the black box. When I heard of the murder——'

'When did you hear of the murder?'

'I heard of it on Tuesday, and next day I heard that some of her clothes were a-wanting and, having them in my possession, I got frightened; so I put them in the black bonnet-box and sent them up to Ayr. . . .'

'Addressed to Mrs Darnley?'

'Yes, because I knew Mrs Darnley and I could explain to her. I sent them to Ayr to be out of the way until I could see her and talk to her.'

'But you changed your mind?'

'Yes, on Thursday night I got frightened about them lying there where anyone might examine the box, and I told my husband about them and asked him to take them to Greenock, to his sister. He wanted me to go to the Fiscal's office and tell about them,' said Jessie loyally, turning the other cheek to his treachery, 'but I felt frightened.'

'Where did you get the black japanned box?'

She had bought it, she said, 'for general use'—just a Useful Box to put things in as Winnie the Pooh would have said?—and paid five and sixpence for it; and the sealed labels referred to in the foregoing, etcetera, etcetera: and all of which she declared to be the truth. . . .

And this also, commented Jno. Gemmel, Peter Morton, Bernard M'Laughlin, old Uncle Tom Cobley and all, was freely and voluntarily emitted by the therein designed Jessie M'Lachlan while in her sound and sober senses: and all the rest of it.

CHAPTER ELEVEN

And so the days went by. The world wagged on—a large Monkey or Baboon escaped from a sailor down at the docks and made a Frightful Attack upon a mother and child; the *Glasgow Herald* fulminated against the indiscriminate use of Turkish Baths; the Beautiful very Fast Sailing Clipper ship *Edouard et Julie,* newly coppered, was still actively Loading and would soon set sail for Singapore. In Paris an old gentleman who thought he was Robespierre was visited by a relative unaware of his peculiarity and, crying out 'He is the gendarme Metra, behind him is the coward Louis Bourdon!' jumped out of a window and killed himself. You could go by Cheap Midday Sail to Renfrew, Bowling, Greenock and Dunoon, fares for the round one shilling, steerage sixpence. . . .

On the Tuesday, Mrs Reid, James M'Lachlan's sister, who was closest to her brother and evidently devoted to him, decided to go to the Broomielaw and bring back his little boy, who all this time had presumably been still in the care of Mrs Campbell. But her brother met her in Glasgow and warned her not to go near the house; it was swarming with police, she'd only be arrested herself (for her part in harbouring the box of clothes?) and she had better go back home. So she returned to Greenock alone. And poor Jess M'Pherson was buried, up in the Sighthill Cemetery, with, despite all efforts to keep the time secret, a vast mob of people following her coffin out of curiosity—a tiny handful out of respect and love. It is said that her father, who till now had never owned her, turned up and tried to claim her possessions; but Jess was gone now, beyond petty greeds and resentments. Later on in the year a letter appeared in the Press. A stone was to be placed on her grave, 'Erected by Mary Downie in memory of Jessie M'Pherson, murdered at Sandyford Place, July 5th, 1862'; and the writer asked if the public might not like to subscribe to it. There is no record of any response, so perhaps poor Mary Downie paid the whole cost herself. She had been a great friend, as great a friend as Jessie

M'Lachlan. It was she who had set up with Jess the little grocery shop that failed because their hearts were too kind. She probably didn't mind, even if she did have to pay the whole.

By now, two weeks after the murder, interest in it was already at fever pitch, as it was to remain, with brief intervals, over almost a year. Crowds besieged the house in Sandyford Place, feeling on this side or that ran high. The newspapers, of course, were packed with information, correct or incorrect, with rumour and comment, reports and misreports of the doings and sayings of anyone however remotely connected with the case. The editors bribed the clerks at County Buildings, and their editors waylaid the witnesses at the Fiscal's hearings, which of course were held in secret, and bribed the clerks; full reports of the proceedings were published with editorial comment, biased according to which side the papers had chosen to uphold: it was all M'Lachlan *v.* Fleming. So flagrant were these breaches of official confidence and so biased the comment, that the Sheriff of Lanarkshire had to write round to the editors begging them to refrain from further notice of the case, otherwise the accused would not get a fair trial. 'Some people,' writes Mr Roughead, 'treated the "wretched woman" already as a convicted murderess, while shedding tears of ink over the unmerited sufferings of virtuous Mr Fleming; others clamoured for his blood and canonised the prisoner. One journal, being very certain that the rum bottle found in the house contained laudanum, insisted on an immediate analysis. A worse instance occurred with reference to certain superficial marks on the prisoner's hands, caused, as she explained and as the Crown doctors believed, by the bite of her own small dog. This paper knew better—"they had been inflicted by Jessie M'Pherson in her death struggle." ' These factions were led by two rival newspapers, the *Morning Journal* for the 'M'Lachlanites' and the *Glasgow Herald* for the 'Flemingites'. Had Jess M'Pherson been savagely slaughtered for the price of a few well-worn clothes and 'a handful of silver' by a delicate, gentle young woman, her closest friend—or by an old gentleman with no apparent possible motive, confessing to eighty-seven years? The puzzle 'was to disturb the peace of families and agitate a generation.'

In this atmosphere the Glasgow authorities took their first big decision; and a momentous one it was.

By Thursday, July 17, old Fleming had been in custody for

eight days, Jessie M'Lachlan for five. Jessie, as we know, had already made two lengthy statements, Mr Fleming also had been under examination, 'with the object' as the *Journal of Jurisprudence* would say 'of allowing him an opportunity to make some explanation of the circumstances which seemed to weigh upon him.' What explanation he made at this stage we are unable to discover; 'in Scotland,' Mr Roughead says, 'the secrets of a criminal investigation conducted by the Procurator-Fiscal (the official who collects evidence and reports to the Lord Advocate as Crown Prosecutor) are, unfortunately, inviolable.' Jessie's declarations, of course, are now no secret; they were duly, despite the arguments of her counsel as to the monstrous unfairness of their elicitation, produced in court.

The circumstances at this time certainly known to the Fiscal which would seem likely to have 'weighed upon' old Mr Fleming were these: that, having admittedly heard screams in the night and woken next morning to find Jess M'Pherson mysteriously absent and her door locked, he had lived in the house for three days and yet done nothing at all to try and trace her—though the key in the adjoining door fitted the lock of her room; that in all that time he had not mentioned to a soul that she was missing; and that, furthermore, in the basement, where he spent much of his time, there were evident signs of blood—and of blood-stained floors having been so recently washed as to be still damp on the Monday. They seem to have weighed upon him remarkably lightly. He had entered prison 'hale and hearty', and remained there very calm and declaring that the Lord would send light which would soon clear him. Nor was this confidence entirely misplaced.

The case against Jessie at this time was that she had admittedly started off that evening to see Jess M'Pherson; that she had pawned a quantity of silver missing from the house; that she was in posession of certain of the dead woman's clothes, some of which she had concealed, some of which she had altered, most of which she had lied about; and that two naked footprints in blood on the floor of the dead woman's room could have been made by her. And finally that up to the evening of the murder she was believed to have been short of money. . . .

Youth, albeit frail and delicate youth—or crabbed old age? Mr Sheriff Strathern and Jno. Gemmel, Procurator-Fiscal, 'proceeded to Edinburgh' and there held consultation with the Solicitor-

General and the Advocate-Depute. They came back to Glasgow and next morning the pro-Flemingite *Herald* was triumphantly jubilant. 'The old innocent' had been set free.

And this decision was momentous for this reason: had he been charged with Jessie, he could not have testified against her; he had been liberated so that he might do so and was now by Scots law—though this was later questioned in the House of Commons—immune from further prosecution. Let Jessie M'Lachlan be found innocent of the crime as her own child—as indeed she cried out in court that she was—James Fleming was no longer in danger from the law. The old hypocrite was free; his innocence, said the *Spectator*, a M'Lachlanite organ, assumed as an axiom by the law, and the object of the prosecution apparently not so much to prove Jessie guilty of the murder as to demonstrate that Mr Fleming had no concern with it whatever. . . .

What on earth can he have said in that secret examination as to 'the circumstances which seemed to weigh upon him'—and despite what his *Glasgow Herald* called the strongest prejudice and gross perversion of the facts against him—what on earth can he have found to say to persuade Jno. Gemmel and the rest of them to this abrupt and totally conclusive decision? Whatever it was, he must have forgotten it by the time he came into court; but of course, dear old innocent, it didn't matter by then. Not to him, anyway. Hale and hearty as ever, he was hustled out by a back entrance to avoid the crowds. Mr Fleming was free.

It is alleged that at about this time Jno. Gemmel paid a private visit to the Fleming family which lasted a very long time.

Jessie meanwhile, all unaware of what was going forward, continued to live out her weary days with Agnes Christie and Catherine Fairley in their prison cell; secure at least in the belief that the old man was in custody also, to bear the brunt of accusation. She knew all about the milk boy having called at the door—they supposed she had read it in the papers before she was brought to prison, said Agnes Christie—and the old man answering and saying they wanted no milk; and about 'the lad from the country' calling and being told on two days running that Jess was 'not in'; and she told them that shirts, a vest and a pair of trousers of the old man's had been found in his wardrobe, all stained with blood. Old Fleming had offered to marry Jess, she said, and 'put her in a house of three rooms and a kitchen'; but Jess had said that she was going to Australia, and the old man was spited of her wishing to go there and refusing to marry him—and that was the motive for his killing her. She was sorry for poor Jess—she had been a nice person and they had been on good friendly terms. . . .

But the prison life was telling on her. She could not eat. She was growing daily more thin and haggard; already a shadow of the woman who, pale but calm and steady (James M'Lachlan was said to have been far more visibly distressed) had surrendered to the police less than a week ago.

Up in Hamilton the two little girls had been talking and the police set off towards the Tommy Linn Park to investigate, P.C. Stewart taking with him 'a wee boy' whom he presumably thought fit companion in the macabre treasure hunt upon which they were embarked. With the wee boy's assistance, he found thrust away under the roots of a hedge the brown coburg dress, all torn to ribbons and with one sleeve missing; and under another hedge a flannel petticoat torn into thirteen blood-stained pieces, and under yet another, opposite, a wincey petticoat also torn into strips. P.C. Cooper, without the advantage of the wee boy's help, found only a single petticoat—in a field called Hollandbush, near Low Waters, where the stranger had called for her glass of whisky at the public-house. It was not until the following Monday, however, that Jessie was confronted with these trophies. The authorities had other things to think about. For this was the day—though they had not yet heard of the discoveries at Hamilton—that they had decided to set James Fleming free.

Five days later, the authorities having meanwhile happily plied their investigations in the light of these new discoveries, Jessie was hauled up again—for the third and last of her celebrated examinations.

This time, despite the reticence of the Fiscal, she was in some sort prepared. The prison grapevine had been at work and, while exercising on the green, Agnes Christie had heard that a bundle of bloody clothes, supposed to refer to the Sandyford murder, had been found in Hamilton. (There is never any mention of Jessie joining these exercisings on the green, which seems to suggest that her health prevented any exertion.) Back in their cell, Agnes Christie asked if Jessie had any acquaintances in Hamilton; even Miss Christie, it seems, was not unsuspicious and walked warily. Jessie said she had no friends there, but she had acquaintances, with whom, however, she kept up no correspondence; and enquired why she asked. 'Because a bundle of clothes has been found there,' said Agnes; on which 'she looked amazed and confused, but I did not put it to her whether she had placed the bundle at Hamilton and the conversation turned to another subject.' It would be fascinating to know what subject transcended this in immediate importance; and whether it was through lack of curiosity or through the merciful courtesies of one unfortunate to another that Agnes Christie was content to let it lie.

Mr Sheriff Strathern and his associates were naturally not so considerate. 'Compeared, Jessie M'Intosh or M'Lachlan, presently a prisoner in the Prison of Glasgow, and the declarations emitted by her in the presence of said Sheriff-Substitute on the 14th and 16th days of July current, being now read over to her, after being again judicially admonished, and being examined, declares and says—I adhere to said two declarations as being correct. And being now shown thirteen pieces of flannel, to which a label is attached; as also six pieces of wincey cloth, to which a label is attached; as also twenty pieces, or thereby, of merino to which a label is attached; and, being interrogated, declares—None of said articles now shown me belong to me and I never had any of them in my possession. I was not wearing a gown of the colour of the pieces of merino shown me on Friday the 4th July current. I am shown a piece of merino, apparently part of the sleeve of a gown, to which a label is attached. Declares that it is not the sleeve of any gown belonging to me that I know of. I had at one time a gown of the same colour as that sleeve, the skirt of which I gave to the Washerwoman, Black or Adams, as I have mentioned in a previous declaration. I never had a gown of the same colour except that one. The body of the gown was worn done, and I gave it away about a twelvemonth ago to a poor woman who came to my door; or perhaps, for I am not quite certain, I may have thrown it into the ashpit. The several labels above referred to are docquetted and subscribed as relative thereto. All which I declare to be the truth.

Signed: Jessie M'Lachlan.
Alexander Strathern.'

The foregoing declaration, etcetera, etcetera, was signed by P. Morton and Bernard M'Laughlin as usual, but Jno. Gemmel was replaced by William Hart, writer in Glasgow. Jessie must have quite missed Jno. from those merry meetings—of which, alas, there were to be no more.

It would be a clarification perhaps at this stage to trace the comings and goings of all these clothes and, stepping for a moment from the chronological order of events, foreshadow something of their significance. Shorn of Mrs M'Lachlan's denials and evasions, it is all a good deal more simple than at first it seems.

One could make a simple division perhaps—as Jessie herself did —between the small trunk which the little girl, Sarah Adams, saw being packed in the basement, and which she later carried for Mrs M'Lachlan to the Hamilton station, and the black japanned box which Jessie bought on the morning after the murder and sent off to Ayr.

The contents of the trunk, which were found scattered about the countryside by the Hamilton police, added up to three petticoats and a brown coburg dress—all blood-stained and all torn to shreds. One petticoat had belonged to the dead woman, the other two were Jessie's own—a thick woollen one made out of a blanket and designed to be worn over crinoline wires, and a wincey. The dress was her own dark brown coburg with the flounced skirt, which she had worn when she set out from the Broomielaw that Friday night. One sleeve was missing.

The black japanned box contained six garments, intact and in good order, which were found to be those missing from the chest in Jess M'Pherson's room—a silk cloak, a velvet cloak, a black silk dress and a brown 'changing-colour' silk dress, a silk 'polka' and a black plaid—all wrapped in a piece of cotton twill. The black japanned box is, of course, the one which Jessie bought on the Saturday morning after the murder. She left it at the shop, locked and labelled 'Mrs Darnley, Edinburgh, to lie till called for', promising to come back that afternoon. She did not in fact return till the middle of the following week, when the box was re-addressed 'Mrs Darnley, Ayr, to lie till called for', and sent off. It was reclaimed from Ayr station after her apprehension by her husband, James M'Lachlan, taken back to his sister's house in Greenock and there unpacked; later it was repacked and addressed, this time to 'Mr Thompson, County Buildings, Glasgow, to lie till called for', and once more sent on its way, and so came through James M'Lachlan's own confession into the hands of the police.

These then were the contents of the two boxes—Jessie's own clothes, torn and blood-stained, in the trunk; and the dead woman's best cloaks and dresses in the black japanned box.

There was further missing from Jess M'Pherson's room her everyday dress, a cinnamon brown merino, trimmed with blue; it was a cinnamon brown merino that Jessie was wearing when she arrived home on the morning after the murder. Later that day, having redeemed her blue and black shaded poplin, she changed into it and took the cinnamon merino to be dyed black. At the same time she arranged for her light grey cloak to be cleaned, went away for half an hour, returned wearing a black plaid and handed in the cloak. She showed Mrs Campbell the plaid a couple of nights afterwards and said she had bought it very cheap at three or four shillings.

The inference to be drawn from all this was only too plain. Wearing her light grey cloak and brown coburg dress, the accused went on that Friday evening to Sandyford Place, and there in the course of the night she murdered Jess M'Pherson and broke open the chest in her room and stole its contents—the two cloaks, the two silk dresses, and the polka and the black plaid. Finding her dress blood-stained, she changed into one of the dead woman's, the cinnamon brown, wrapped her own brown coburg in a bundle with the stolen clothes (including Jess M'Pherson's blood-stained petticoat perhaps by mistake) and took them all home. So much of her personal wardrobe was in pawn that she was obliged to continue wearing Jess M'Pherson's dress till she could redeem one of her own—the blue and black poplin. Having changed into this she sought to disguise the cinnamon merino by taking it to be dyed black; at the same time, lest it show traces of blood, she left her grey cloak to be cleaned, buying with her ill-gotten gains a black plaid to replace it. Her own blood-stained dress and petticoats and the dead woman's petticoat which she had brought home by mistake she tore to pieces—either with the idea of trying to dispose of them bit by bit or of disguising them lest they be discovered. She sent the rags off to Hamilton in the trunk and later reclaimed them and hid them under hedges in the countryside outside the town. A sleeve of her brown coburg, however, got left at home by mistake; it was later proved to match the dress found at

Hamilton. The covered crinoline wires of her woollen petticoat being also bloodstained, she tried to eliminate the marks by burning and, not aware perhaps that this had not entirely succeeded, gave the wires to Mrs Adams for the little girl Sarah, with a story of the wire having been pushed against the fire by her little boy.

It was a formidable case to have to answer.

CHAPTER TWELVE

In the week following that of her committal William Wilson, a lawyer—variously called in Scotland a writer, a procurator, a law agent or simply an agent—visited Jessie M'Lachlan in prison, and from then on represented her as her legal adviser, together with Mr Dixon and Mr Strachan, also Glasgow solicitors. Immediately upon Jessie's arrest she would be by law entitled to legal representation, but how this particular firm came to be chosen is not apparent. They were all three quite young men. Mr Wilson had been qualified only three years, Mr Dixon two, and Mr Strachan less than a year. Their average age was probably not more than thirty. Later many subscriptions were raised 'for her defence and escape'—there is no record of how or whether the money was used to this purpose.

Their consultations were held in a private room and Jessie's friends in the prison therefore knew nothing of what took place, except what she told them. After the first interview she said she had explained to Mr Wilson all about old Fleming bringing her the silver to pawn; but later she grew less talkative and said her lawyers had advised her not to discuss her case; indeed, she said on one occasion they had told her that but for her declarations made at the County Buildings before the Sheriff she wouldn't be still in prison. 'I wish,' added Jessie, 'that the County Buildings would take fire and be burned up, books and declarations and all.' She did not, in saying this, suggest that the declarations had been anything but the truth, but, said Agnes Christie and Catherine Fairley, she used to sit writing a great deal before the interviews, and she said she was trying to remember what she had said in the various statements. Agnes and Catherine were unable to say more positively what these anxious scribblings contained: like Sarah Adams, they couldn't read writing.

So things were a little less exciting for Agnes and Catherine till one day, about three weeks after Jessie's commitment, something occurred to jolt her out of her reticence. She learned that old Mr Fleming had been set at liberty.

Agnes Christie says it was she who gave Jessie this news, having learned of it herself that day on the exercise green. Jessie's lawyers, Messrs Wilson, Dixon and Strachan, say it was they who told her.

The position of these three gentlemen at the time was this: Mr Wilson was on the point of leaving the case and handing it over to his colleagues, and was already immersed in other business; Mr Strachan had only just come into it; Mr Dixon, when Jessie urgently wanted help, was the one she seems to have thought that she should turn to. Mr Dixon, alas! did not return this confidence; he had told her frankly that he did not believe her declarations before the Sheriff, and his general impression of the case had been that in fact she was guilty. Mr Wilson seems to have shared this opinion, for when later she wanted to 'tell him all about it' his immediate reaction was that she was going to make a confession.

They had seen her two or three times already; twice, at least, reiterating that (a) her statements were true and (b) all would come right in the end, for old Mr Fleming 'would surely clear her.' She did not say how, and the three lawyers maintained what must have been a rather chilling silence.

Why they had not told her long ago that the old man had been set free—for he had by now been at liberty for more than three weeks—one can't imagine. It was not until August 7, however, that (so he says), on her saying once again that Mr Fleming would clear her, Mr Dixon repeated what was then a popular rumour, that old Fleming denied knowing her at all; and told her that anyway he had been released. He says she expressed the greatest astonishment and said, 'Out, and left me here—I canna' believe it!' And Mr Wilson confirms this and adds that she questioned the prison matron, who, however, was prevented by the regulations from confirming or denying it.

It seems likely that these three busy men—who were afterwards all a little hazy as to the sequence of events—were not strictly accurate and that Agnes Christie, who had less to occupy her, was correct. What in fact happened probably went something like this: Agnes heard the news through the grapevine and came back and told Jessie; Jessie could not believe it, tried to get the wardress to confirm it (Agnes, too, says she did) and, failing, turned to her lawyers—probably introducing her doubts tentatively by a reference to the old man instead of asking flat out. This sequence would account for her astonishment when Agnes gave her the news and for her still being surprised when Mr Dixon repeated it: she simply had not believed up to then that it could be true. When at last she was convinced, Agnes says and Catherine Fairley confirms, she burst into tears and remained for the next two days in a mood of bitter depression. James Fleming was an old rascal, she said; he was an old murderer. It was he who had killed poor Jess, and now he had set a trap for her, for Jessie, and so the guilty was set free from prison and the innocent kept in. If she had had money, she said, she too would have been let go; but she still maintained that she would be freed at last.

Even now she fought against the facts. Ignorant and bewildered, chilled perhaps by their lack of genuine sympathy—for they privately believed her a cruel and violent murderer—she may have been suspicious even of her own counsellors. At all events, she now asked to see her husband and besought him to go and find out exactly what had happened. He confirmed the truth and on August 11, four days after Mr Dixon had told her of Mr Fleming's release, he called round at Mr Wilson's office and said that his wife would like to see Mr Dixon.

Mr Dixon and Mr Strachan were both out of town; one may think it was with something of a sigh that Mr Wilson went round late the next afternoon to the prison. (As has been said, he was at the point of retiring from active interest in the case.) In these unpromising circumstances she explained that she had not fully realised that old Mr Fleming was really exonerated and set free; but now that she knew it she could not rest till she had told her lawyers all her story. Mr Wilson, afraid that she was going to prejudice her case yet more by making a confession to him, told her outright that she had better not do so; if she did, she put her advisers in a very difficult position. She protested that she was not going to incriminate herself, and suggested that he should write down what she told him as he 'wouldn't be able to remember it all.' Mr Wilson preferred to rely upon his memory, and must have regretted it, for he got into something of a tangle when, six weeks later, it became urgently necessary for his credit as well as everyone else's that he should recollect exactly what had passed.

So Jessie settled down and recounted to him what has been described as one of the most extraordinary stories ever to be told in a court of law: the story of that night of July 4 at 17 Sandyford Place.

Mr Wilson was considerably shaken. The more he thought of it, the more circumstantial the story seemed and the more he thought that some of it at least must be true. In a state of 'suspense and perplexity' he went back to his office, and must have been thankful to discover that Mr Dixon had returned to town. He told Dixon what had happened; some of it sounded like lies, he said, but some of it sounded like the truth—he thought Mr Dixon ought to go and see the woman and get something down in writing. After all, it was he she had asked for in the first place. We can see Mr Wilson with another sigh, this time of relief, washing his hands from now on of Mrs M'Lachlan. If this was his intention, however, he was a bit previous; Jessie was to rise up again one day and make him look a bit of a muddler.

Mr Dixon whizzed off to the prison, probably in some small excitement, for here was a case which must have seemed pretty dead showing signs of life after all. Jessie once again recounted her story; as far as he could recall, it differed from what she had told Mr Wilson only in being rather more detailed. He scribbled it all down in pencil, in his tiny, close handwriting, on a folded double sheet of blue foolscap. He was to say later that, from the way she told it, he had every reason to believe it a spontaneous narrative and in no way made up of information derived from others. Neither he nor his co-agents, he solemnly affirmed, had given her advance information which might have helped her.

Nor could they have done so. The indictment had not yet been served, was not to be served till almost three weeks later; no one knew what evidence would be brought against her. They had so far examined very few witnesses in the case, and those mostly concerned with the leather trunk and the discovery of the blood-stained clothes. There seems to have been some attempt to identify Mary Adams, the washerwoman, as the woman who had been up in Hamilton. It was her child who had presented herself at the station with the leather trunk; she had been concerned with much of the pawning and redeeming of articles, she was in possession of the blood-stained crinoline hoops, and she and Sarah were in and out of the house in the Broomielaw and familiar with Mrs M'Lachlan's friends and affairs generally. She knew Jess M'Pherson well and had probably seen old Mr Fleming when he visited Jessie, as he now and again had done, at the Broomielaw; so she might quite conceivably have gained entry to Sandyford Place. Some more or less delicate probing and fencing went on. She was confronted with Mr Dunlop, who had sold the black bonnet-box, and by Aaron Wharton, who had handed over the box at Hamilton station to the woman and the boy, James Chassels; and finally with Mr and Mrs Gibson from the public-house at Low Waters. Mr Wilson and Mr Strachan, having heard a description of Mrs Adams and the description given by the Gibsons of the poor wanderer who had applied to them for half a glass of whisky on that hot afternoon in early July, had persuaded themselves that the Gibsons 'had Adams in their eye'. (But of course they hadn't; and, as has been said, Jessie, though she later admitted her peregrinations in Hamilton, always denied that this visit to the public-house had ever taken place.) They also had up Sarah Adams and questioned both mother and daughter, though Mr Dixon is careful to make the distinction that this was a skirmish to try to prove something against the Adams's and not a formal examination of them in regard to the prisoner; that is to say, they were not then asked for evidence as to Jessie's movements. Mrs Adams seems to have borne it all with fortitude, even consenting to having her foot measured, with a view to comparison with the bloody print in dead Jessie's room; but when Mr Wilson touched on the earlier case of M'Kay, where ten-year-old Sarah had told her tarradiddles, then the affronted mother 'got up in a passion' and refused thenceforward to answer any more questions.

Apart, therefore, from these brief encounters and from newspaper reports and general talk among the police, the lawyers at this stage knew next to nothing themselves; so, the inference went, even had they wanted to, they couldn't have prompted Jessie. And, indeed, why should they want to? Till she made her statement, they believed her in their hearts to be guilty of atrocious murder; and though they were, as her advisers, concerned to present her case in the best light possible, this is a different matter from seeking by fraudulent means to pervert the ends of justice on her behalf. In the prevailing spirit of the times regarding the case they were obliged to protest their honesty; but at this distance we may almost certainly simply and absolutely accept their word, backed up as it was by the facts. The prisoner made her statement in such a way as to convince them—prejudiced as they were—that she made it untaught and spontaneously; and they themselves contributed nothing to it, if only because they could not.

So for the second time Jessie told her story; and we can picture Mr Dixon sitting when she was done staring down at those tiny scribbled, close lines on the blue fold of paper, staring into the face of the woman before him, and staring at the paper again. He had perhaps been sceptical of Mr Wilson's report—Mr Wilson was, in part at least, sceptical himself. Now—he had heard Jessie herself tell the story. He had arrived still believing her guilty; now he was confounded—he did not know *what* to think.

He left her and went back to Mr Wilson. Mr Wilson, as we know, had washed his hands of M'Lachlan, and he was very busy —with other affairs. Mr Dixon began to read out the statement, but it seemed to Mr Wilson very long and minute, and when there came a merciful interruption he said just to leave it and he'd read it over some time for himself. But when he and his clerk came to look at the pencilled notes they found the writing so small and so close that really, said the clerk, it looked as though it were the Lord's Prayer written on a sixpence. But it was only Jessie M'Lachlan's prayer, written in a prison; and Mr Wilson never did get around to reading it, but was content to have it collected by Mr Strachan the next day—or it may have been Mr Dixon, he couldn't remember—and in future just to hear snatches of their ceaseless discussions on the subject. And anyway they—Strachan and Dixon—were all for dashing here, there and everywhere making enquiries, while he was for refraining from interference till the Fiscal had concluded his own investigations.

It was Mr Strachan, in fact, who had collected the notes from Mr Wilson's office. Mr Dixon had gone round to see him the morning after his interview with Jessie and had told him of her latest 'extraordinary statement'. Mr Strachan read through the notes with the greatest care; but now a division arose in turn between him and Mr Dixon. Dixon thought they should place the statement immediately as a fourth Declaration before the Sheriff; Mr Strachan thought they should probe about first and see how vulnerable it might prove to investigation. Mr Dixon had so far been the Doubting Thomas; now all was changed. But then Mr Strachan hadn't, like Mr Dixon, had the advantage of hearing Jessie herself tell the story.

By this time, however, Mr Strachan whether he believed in

Jessie or not, was infected with Dixon's new-born enthusiasm. They had another long consultation next day, but still couldn't agree. Strachan was going to the theatre that night, but he made up his mind to call round on Dixon afterwards and go on with the argument and, meeting Mr Gordon Smith, a fellow lawyer, at the theatre, he confided the whole story and persuaded him to come along too. Mr Dixon was out but they walked about the streets for two hours talking and talking, and at midnight tried again. This time Mr Dixon was at home and they all sat up till four o'clock in the morning in deep consultation. Mr Dixon had by now laboriously traced over his pencilled notes in ink. One would have thought it less trouble to have simply made a fresh copy of them, and so at least have had two—the first remained for a long time the only one, and for a fortnight at least was just carried round in Mr Dixon's pocket; nor was it so valuable as an original but that he chucked it away when at last they did get a copy.

Mr Gordon Smith's advice was that, as they couldn't be sure of getting corroboration of the particulars of the statement, it would for the present be dangerous to adopt it as a line of defence. (When, later, they found corroboration he was all for their going ahead and using it.) Still not content, Mr Strachan further canvassed the opinion of a Mr Galbraith, a procurator of the Court, 'standing high in his profession'. Mr Galbraith supported his own contention, that it would be hazardous to use the statement until they were much more sure than they could be at present, that it was true. So Mr Dixon was in a minority of one and Mr Rutherfurd Clark, whom they now briefed as counsel for Mrs M'Lachlan's defence, left him still alone on the side of 'publish and be damned'.

Or perhaps it would be truer to say a minority of two: for the prisoner throughout was anxious and urgent that in some way or other the statement should be brought before the Court; and indeed on the last day of her trial, sent for Counsel and begged him whatever the outcome of the trial, to put her statement before the Court.

Andrew Rutherfurd Clark, Sheriff of Inverness, Senior Counsel for the defence in the case of Her Majesty's Advocate against Jessie M'Lachlan, was at that time still a young man, thirty-four years of age, keen, clever and conscientious, an accomplished scholar and conversationalist and a most able lawyer who was to become Solicitor-General and in due course be raised to the bench; and under a certain affectation of manner there was, we may deduce from a something about his whole conduct of the case, a true integrity and tenderness of heart. He entered with enthusiasm into the rising excitement of the two solicitors from Glasgow who arrived for their first consultation bearing the increasingly precious notes of their client's latest statement. It must have seemed to all of them that out of the mire of a sordid and brutish murder with gain as its object and with the verdict a foregone conclusion, had sprung a new and thrilling promise: that their client was after all quite possibly just what she seemed— a frightened and innocent woman with no knights to ride to her defence but their three selves. As the days and weeks passed, it becomes more and more apparently their passionate determination to see that the victim, trapped and helpless, should be recognised for what she was, and set forth free.

Mr Rutherfurd Clark will no doubt have been acquainted by the time the three met, with the outlines of the case against the accused. Mr Strachan read aloud from Mr Dixon's notes Jessie's answer to that case.

Mr Clark's first reaction was to insist on a thorough and immediate investigation all round, to try to get the facts of the statement corroborated.

Mr Dixon and Mr Strachan concentrated on the information offered by Donald M'Quarrie—of whom they had heard nothing up till now, except for a rumour in one of the papers that a milk-boy was declaring that he had seen old Fleming at the door of Sandyford Place early on the morning of the murder; and on enquiries of Mr Littlejohn who kept the liquor shop in North Street. Had Mr Littlejohn heard a knocking at his door on the Friday evening at a little past eleven, after he had closed the shop? Unfortunately Mr Littlejohn couldn't oblige; and by the very nature of the story she had told there could be no other witnesses in their client's defence. Only 'the heroic milk-boy' remained to stand in staunch 'support of Messrs Clark, Strachan and Dixon to the end.

So it had to be faced: they had the statement but it must stand almost totally uncorroborated.

Rutherfurd Clark grasped the nettle.

It was not until 1898 that a prisoner was permitted to give evidence in his own defence. This reform in the law has not necessarily proved a blessing to all so privileged. The witness box is a strangely revealing place—and yet to avoid it is to subject the accused to adverse comment; for if he be innocent, why not give evidence, what has he got to fear? In 1862, however, this doubtful benefit was not open to Jessie M'Lachlan. To use the statement, it would be necessary either to declare it in advance before the Sheriff and put it in with the earlier statements, or to read it after the verdict—if it was then necessary—when the prisoner was allowed, at last, to speak.

To put it in with the other statements must, of course, be to base the defence upon its contents. To keep it to the end meant simply a last-ditch appeal which would have to be dealt with by higher authorities; once it was declared, the verdict of the Court could not be altered by anything the prisoner might say.

The essence of the earlier statements had been that Jessie had not been to Sandyford Place at all on the night of the murder. The reader may deduce in advance that the new statement acknowledged it to be untrue. To base any defence upon such an admission, however, was fraught with danger. It would resolve itself simply into a struggle between Jessie and the old man—which had committed the murder? But she would by her own present admission be known to have made lying statements: *his* story had been accepted by the authorities, and so thoroughly as to have induced them to release him and put him outside further reach by the law. Her new version was impossible of corroboration: James Fleming was now free to testify that it was yet another pack of lies—had been set free for this very purpose. To succeed must entail over-setting this verdict-in-advance in the old man's favour: and even then, to lay the prisoner open to a charge of accessory before or after the fact. To fail would be to fail absolutely and utterly.

The only alternative was to go all out for a total acquittal on the score that it could not, on the evidence, be proved that the accused had been in the house that night.

But the statement, the wonderful statement?—which, after all, had convinced *them*—had shaken their presupposition of guilt, three hard-headed solicitors and now Andrew Rutherfurd Clark himself. . . .

We must keep it for the end, said Rutherfurd Clark, in case things go against us. And meanwhile, we must slant our whole case, our speeches, our examinations of witnesses, so as to lend support to it, if it has to be used at last.

Only Jessie herself, who knew nothing about the complications of the law, was clamorous to the end that the statement should be used. She had told so many frantic fibs which no one could be expected to believe: now here was the truth—or so magnificent a lie that she seemed to think everyone simply must believe it. But either way, she never lost faith. She discussed her case much less nowadays with her prison companions and never to either of them mentioned the statement or hinted for a moment that she hadn't told the truth when she said she was not at Sandyford Place that night. But she spent a lot of time writing on a slate and learning something by heart—she said it was a chapter of the Bible which she was going to recite at her trial—which chapter it was she did not say, nor what good such a course was supposed to be likely to do her; in all probability it was her statement, which she then thought she might have to speak to the Court herself. She said her agents had assured her that all would be well; that she was to keep herself very calm, and that when old Fleming was giving evidence against her, she was to rise up and confront him, saying, 'Mr Fleming, was it me that did the deed?' There would be no doubt, her agents had told her (said Jessie) that the old man would shudder at it and that it would be seen that he had done it.

But when the time came Mr Fleming was not so dramatically put to the test; and Jessie rather more prosaically concluded her forecast by inviting Agnes Christie to tea at the Broomielaw when they should both be seeing happier days.

CHAPTER THIRTEEN

The trial of Jessie M'Lachlan opened in the Old Court, Jail Square, during the Glasgow Autumn Circuit, on Wednesday, September 7, 1862, before the Honourable Lord Deas, one of the Lords Commissioners of Justiciary. The venue was highly prejudicial to the accused. There was enormous local excitement about the crime; it must be impossible to empanel an unbiased jury; such a trial should by every right of justice have been held in Edinburgh where it would have been presided over by the Lord Justice-Clerk and two Lords of Justiciary. As it was it was dealt with by a single, and hostile, judge. British justice blushes for the conduct both before and during the trial of the Jessie M'Lachlan case.

Lord Deas was at this time fifty-eight years of age: a man of 'dry looks and air'. Keen, cold, clever, 'incapable of display himself and a great enemy of all forms of judicial sham', he is described by a contemporary as the most striking personality in Scotland. Mr Roughead records a story of Lord Young who once remarked on the over-long prayer of the minister at the opening of the Court, 'I suppose when Deas is on circuit they think it right to call the Almighty's attention to the fact.' He had a very broad Doric accent which he made no attempt to soften. He called an issue an 'ishy', for example, and it is told of him that on one occasion after something of a turn-up with counsel, he asked irritably, 'Di ye ca' that an ishy?' 'No, I don't,' said counsel, 'I call it an issue.' His conduct of the case of Jessie M'Lachlan was to be described later by the leading English legal journal as 'putting his foot fiercely into one scale and kicking against the other.' At the receiving end was Mrs M'Lachlan. It was during her trial that his nickname became 'Lord Death'.

Counsel for the Crown were Mr Adam Gifford, Advocate Depute, and Mr Andrew Mure; Counsel for the Pannel (as the accused is called in Scotland) Mr Andrew Rutherfurd Clark, Mr Robert MacLean and Mr Adam Bannantyne. Her solicitors as we know were Mr Joseph Anthony Dixon, Champion of Champions, Mr John Strachan, second only to Mr Dixon, and Mr William M'Whirter Wilson—also ran.

The Old Court no longer stands and nowadays Jail Square is called Jocelyn Square. It had originally been intended as the Glasgow Municipal Buildings but was subsequently taken over, and housed not only the criminal courts but a prison as well. Built in 1814, it was in the Doric style with a double row of fluted columns with frieze and pediment over the splendid entrance. The court room itself was 'laid with great taste', lighted by seven great windows; like the present court it was built in the shape of a horseshoe, with a large circular table below the bench, where counsel sit, moving to a spot between the jury and the box to examine witnesses—the jury sits facing the box. The bench and table are of fine pale mahogany and a huge goblet of engraved glass stands in the centre of the table, holding, by tradition, the names of jurors to be picked out at random. The walls were ornamented with Ionic columns with appropriate frieze and cornice, 'the ceiling in stucco handsomely executed'—it must all have been a great comfort to Jessie. However, much attention had also been paid to the care and convenience of the prisoners in the jail which was housed behind the splendid façade. The authorities had visited the principal prisons in England and 'received many useful hints'. The cells were ten feet square, each with a window, and on every floor there was a w.c. which 'tends much to the accommodation and cleanliness of the prisoners'. The condemned cells, however, in one of which Jessie would be housed if she were convicted, faced inward on to a court and received their only light from its well. Let us hope she need not know that the court was paved with the flagstones, initialled and dated, which covered the graves of all those hanged in the square beyond. Still, she would see little of it. The cells were in the basement, made entirely of cast iron built round with stone, lit by a tiny barred window in the three-foot-thick wall and with no fourth wall but only heavy open iron bars. Much attention, however, the records assure us, was paid to the health and comfort of the Unfortunate. But their entrance in the West front was indescribably gloomy, compared with the lovely columned portico on Jail Square, with only 'a frieze executed in droved rustic work'—whatever that may have been. (The author was shown a short flight of steps and small doorway, said to be a remaining part of the old building, where the condemned were led out to execution. In the street outside, where this door, now half built up, was visible, a flight of starlings chittered and chattered as they do all over Glasgow: and a woman appeared, not very old and rather pretty, with a round, rosy face, and began to feed the birds. It was an odd and touching little incident, directly outside this terrible doorway that had known so much torment of terror and pain; until suddenly the little woman lifted up her head and began to sing, hopping about with a grotesque little dancing step. She was mad.)

In the great square beyond, nearly seventy men and women had so far been publicly hanged: and here Jessie M'Lachlan—it is incredible, but it is true—if she is found guilty will also be publicly hanged. For it is only 1862; and the last to die there in public was to be the infamous Dr Pritchard who was not executed till 1865. The gallows, or the 'wuddie' as it was familiarly called, were dismantled and kept handy in the vaults below the prison. ('Gang along up the wuddie, Donal',' an old woman is said to have urged her reluctant husband, 'and be hanged like a man and no anger the laird.') The hangings, of course, were the principal entertainment of the day; but Jail Square, or Jail Green, housed also the Bird and Dog Market, and the Glasgow July Fair was for a long time held there each summer. It had been prophesied by Alexander Peden that in the nineteenth century 'lions would be whelped on Glasgow Green' and when a lioness in Wombwell's Wild Beast Show did in fact give birth to twins, every auld wife in the city, it is said, paid her sixpence to see them.

There was something not very far removed from a wild beast show in Jail Square on each of the four days of Jessie M'Lachlan's trial. A wild mob surged, fought and struggled for entrance or for only a glimpse of the great ones going out and coming in. The court was crowded to bursting point. In the galleries was 'a preponderance of the fair sex' representing the inevitable fashionably dressed women inseparable from any newspaper account of a sensational trial; 'numberless gay bonnets nod' and the few gentlemen present are there possibly less from curiosity than from the need to protect their ladies (reports a gentleman). The newspapers held their breath in anticipation: even the advertisements that day are rather dull, though there is an agreeable propinquity in 'An experienced girl wanted', following very closely upon 'Two experienced Vice Men needed immediately'. But there are some splendid sailings, for Ceylon, San Francisco, Demerara, the Cape of Good Hope . . . The Carra Linn, Knight Templar, Henrietta, Maid of Orleans, Wolverine, Mountain Ash, Berbice, Alhambra spread wings of sail or are newly coppered and actively loading. . . .

And through gloomy basement corridors, Jessie is being brought to sit two hours waiting in a cell beneath the court.

Representatives of the press from all over Scotland—more than had ever before attended a Glasgow trial—were assembled: placed in the court, however, one of them acidly reports, in as suitable a position for seeing and hearing nothing, as could conceivably have been devised. If the acoustics were anything like those of the present courts, they may, indeed, well have had difficulty in hearing, and the soft Highland voices, often heavily accented, would not have made matters easier. It may be for this reason that their reports in so many details differ. (Rather than irritate the reader with innumerable alternatives, we have in the following account, chosen in each case the version most likely to be correct, or taken from the most reliable source, except of course where the alternatives materially affect 'the ishy'. The actual report of the evidence and speeches has been taken from that edited by Mr William Roughead in the Notable British Trials series; compiled by him with much care and toil from various sources. He notes that the reporting of old Mr Fleming's evidence in the vernacular is the only such instance he knows of.)

As the clock struck ten a blare of trumpets echoing through corridors and ante-rooms, heralded the approach of Lord Death. In the floor of the big dock, a trap door opened and the prisoner appeared, as though rising up out of some tomb to which, in too hasty anticipation of an adverse decision, she had been prematurely confined. The matron of the prison and a female turnkey attended her. She wore the lilac gown and little black shawl and the straw bonnet trimmed with white ribbons, a short black veil covering the upper part of her face. She was deathly pale and very thin and haggard after the long and anxious incarceration, the heart-rending separation from her delicate baby; but she was marvellously controlled, 'a rare fortitude', scribbled the reporters, 'magnificent resolution', 'an iron strength'. This outward calm she was to maintain throughout the four days, sitting quiet and still, looking down at her hands and, when obliged to face a witness, doing so frankly and steadily without any sign of shrinking.

Red robed, bewigged, the judge took his seat. The Sheriffs of Dunbartonshire, Lanarkshire and Renfrewshire were in attendance. The minister spoke a prayer beseeching the Almighty to grant that justice tempered with mercy might prevail in that court that day—as it transpired either God or Lord Deas was not listening, perhaps because his lordship had already made up his mind; but no one was to know that as yet. There were a few minutes of preliminary whispering and consultation, all eyes were on the ashen-faced woman in the dock. The clerk of the court gave the signal for the macer to read out the indictment.

The Indictment is a long and flourishing affair with some splendid bits of legal phrasing; accusing the Pannel that 'albeit by the laws of this and of every other well-governed realm, murder, as also theft, are crimes of an heinous nature and severely punishable; yet true it is, and of verity, that you, the said Jessie M'Intosh or M'Lachlan are guilty of the said crime of murder, of the said crime of theft, or of one or other of the said crimes, actor or art or part' inasmuch as she did wickedly and feloniously attack the said Jessie M'Pherson 'on the fourth or fifth day of July 1862 or on one or other of the days of that month or of June immediately preceding or of August immediately following'— they were taking no chances on any argument about the date: still, at least they got the year pinned down—'in or near the house or premises in or near Sandyford Place, in or near Glasgow, then and now, or lately, occupied by John Fleming accountant, now or lately residing there'—nor was there going to be a slip-up as to where the crime was committed; though one might have thought 'in or near Glasgow' was erring on the side of cautiousness. And that, having 'with an iron cleaver or chopper or other similar edged instrument, to the prosecutor unknown' struck and killed the victim, she 'farther had wickedly and feloniously stolen and theftuously taken away' a list of articles, to wit the silver found in Lundie's pawn and the seven articles of clothing belonging to the dead woman which had been left at Bridge Street Station in the black japanned box. 'All of which or part of which', concludes the indictment, 'being found proven or admitted by the Pannel's judicial confession, OUGHT to be punished with the pains of law to deter others from committing the like crimes in all time coming.'

The Pannel, in her lilac gown, her straw bonnet and her little thin black shawl—either showing no trace of agitation, or flushed with emotion according to which newspaper was reporting her—pleaded not guilty: and without prejudice to that plea specially pleaded that the murder alleged in the Indictment was committed by James Fleming, 'now or lately residing with John Fleming, accountant, in or near Sandyford Place, Glasgow.'

The jury, chosen after several rejections, three of which were upheld, were fifteen good men and true of Glasgow and the country round Glasgow: a commission agent, two grocers, a saddler, a ship's chandler, a brass founder, a coalmaster, a colour merchant, a cartwright, a farmer, a merchant and two dealers in spirits; and Messrs John Stalker and Alex. Phillips, occupations unknown or undeclared. We have the word of Lord Deas for it that the case received from them as great attention as ever he had seen paid by any jury. They were furthermore men of despatch. The trial had taken three days and a half, sitting from ten in the morning till nine at night, a total of nearly forty hours. They took just fifteen minutes to come to their verdict. And as has been said the verdict was both unanimous and unequivocal. There was no question of 'not proven.'

The opening of a murder trial is, by any reckoning, an extraordinary moment. A life has been taken, a man, woman or child lies dead. It is as though a stone has been thrown at the mirror of a life smashing it to pieces; as though those pieces, correctly reassembled, would mirror, not the life that has been taken, but the image of the murderer. Piece by piece, the broken bits are gathered together, a great heap of fragments to be placed before the court. Rightly juggled—this discarded, that retained, this displaced, changed about, found to fit in another corner altogether—they begin to form a recognisable reflection. By subtle readjustments here or there, each side seeks to dull or heighten a resemblance. The last piece in place, the judge holds up the patchwork mirror to the jury. Chipped, scratched, clouded, cracked-across, a piece here missing, a piece there not well-fitting—is there yet enough for you to say without reasonable doubt that here is a reflection of that man in the dock? If not—dismiss him: don't take any chances. But if you are reasonably sure—then this is the face, members of the jury, of a murderer. Just use your good sense, as ordinary people. Are you reasonably sure? It is for you to say. Yes or no? We will do all the rest.

Weeks, months, perhaps of patient assembling of the pieces of a giant patchwork that will take days to complete. And then— all of a sudden the moment has come and gone; almost before anyone noticed it, the first piece of the jigsaw has been placed on the board. It is the strangest mixture of excitement and anti-climax: not least to the quailing heart at the centre of it all. Guilty or innocent—for mistakes have been made before now— will this panel of men playing this fantastic game, declare that mirrored image to be my own?

In Scotland there is no opening address to the jury. The first piece in the game, Her Majesty's Advocate *v.* M'Lachlan, was thrown down therefore by the Sheriff-Substitute of Lanarkshire, Alexander Strathern. All he had to say was that 'shown declarations of the prisoner, dated 14th, 16th, and 21st July, these were emitted by her in my presence, freely and voluntarily, in her sound sober sense and after receiving the usual warning.' The Court seemed settling down into the jog-trot of its opening stages. But Mr Rutherfurd Clark was up on his feet, fighting to have this very first piece removed altogether from the board. Had not the prisoner's husband been apprehended also, on a warrant? Were not husband and wife included in the same charge? Was it not true that the husband had left Glasgow on the morning before the murder was committed and did not return till late the following week? And: *when had it come to be known to the Sheriff-Substitute that this was so?*

Mr Strathern 'could not answer that distinctly'. But a moment later, he did answer it at least fairly distinctly: he said he thought it was in the course of the husband's examination—which lasted something under an hour.

The examinations of the prisoners had been 'taken in the usual way'. The Procurator-Fiscal asked the questions 'as far as I allowed him, and I dictated the answers to a çlerk'. Mrs M'Lachlan was a second time examined, some articles having been found in the interval bearing on the case. 'The second examination was conducted in the same way as the first, but she

127

volunteered an explanation which I thought it right to take down.' It all sounded nice and smooth until Mr Clark pounced with his next question: at what stage was it made known to the prisoner that the articles had been found? Some introductory interrogatories were put first, admitted Mr Strathern, but these lasted only a few minutes.

They must have lasted, in fact, for at least two hours while poor Jessie painfully unfolded her gabble of lies about her movements up at Hamilton; they ended with her categorically denying, under questioning, that she had ever seen the articles—which at that moment the Sheriff-Substitute had in his keeping, in the black japanned box. Only then was she told that they had been found.

It was Jno. Gemmel's turn next. The Procurator-Fiscal came in for a pretty bad time, and wriggled most painfully on the hook of his knowledge or ignorance of James M'Lachlan's absence from Glasgow at the time of the murder. 'It was not known, though reported. . . .' 'We had no means of ascertaining it. . . .' 'I did not personally make enquiries after her husband but I got reports from some of the criminal officers. . . .'

'Had you not got reports from some of the criminal officers prior to the examination?'

'I may; and personally I made some investigation before he was examined.' (No one seems to have commented that he had just stated the exact contrary.) 'I had no reason to believe that he was out of town before that period.'

'Had you any reason to doubt it?'

'I cannot say that I had any reason to doubt it.'

The judge here intervened. 'Can you state whether in fact you doubted it or not?' But Jno. said no, he couldn't. He was not satisfied that M'Lachlan was out of town. 'It was stated by some persons in the house where the husband was. I had reason to doubt it, because I was not satisfied that he was out of town.'

Mr Clark: 'Did you not say that you had no reason to doubt it? Didn't you say so?'

Mr Gemmel: 'I think I did.'

Mr Clark: 'And now you say you had!'

Lord Deas wound the whole thing into a not very neat cocoon. Would it be correct, he asked Mr Gemmel, to take him down as having said: 'I heard he had been out of town from the morning of the fourth, and I had no reason to doubt he had been so. I was not satisfied it was true.' Jno. grasping eagerly at any form of words which would end this back-and-forth argument, said yes, it would.

Mr Clark asked a few more questions, got him tangled up as to when he had made enquiries at the ship's agent in Glasgow and finally let him go. He must have been considerably the worse for wear.

Mr John Fleming succeeded the Procurator-Fiscal in the box and gave evidence of his return from Dunoon and the discovery of the body, his own precipate flight from the house in search of help and comfort, his return with Dr Ebenezer Watson. 'He came with me and I took him downstairs and showed him the body. He put his finger on the hip and said, "Quite cold; has been dead for some time," and asked me if I had sent for the police.'

Mr Rutherfurd Clark's first questions showed clearly how the defence was to be conducted. They related entirely to old Mr Fleming. Did your father attend your office? Did he collect rents for you? Was this his occupation early in July, at the time of the murder? What was his usual state of health? What was his state of health when you left for Dunoon on Friday? What was his state of health when you returned on the Monday?

His father was quite well, said Mr Fleming. 'He was often ailing with cold, but he was quite well, I think, that morning. I think he was quite well when I returned on Monday.'

He described his first attempts to get through the pantry window and so into the area and in again at one of the bedroom windows: he had forgotten that those windows were barred. Then he had noticed the pantry key and tried that in the lock.

They came to the curious business of the key in the lock of the bedroom door.

Mr Clark: 'When you put the key into the lock did you press out any key inside?' 'I don't think so. The key went in freely; I didn't hear any key fall inside.'

'Have you always thought so?'

'I don't know how to answer that question.'

'I will tell you how to answer—have you expressed that opinion to anyone?'

Mr Fleming had expressed that opinion to P.C. Cameron and also to Dr Watson as they hurried back to the house (and to Chrystal the grocer too, Mr Clark reminded him, which was rather naughty, as Mr Chrystal was not called to give evidence and therefore should not have been quoted). Mr Fleming now denied it, however, or rather, in his eminently fair and honest way, simply reiterated, 'I don't think I did.' He could swear that the door was locked; but he really could not say whether or not there had been any key inside. Under re-examination by Mr Gifford, for the Prosecution, he repeated that he had seen no key of the bedroom door when he got into the room, and if there had been one, he thought he would probably have stepped on it. 'I was a good deal excited and if it is thought I said anything about finding a key inside the servant's bedroom door I must have been misunderstood. I really cannot recollect saying anything at all about it.' It is an odd little incident; but probably, in the end, Mr Fleming's own explanation is correct enough—he was over-excited and was misunderstood. There seems no earthly reason to suppose that in fact there *was* any key inside the lock. It would, of course, have been to old Fleming's advantage to have proved that there was: but his son certainly did not suspect him at this time, nor was he sufficiently calm to have made up this incident to protect the old man. And now that it might be a point in his favour, we find the son nevertheless honourably denying it.

The only way to get into the area, said Mr Fleming, in reply to Mr Clark, was by climbing over the railing, jumping down into the area and getting in through the pantry window. There was a padlock to the pantry window but it had not been in use for some time. There was a 'snib' upon it, but he couldn't remember whether or not it was fastened that day. The window opened quite easily.

A juror, apparently infected already by the judge's habit of asking what, from a reading of the trial, would appear to be largely unnecessary questions, here enquired whether it was possible for a person to get into the house by the window if they were to get over the railing. Lord Deas very properly pointed out that the witness had that moment said that it was.

He himself asked Mr Fleming, before they let him go, if he knew what his father's age was. 'I believe,' said John Fleming, 'that he was eighty-seven on the ninth of August last.'

And that in turn showed how the prosecution—in the capable hands of Lord Deas—was to be conducted.

John Fleming, junior, followed his father. In the course of his brief examination, the prosecution were assisted by no less than eleven questions from the bench, every one of which might safely have been left to counsel. Mr Rutherfurd Clark asked him only three questions. Two were about the 'smell' in the basement which had caused him to go down the passage and throw open the back door. But it was not a smell, said John, just a closeness.

Mr Clark: 'Was there any word of Jessie going away on the Friday?'

'No,' said John.

But that might make it look even odder that old Mr Fleming had apparently been ready to believe that she *had* gone. His lordship came to the rescue. 'Not that you heard of?'

'Not that I heard of,' agreed John, obediently.

Young Fleming stepped down; and—'nimbly', reported the *Morning Journal,* leading organ of the M'Lachlanites—old Fleming stepped up.

Sensation in court.

A drawing of him made in court shows a thin, rather bent old man, apparently using a stick to support himself; with a bald head, surrounded by a thick fringe of white hair and long white side-whiskers. His nose is high and thin with a tendency to 'nut-cracker' with his chin; his mouth is thin and his eye has a rather leery sideways look. There is nothing about the picture of doddering or senility, nothing to suggest a man of nearly ninety years—nothing, indeed, to suggest any great age, except for the stoop, the white hair and the suggestion of a stick. It must be added, however, that it was fashionable among the M'Lachlanites to believe him to be in fact seventy-eight and not the other way about, and the nasty, thin-lipped, sly face depicted would lead one to suppose that the drawing was made by an artist not too favourably inclined—a M'Lachlanite, perhaps, who would not go out of his way to make 'the auld devil' seem more frail— or any more attractive—than he really was. He does seem, never- theless, to have been pretty spry as he mounted the steps to the box and to have had all the appearance of excellent health and spirits. His conscience, at any rate, was in splendid condition. He had been visited by his pastor, the Reverend John Aikman, a few days earlier, who had had a long private interview with him. He had given, that gentleman later declared, precisely the same account of his actings during the crucial days as he gave the Court—the reader will judge in due course how possible this can have been—and had assured him that he had been praying away like anything. Mr Aikman accepted this as a matter of course. 'Ay, but yae prayer,' said the old man. Mr Aikman looked him sternly in the face (or searchingly in the face, he couldn't afterwards be sure which) and asked him what the prayer was. That God would strengthen his recollection, said old Mr Fleming, so that he could tell all he knew about this awfu' business; for really his memory was terrible, 'I lay things out of my hand the yae minute and forget them the next.' (No one else mentions this peculiarity; but Mr Fleming's faculties, hitherto remarkably good, had suddenly taken a turn for the worse all round—he had grown hard of hearing, taken to spectacles and now here is his memory growing treacherous.) Mr Aikman went on looking him sternly (or searchingly) in the face. 'But what about your conscience in this matter?' he suggested. Mr Fleming said that he had many sins to answer for but on this he was perfectly clear. 'Would you feel perfectly comfortable in your mind,' insisted Mr Aikman, 'if summoned from the witness box to that Judgement Bar where the secrets of the heart are known?' Mr Fleming drew himself up 'with manifest indignation and surprise' and said crisply, 'Perfectly, so far as that's concerned.'

Mr Aikman could hold out no longer. The impression produced upon his mind, he declared, was that the old gentleman looked with horror upon the murder but was entirely ignorant and therefore innocent of 'the circumstances attending the commission of the crime.'

Mr Fleming fortunately survived his ordeal in the witness box and it was not till several years later that he was called upon to account for himself before any bar higher than that over which Lord Deas now presided. Let us hope that when the time came, justice was tempered with as much mercy as was now showered upon him by a temporal judge.

He took the oath in a loud clear voice that could be heard distinctly all over the court.

Mr Gifford, prosecuting, came to the point at once. 'Mr Fleming—how old are you?'

'I was eighty-seven on the ninth of August last.'

'What is your employment?'

'Eh?' said the old gentleman. 'I'm a little dull o' hearing, sir.'

'We'll try to make you hear,' said Mr Gifford indulgently. 'How were you employed?'

The old man explained his work in his son's office; he was employed 'to be generally useful'. He lived with his son at Sandy-ford Place; he had lived there all the time his son had—two or three years. Yes, he knew Jessie M'Pherson.

'When did you know her?'

'She was a servant wi' Mr Fleming, and cam' back the second time. I first kent her when she cam' the first time to be a servant wi' my son.'

'How long ago is it since Jessie M'Pherson came to be a servant?'

There was no reply to this and Mr Gifford rephrased it. 'How long is it since she left?'

'She gaed to keep a bit shop for hersel'. It will be—my memory is no very guid; I can't tell you exactly. She gaed ony way, her and anither comrade, and took up a bit shop and sell't grocery goods. It's a few years ago. She cam' back again.'

'How long ago is that?'

'It's—let me see—a year ago.'

'In July last was your son residing part of his time at Dunoon?'

'Yes; he has a cottage there, and spent part of the week in Glasgow and part in Dunoon.'

'Who had charge of the house?'

'Jess M'Pherson. She had the whole charge.'

'The other servants were at Dunoon?'

'Yes; but there was anither servant at hame besides Jess. It was anither servant that assisted her in the kitchen.'

'Did she go with the other servants to Dunoon?'

'No, she is a witness here the day. I canna tell ye her name.'

'Martha M'Intyre?'

'I daursay yes.'

'Or is it Margaret M'Innes; which?'

There was again no answer; and the judge interrupted. 'No matter; she will tell you herself.'

There was some muddle here: Martha M'Intyre had in fact left the Flemings' service some months earlier, nor was any servant left except Jess in the house in Sandyford Place.

Mr Gifford resumed. Yes, the old man remembered the fourth of July last; yes, he had breakfasted at Sandyford Place, but he didna' recolleck whether his son had left for the office or not.

'Did Jessie M'Pherson serve you that morning?'

'Yes.'

'Where did you go upon that Friday?'

Mr Fleming did not answer him directly. He burst into a description, instead, of Jess M'Pherson's day and gabbled away until Mr Gifford had almost to beg him to stop. 'She had been thrang for three days wi' a washing, and she was finishin' the shirts and dressin' them that day——'

'What a clock——?'

'—and her maister's were laid by, and mines were finishin', an' they were hangin' on the screens, ye ken, at the side of the fire, an' I cam' hame to ma dinner at the usual time, aboot four o'clock, an' took ma dinner: an' after I took ma dinner I had a custom of going up to the West End Park an' takin' a walk after dinner. This was Friday an' I went away the fecht o' couple of hours——'

'Stop a moment!'

'—It was vera wat thae days. I was vera much fasht wi' cauld feet and there was no fire in the room, and I went doun to the kitchen fire to get ma feet warmed, and Jessie M'Pherson made ma tea.'

'What o'clock?' said Mr Gifford, making himself heard at last.

'I reckon it wad be weel on eight o'clock. She made ma tea and she poored it oot and took a cup along wi' me; and after the tea was by——'

Lord Deas: 'Was it in the kitchen you got the tea?'

'Ay.'

'Well?'

'Then after I got my tea by, I yoked to the readin'; I had always the papers in ma pouch; and then I stopped till half-past nine o'clock.'

'In the kitchen?'

'At the kitchen fire. At that hour, I said I would go and mak' ready for bed: and I went awa' to ma bed up the stair. I left Jess

M'Pherson working away in the kitchen, ye ken; and in the mornin' I wauken't wi' a lood squeal.'

Mr Fleming paused again on this dramatic note, and no doubt there was a further sensation in court. Mr Gifford started him off again. 'Where is your bedroom? What flat [floor] of the house is your bedroom on?'

'It is a flat above the kitchen, ye ken. Weel, I was sayin' I was wauken't i' the mornin' wi' a lood squeal; and after that followed ither two, not so lood as the first ane. But it was an odd kind o' squeal I heard and I jumped oot o' bed, and I heard no noise. A' was by in the coorse o' a minute's time; in a minute a' was quate, and I heard naething nor saw naething. I took oot ma watch—I kept the time beneath ma pillow—and looked what o'clock it was. It was exactly four o'clock; a bonny, clear mornin'.'

'A lovely morning, still and calm,' Peterina M'Clean had called it: pausing with her two sisters, strolling home from their wedding party, to listen to the small birds singing in the trees opposite the houses in Sandyford Place—observing, at four o'clock in the morning, the lights of the gasolier burning in the ground floor front room of No. 17.

'So—what did you do?'

'I gaed awa' to ma bed again,' said the old man. But even he must have thought this needed some elaboration for he explained reasonably: 'A' was quate.'

'What did you think had happened?'

'I thocht she had got somebody to stay wi' her. There was a woman she ca'd a sister o' hers—she bood to be in her room.' ('She bood' would mean here 'behoved', in other words, she must be in her room; but this answer is elsewhere reported as 'There was a body she ca'd a sister and wis stopping wi' her or else some ither body.' It may be said here that Jess's foster-sister later stated that she had never in her life spent a night at Sandyford Place, and 'the old man had no reason in the world to say that I ever did.')

'So when I heard a' was quate and no noise, I gaed away to ma bed again and wisna lang in it till I fell asleep again.'

'How long did you lie?'

'I lay till about six o'clock o' the morning, and she always used to come up. I lay wauken after that. She always used to come up with a little porridge about eight o'clock.'

'And this morning—did she come up?'

'She did not come up that morning and I was surprised she didna come. I wearied very much for her. I lay still till nine o'clock——'

'And then?'

'Then I raise and put on ma claes. I forget whether I washed masel' before I went down; but I gaed down to her door and gied three chaps that way. . . .'

He knocked three times on the ledge of the witness-box with his knuckles; and the sound must have rung through the court-room like the knocking at Macbeth's castle gates. But here was none to answer. 'I tried the sneck of the door and fan' that the door was locked. There was no key in the door and sae I gaed up till the store-room' (i.e. 'I went into the pantry').

'The store-room is adjoining the maid's bedroom?'

'Ay, the store-room and her bedroom was just adjoining ane anither maistly.'

'And in the store-room——?'

'I gaed into the store-room and then I found what was a bit window in the area standing open.'

'Is that window usually open?'

'Nae, it did not use to be that way.'

'Then what did you do?'

'I drew it to and returned to the fire again. The fire was wake. I put some coals on the fire.'

'You say the fire was low; but was it still burning?'

'Ay, it was still burning.' He added, presumably inconsequentially: 'That was Saturday morning, ye ken.'

'Saturday morning, yes. And then?'

'And then after that the main door bell was rung. I went to the door. It was Mr Stewart, the next-door neighbour's servant. I dinna mind her name. She wanted the len' o' a spade to clean the back door. She said her people were all away to the coast the nicht before.'

'Did you give her the spade?'

'I gaed doun to get the bit spade to the washing-house, and when I got to the washing-house there was nae key in it. I could not get the key and the girl did not get the spade.' He added with another of his apparently inconsequential turns: 'At the same time, ye ken, when I got out to give the girl the spade, the back door was locked, and the key on the inside o' the door, ye ken. That was the way I gaed down to look for the spade.'

'What o'clock was it?'

'Eleven o'clock,' said the old man. 'After that Mr Watson, the baker's man, cam' wi' his van and the bell was rung and I gaed up.' Mr Watson is not mentioned elsewhere and was not called to give evidence; but here is yet another visitor to whom apparently Mr Fleming did not think fit to mention the odd disappearance of the maid. The same thought may have occurred to him, for he switched again. 'But did I tell you first about the main door not being locked?'

'No,' said Mr Gifford, doubtless delighted. 'Tell us about that.'

'It was not locked. The key was in the inside o' the door and the door was on the latch; just snecked, ye ken, not locked. Sae whaever had been in,' elaborated Mr Fleming, 'they had got out by that door; there is nae doubt of that.' But that brought him back to his reason for being at the door. 'An' so Mr Watson, the baker's man, ca' wi' his van shortly after that servant girl was seeking for the spade, and I took a half-quarter loaf.' But perhaps, after all, he wouldn't have been able to confide in Mr Watson about Jess. 'The man was sitting upon the cart; he had a little boy that handed me in the loaf at the door.'

'And so then?'

And so then, Mr Fleming is reported as saying—and elsewhere not reported as saying—'always looking and wearying, windering what had become of Jessie that she did not make her appearance', he had stopped in till about twelve o'clock and then thought he would go to the office. 'I looked for the check key and got it on a shelf in the pantry, and I locked the door and went away to the office in Glasgow, and stoppet a wee while there and then I gaed awa' down to the Briggate to see a property that I had charge of. A water-pipe had burst there two or three days before, and I went down to see if it was all right and to see whether they had plaistered it up—it had to be plaistered up wi' lime, ye ken. All was right and I cam' awa' up again to the office and stopped till about two o'clock.'

'And then?'

'And then I took the bus and gaed up to Sandyford, thinking maybe that Jess would be waiting till I gaed up. But when I got up all was quiet and no appearance of Jess.'

'What did you do?'

'I did not go out again that night. I made masel' a bit o' dinner.'

'Did you see anyone?'

'Ay, about seven o'clock at the night the bell was rung and a young man came to the door. He said he was from Falkirk and his name was Darnley. He said he had promised to call on Jess when he was in town. I said she was not in. He went away.'

'What did you do next?'

'My shirts—there were a dozen of them—were on the screens in the kitchen, set on the side of the fire. I laid them by, one by one, off the screens, which were laid against the pantry door——'

'Against the pantry door?'

The old man was apparently accustomed to call the true pantry —the small room next to the maid's room, looking on to the area —the store-room. By the pantry he probably meant the large built-in cupboard in the kitchen. The screens were lying in the kitchen beside the pantry door, he repeated; they had been 'laid or driven down'—he meant that the screens or clothes-horses had been overturned. 'There was a pantry door they keep their things in and the screens were either laid or driven ower upon it. So I took my shirts off the screens.'

'Very well. Then what did you do?'

'There was a room off the kitchen that my drawers and kist [chest] stood in, I laid by my shirts.'

'Did you observe anything about your shirts?' asked Mr Gifford, skipping over it, perhaps, with a carefully casual air. (But it would have to come out!)

'Ay; there were two marked with—like—blood upon them.' He had laid them by, he added, probably just as casually as Mr Gifford, on the tap o' the ithers.

'Did you get any supper that night?'

'I made masel' a cup of tea.'

'What time would this be?'

'It would be eight o'clock. I thought if Jess had gone awa' with any of her acquaintances she would make her appearance.'

'But she did not?'

'Na, she did not. I sat up till after nine and then went to bed.' Next morning, he added, the Sabbath, the bell was rung by the milkman; but he did not answer.

'What did you do then?'

'Well, I made ma breakfast again: a cup of tea and a boiled herring to it, that was ma breakfast.' And then he had gone to church—'Mr Aikman's church in Anderston.'

'And then?'

'And then after the church skailed I went straight hame.'

'Did you speak to anyone that morning?'

'When I was going to the church Mr John M'Allister, who was coming out of his house door to go to the church, spoke to me.'

'And in the afternoon——?'

In the afternoon the pious old gentleman had gone to church again.

Now another visit from Darnley must be faced. Mr Fleming took it straight. 'After I was hame, the lad Darnley, who had ca'ed before, ca'ed again and asked if Jess M'Pherson was in. I said no. He asked, "Is she at church?" I said, "I don't know." Says he, "If she comes out the town, will she come this way?" I said, "I suppose she will." He went away. I had no more calls that night that I recollect, and at half-past nine I went to bed.'

So ended the second day of the servant's being missing; and no word of her disappearance to anyone. Mr Gifford's heart must have sunk at the thought of conducting his garrulous witness through almost the whole of yet a third. One face in court, however, will have reassured him. The judge would be at hand to help out whenever the old gentleman got into a bit of a tangle. Lord Deas was already quite evidently all for Mr Fleming.

'We come then to Monday morning . . .?'

On Monday morning, said Mr Fleming, he had risen at eight o'clock as was usual and went about his business. 'I afterwards went to the office and gied in what cash I had gotten. I then gaed awa' hame to Sandyford——'

'What o'clock would this be?'

'This would be about one or two o'clock. All was quiet and I heard naething.'

'What did you do?'

'I kent that Mr Fleming would be hame after he came up frae doun the water and that he would be out for dinner——'

'And when he came?'

'About four o'clock young John came in, and his father followed him.' He described the discovery of the body. 'Her head was covered either with a skirt or white sheet, which was all blood, and her body was naked as she was born, downwards; she was lying on her face. He was in an unco' state tae, and he ran out and got in some neighbours, Mr Chrystal and some ithers, and went to the Police Office.'

'Did the police come?'

'The police officers came directly and took possession of the body. Dr Fleming and Dr Watson were also brought to the spot directly, but their presence was of no avail, ye ken, the woman was gone.' Some observers report that the old gentleman added approvingly that 'it was regular that they should be called.' This was not the moment to remark that he might have thought of it himself three days earlier.

'From the Friday night to the Monday morning, did you make all your own meals?'

'I was not verra particular but I made all that I needed.'

'Did you use any silver spoons or forks?'

'I dinna think I did. If I did, I only used a teaspoon; but I dinna mind.'

Mr Gifford asked that exhibits eleven to eighteen be shown to the witness; these were the articles of silver recovered from Lundie's pawn which, Jessie's first statement declared, the old man had brought to her to be pledged. He identified them as his son's property: they were in daily use when his son was at home. Mr Gifford, on happier ground at last, asked solemnly: 'Did you take any of that plate out of the house?'

Mr Fleming, also on more comfortable ground, had lost his rather senile garrulity. For almost the first time so far in his examination he answered with one word: 'Never.'

'Did you give them to anybody on that Friday——?'

'I did not.'

'Or that Saturday, Sunday or Monday?'

'I never gave them to any person.'

'Look at the prisoner: do you know her?'

They confronted one another, those two. But if Jessie hoped that the old man 'would shudder at it', she was disappointed. He said simply that yes, he knew her; he had known her first when she was servant to his son John.

'How long is that?'

'She left when the ither girl (Jess M'Pherson?) came back, ye ken.'

'It is some years ago?'

'It will be three years ago, I'se warrant, but my memory is not sae good.'

'Have you seen her since she left your son's service?'

'Yes.'

'Where?'

Mr Fleming's memory was certainly rather peculiar. He could describe three or four specific occasions when he had seen her, more than a year ago, but had apparently forgotten his habit of dropping in at any odd time at the house in the Broomielaw— Jessie's sister, who had lived with her for eight months in the previous year, had seen him there at least half a dozen times; and we know that the reason that Jessie had taken to timing her visits to Sandyford Place very late was because, if he was still up, she had to see him. 'She came up along wi' her husband to pay a visit to Jessie M'Pherson; I saw her that night in Mr Fleming's house, Sandyford Place; that is twelve months ago.' But Jess M'Pherson's foster-sister, Mrs M'Kinnon, had seen Jess only a month before her death, and Jess had told her then—so surely it must have been a fairly recent thing?—that, when Jessie M'Lachlan and her husband had come round, 'not to give the old man satisfaction' she had taken them to her own room; but he had come into her room and said, 'Oh, Jessie, is that you?' and Jessie had said, 'Yes, who did you think it was?' and he 'had sat them out on that occasion.'

'Did you ever see her anywhere else?'

'Yes, she invited me to see her house.'

'When?'

'A twelvemonth ago.'

'Did you ever see her on any other occasion?'

'I saw her in her own house at another time; that was before she flitted to that other, her last house.'

'How long ago?'

'It would be two or three years ago.'

And he had seen her also at the examination in the County Buildings. 'The Sheriff showed her to me there.' On that occasion, or at least so it was reported, he had denied knowing her at all— Mr Wilson had told Jessie that he had done so. Reminded that she had once been a servant in John Fleming's house—for two years; and, after all, she knew him well enough to address him as 'Grandpa'—he had replied that he wouldn't have taken her for the same person.

'Excepting at those times you have mentioned, you have never seen her, did you?'

'Not since she left my son's service,' reiterated old Mr Fleming, undeterred by this curious ellipse of grammar.

'Did you give her these articles?'—referring to the silver plate.

'No, never.'

'Did you ever tell her to pawn them?'

'No, never.'

'Did you see her on the Friday evening that Jessie M'Pherson was a-missing?'

'No.'

'Did you ever get any money from her?'

'Never.'

'Did you give her any money on that Friday or Saturday?'

'I did not.'

'Did you ever call at her house excepting on the occasions you have told us about?'

'I only called twice to my recollection.'

'And these are the two occasions you have already referred to?'

'Yes.'

'Have you any money in the bank?'

'Yes, a little.' A hundred and fifty pounds in the Savings Bank, he said, and thirty in the Royal Bank; he identified his two bank-books, exhibits 58 and 59.

Mr Gifford took him back to the business of the pantry window or 'wicket' which he said he had found open on the Saturday morning.

Old Fleming's motive, if he were lying in this matter, would obviously be to suggest that the murderer had entered by this window, climbing the railings, dropping down into the area, and getting through into the basement via the pantry; killing and robbing the maid, going on upstairs and taking the silver and letting himself out by the front door—which door he said he had found only latched, not locked.

It is a little difficult to visualise the arrangement of the pantry window. There seems to have been this small barred door or 'wicket' leading into the area, with a smaller glass window, working up and down on sash-cords, let into the door. 'You told us, Mr Fleming, that on the Saturday morning you went into the pantry and found the wicket open?'

'Yes.'

'Did you open the glass window?'

'No.'

'You say that you drew to the wicket?'

'I did.'

'Tell us how you got that done.'

'It was straight open. It opens outwards.'

'Did you put out your hand to pull it to?'

'Yes.'

'To do that had you to lift the window?'

'It was a little window, ye ken, inside of the big window.'

'How did you get hold of the wicket to draw it to?'

'I put out ma hand and drew it tae.'

'Did the glass window not prevent you?'

'I forget,' said Mr Fleming.

'Is there not a glass window to the pantry?'

'Yes.'

'Was it open or shut when you went into the room?'

'It was open.'

'The glass window was open?'

'Yes, or I could not have got out my hand to draw it tae, ye ken.'

'Well, did you open the glass window or did you find it open?'

'I found it open.'

'The glass window?'

'Yes,' said the old man. He added, according to one source, 'I opened naething, but just put oot ma hand and drew it tae.'

Mr Gifford sat down and Mr Rutherford Clark rose to cross-examine.

The opening question in a cross-examination is often of paramount importance. The witness has come through his examination-in-chief—a little battered, it may well be if he be not telling the truth, and thankful to have such an ordeal safely over. He relaxes, breathes a sigh of relief; and before he has had time to brace himself for the shocks in store, calmly, without sign or ceremonial of change-over, the next question comes. One man has sat down, one man has risen to his feet, and that is all. But it is his friend who has sat down; the man he now faces is his enemy.

Mr Rutherford Clark's first question was: 'Was your watch right that Saturday morning?'

The old man must have been taken a little aback; such a casual general question, not apparently leading to anywhere in particular. He answered 'Yes.'

'You know that?'

'Ay, it gangs very regular,' said old Mr Fleming.

'Therefore you are sure about the hour you have given us?'

So that was it!—a point of no particular importance (of no particular danger his heart must have said, if his heart held guilty secrets). He thought counsel referred to the screams he had heard in the night. 'Yes, exactly four o'clock and a fine clear morning.'

But Mr Clark cared nothing at the moment for the screams in the night. 'You are quite sure, then, that you lay in bed till nine o'clock?'

The old man had said so. He had lain from six o'clock to nine, waiting for Jess to bring him up his bit of porridge. He repeated now, 'Yes.'

'You were not out of your bed or dressed till nine o'clock or thereby?'

'I didna leave ma bed till nine o'clock.'

'Who was the first person you spoke to on that Saturday morning?'

The first person Mr Fleming was known to have spoken to— or so Master M'Quarrie would later say in evidence—was the milk-boy, at twenty minutes to eight. But if he hadn't got up till nine, he couldn't have spoken to the milk-boy. 'On Saturday morning? It was the girl for the len' o' the spade.'

'Her name is Brownlie, I believe?'

'I dinna ken. She's Mr Stewart's servant.'

'What time was that?'

This time Mr Fleming definitely said it was about eleven o'clock.

'And until she came there was no one in the house that you had seen?'

'No one that I saw.'

'But was there anyone?'

'No,' said the old man.

'When does the milk usually come?'

'It aye comes betwixt eight and nine o'clock.'

Mr Clark made a neat little swoop. He moved on to Monday. The old man had said he had risen at eight on Monday morning; if, as he now also said, the milk came after eight, he must have been up to receive it. 'When does it usually come on Monday morning?'

But Mr Fleming, though vague enough when he wanted to be, was not so slow either. 'It came aye aboot one time [it always came about the same time], but I didna require any on the Monday morning as I had tae gang awa' tae the toon.' (The milk-boy's evidence was that on all three mornings the old man came to the door—though he was for nae milk.)

'Why did you not require any milk on Monday?'

'I had tae gang awa' to the toon,' insisted the old man, 'and there's a milk shop in our property in the Briggate, an' I went in there an' got a ha'penny roll an' a mutchkin of milk. That was a' the breakfast I got on Monday morning.'

But Mr Clark had his bird netted and they both knew it. 'Did the milk come upon the Saturday morning?'

'I don't think it did,' said old Fleming. What else was there to say?

'It is brought to the front door?'

'Always to the front door. . . .' He embarked on one of his little diversions. 'But it was not locked nor the chain on it nor anything but the latch. . . .'

Mr Clark ignored the diversion. 'Did you hear a ring at the front-door bell at the time when the milk should have come on Saturday morning?'

'No,' said Mr Fleming, brought up short.

'Do you swear—do you *swear* that you did not open the door before that woman—Mr Stewart's servant—came for the spade?'

'Yes,' swore Mr Fleming.

'Did you not open the door to the milkman that morning?'

'No.' But it sounded very bald. 'I don't recollect the milkman coming.'

'Did you not open the door to the milk-boy and tell him that there was no milk required that morning?'

The old man retreated into vagueness. 'There was one that I told that to. I recollect that.'

'You remember that now?'

'I do.'

'Then it was not true that Mr Stewart's servant was the first person to whom you opened that front door on Saturday morning?'

'It was Mr Stewart's servant to whom I opened the door first.'

'Did you open the door for the milk-boy?'

'No, I didn't,' said the old man. 'Mr Stewart's servant was the first that I opened the door to, and then to the baker.'

There is nothing like a nice muddle to confuse the issue in cross-examination, and Mr Rutherford Clark must have recognised with some despair that—intentionally or otherwise—the old gentleman was going to correct and contradict himself till he had them both in a splendid muddle now. He started all over again. 'Did the milkman come to the door on Saturday morning?'

'I'm sure I canna charge my memory particularly about the milkman on Saturday morning.'

'Mr Fleming, you told me a little while ago that you remember him coming on Saturday.'

Mr Fleming played for time. 'I did not require any milk.'

'I don't care about that. You told me that you remembered that the milkman came upon that Saturday. Did the milkman come on Saturday or did he not?'

There was a long pause; the Court, and Mr Clark too, must have held their breaths. But, 'I'm sure I canna answer that,' said the old man.

Mr Clark tried again. 'Mr Fleming—can you tell me whether you opened the door to any person before that servant of Mr Stewart who came for the spade?'

'No, I don't think I opened the door to any person till she came. I am sure of that,' said Mr Fleming, taking heart. 'It was about eleven o'clock that she came, and the baker came shortly after.' (Elizabeth was to say that it was two o'clock in the afternoon.)

'Are you sure, therefore, that the milk did not come that morning?'

But the old man dodged again. 'I am sure I did not get any milk that morning.'

'Never mind that. Are you sure it did not come?'

'I rather think it did not come.'

'Could it have got in that morning without you opening the door?'

'There was no milk brought in.'

'Did you refuse to take milk that Saturday morning?'

What must have been Mr Clark's feelings when the old man at last simply answered 'Yes.'

He pressed his advantage, eagerly. 'Did you refuse to take in the milk that Saturday morning?'

'I refused to take milk. I did not require it.'

But Mr Fleming was getting into deepish waters. The judge hastened to his aid. 'Are you sure, Mr Clark, that he fully understands the question?'

Mr Clark doubtless felt little gratitude for this judicial interruption of the keen flow of his examination, now that he really had things moving. 'I am persuaded that he does, my lord. Did you say to anyone, Mr Fleming, that you did not need any milk that morning, that Saturday? Did you say it to the milk-boy?'

'I told him that I did not need it,' said the old man.

It must have been a moment of tremendous excitement. 'Now, Mr Fleming, don't let us make any mistake about this matter. *Did you say to the milk-boy that you required no milk that day?*'

'Yes, I think I did. This was the morning that I got no milk at all.'

A juryman here interrupted to ask counsel to make sure that there was no mistake about the day. 'I am very anxious that there should be no mistake,' Mr Clark replied fervently, and put the question again. 'You understand, Mr Fleming, that the morning I am speaking about at present is the Saturday morning?'

'Yes,' said Mr Fleming.

He hammered it home yet again. 'Just attend, Mr Fleming. On that Saturday morning you said to the milk-boy that you required no milk at that time?'

'Yes.'

Down came the trap. 'Well—*at what time of day* did you say this?'

Old Fleming took refuge in vagueness once more. The boy would have rung the bell and he would just have said he needed no milk. Lord Deas kindly prompted him: he could have said that without ever opening the door.

'*Could* you have said that without opening the door?'

'Yes; I could take the front door off the sneck [the latch], leaving the chain fastened, and speak to the milk-boy. I think I left the front door on the chain.'

'Are you sure, Mr Clark,' insisted the anxious judge, 'that he fully understands the question?'

'I am trying to make it as plain as I can, my lord,' said Rutherfurd Clark. He added—with what degree of scorn, irritability or umbrage we must judge for ourselves—that he had no wish to take any advantage.

'I have no doubt of that,' said Lord Deas pacifically.

Cross-examination resumed. 'Had the door a chain?' asked Mr Clark—literally and metaphorically in words of one syllable.

Yes, it had a chain.

'Could you have opened the door and spoken to the milk-boy without taking off the chain?' ('Misunderstand' that if you can!)

Yes, he could.

'Did you do so?'

'Yes.'

Well, that was unequivocal enough; except that Donald M'Quarrie was to say that the first thing he heard that morning was the chain being taken down from the door.

'Now, Mr Fleming—do you remember going to the door that morning and opening it to the milk-boy?'

Mr Fleming took refuge in one of his *non sequiturs*. 'No, I did not let him in.'

'Did you see him at the door?'

'It's likely I would.'

'Mr Fleming, do you remember speaking to the milk-boy on that Saturday morning?'

'I would just say to him that I would not require any milk.'

'Do you remember seeing him at the door?'

'Yes, I think I do.'

'Did the bell ring when the boy came?'

'It's most likely it would.'

'But do you remember if it rang?'

'Well, I wouldna have gone to the door if the bell had not rung,' said the old man.

'Well, but do you remember if it rang?'

'I canna mind everything. . . .'

He was retreating again. Mr Clark left him to it and opened a fresh attack from a slightly different angle. 'What time of the morning was it that the milk-boy came?'

It was just about his usual time—between eight and nine.

'Were you dressed?' said Mr Clark.

No doubt it sounded to the uninitiated innocent enough. Old Mr Fleming knew otherwise. He temporised as usual. 'On Saturday morning, do you mean?'

'Yes, on Saturday morning?'

'I canna say that; I suppose I would.' He added: 'I got up about nine o'clock that morning.'

Just what Mr Rutherfurd Clark wanted! 'Well, if the milk-boy came about eight or nine o'clock, how could you be dressed if you didn't get up till nine?'

There was another of those long pauses that at a murder trial are filled, for the unaccustomed spectator at any rate, with a sort of vicarious terror. He said at last, slowly: 'Whether I was dressed or not, I cannot charge my memory. I might not be dressed.'

'But you said that you lay in bed till about nine—and then got up and dressed yourself?'

'Yes.'

'Is that true?'

There was nothing to say but yes again.

And we may imagine for ourselves another pause. Mr Clark would stand for a moment—deliberately, perhaps, to create an 'atmosphere', or simply collecting his thoughts, girding himself for the spring. For this was to be the question of questions, this was to be the point and focus of all that had gone before. Did he bark it out suddenly, or whisper it dramatically, or just put it casually, as if it hardly mattered at all? '*Why did you not let Jessie open the door when the milk-boy came?*'

And: 'Jessie?' said the old man. 'Jessie, ye ken—it was a' ower wi' Jessie afore that.'

Sensation in Court cried the papers next morning; and no doubt that was putting it mildly. Indeed, in the hubbub, the answer was partially lost, and the *North British Daily Mail* heard it as: 'Jessie—we kent it was a' ower wi' Jessie afore that,' or, as they translated it for their readers, 'We knew that Jessie was dead and could not go to the door.'

Into the hushing of the ushers, Mr Clark repeated his question. 'Why did you not let Jessie open the door to the milkman when he came?'

'There was nae Jessie to open the door that morning,' said the old man helplessly.

Lord Deas intervened. 'You had better put the question another way. Ask him why he opened the door himself that morning.'

'Willingly,' said Mr Clark, though it was not precisely the same question, even allowing for different phrasing. He got round that rather neatly. 'Why did you open the door when the milk-boy came—in place of allowing Jessie to open it?'

The old man began to fluff badly. 'I was just saying to him—the chain was on—we did not require any milk. She was deed afore that.'

Mr Clark was anxious to pursue his line of enquiry, but here was an admission that must be noted. 'My lord, there is one matter in this answer which I think is very important. He says the chain was on.' Having got the fact safely into cold storage, as it were, he returned to the immediate attack. 'Mr Fleming, I must have an answer to this question. Why did you go to the door and open it when the milkman came? Why did you not allow Jessie to open the door?'

'On Saturday morning, ye ken,' insisted the old man, 'Jessie was deed. She couldna open the door when she was deed.'

'Quite true. But why did *you* open it? Did you know that Jessie was dead when the milkman came?'

'No, I did not,' said the old man sharply.

'If you didn't know Jessie was dead, then why did you go to the door?'

But he had collected his wits a bit by now. 'I was up, ye ken, and I would just go and open the door to say that we did not require any.'

'Did you leave Jessie time to open the door?'

Lord Deas again. 'You had better ask: Did you wait some time before you opened the door?'

'Well,' said Mr Clark, 'did you wait some time before you opened the door?'

'Oh, ye ken, I went down the stair and through the house before that, and got no answer.'

'How long before the milkman came,' said Mr Clark swiftly, 'would you go through the house?'

'Through the house? I suppose it would be nigh aboot the time.

150

'I knocked three times, ye ken, at her door and got nae answer, and this was after nine o'clock.'

'Are you sure that it was after nine o'clock?' Mr Clark pounced again. The milkman would say he called at twenty to eight, the old man himself had said it was before nine.

The answer was muffled. 'Put the question again,' said Lord Deas. 'Perhaps he misunderstood you.'

'Are you certain that this was after nine o'clock?'

'Yes, after nine. The milkman whiles doesna' keep the appointed time.'

'Did you go downstairs before you dressed that morning?'

The old man said that he might well have done; he would be unwashed and unshaven, and might go down undressed. We may note here that 'downstairs' meant to the basement. One has an impression of coming downstairs from the bedroom floor, but James Fleming slept on the ground floor. It is of course quite possible that he might go down before dressing to get clothes from his wardrobe room, though he does not himself make this point.

Mr Clark was not interested in vapourings about what might have happened. 'I speak about Saturday morning——'

'I can say no more than I have. I have told you everything in my heart. The memory of a man of seventy-eight is not so fresh as a young man's. Be as easy as you can,' begged the old gentleman humbly. 'I am willing to answer every question.'

It might have been more effective had not a juryman jumped up to point out that Mr Fleming had just stated his age to be seventy-eight, whereas he had formerly given it as eighty-seven. Mr Fleming hastily corrected himself. He was born the ninth of August, 1775, he was 'eighty-seven past'. (Only just past; it was now September 17. But every little helps.)

'On Saturday morning—were you down in the kitchen before you put on your clothes?'

The old gentleman thought it over. 'Before I put on ma claes? I might.'

'Did you chap [knock] at Jessie's door?'

'Yes.'

'Had you your clothes on then?'

'I couldna say I was completely dressed. I might have had part of ma claes on. I tried the sneck, but the door was locked and the key awa'. What more could I do?'

'When the milkman came on Saturday morning, was it before or after you had chapped at Jessie's door?'

'I could not be pointed [exact or certain] wi' that question, whether it was before or after.'

Mr Clark went back to the milk. 'Did you take in any milk on Saturday morning?'

'No, I did not require it. I could take ma breakfast without milk as well as with it.'

'Had you your breakfast on Saturday morning?'

'I made masel' a cup of tea.'

'Had the refusal to take milk on Saturday morning anything to do with your not having got porridge that morning?'

The old man was not to be caught with that one. 'No, I could take ma porridge wanting ma milk, and can do so yet. The servant was in the habit of getting in the milk in the morning for her use. She would get a larger quantity when she was alive.'

And that was the last of the milk for old Mr Fleming—except for one question at the end. He would surely have been a more comfortable man at that moment could he have known that this was so.

Mr Clark moved on to other matters. 'When you first saw the back door on that Saturday morning, was it locked on the inside?'

It was locked on the inside said the old man, and the key either in or out of it—no one seems quite sure which he said. But it didn't much matter.

'And when you first saw the front door on that morning, how was it?'

'It was on the latch. There was no lock or chain.'

'You are sure of that?'

'I could give my oath on it.'

He had said, a few questions back, that the chain was positively on; but Mr Clark did not risk any rambling explanations in apparently innocent contradiction. 'You never took the chain off that front door?'

'There was no chain on it.'

'And you did not take it off?'

'No!' said the old man firmly.

'Now, you heard a squeal [a scream] about four o'clock on the Saturday morning. Where did this squeal come from?'

'When I jumped out of ma bed and heard the squeal, I thocht it might be on the street. Next a squeal followed, and then I heard it was down below.'

'How long would it be between the first and last squeal?'

'I think it would be a bare minute; then all was quiet as if it never had taken place.'

'Was it the same voice that squealed each time, so far as you could judge?

'Yes, but not so strong.'

'Was it a squeal as of distress?'

'It was a squeal like as if somebody was in distress.'

'Did you recognise the voice?'

'No.'

'What did you think at the time?'

'I thocht that Jessie had got some person in to stop wi' her, after I had gone to bed.'

'And what did you think had caused the squeal at the time?'

'Och, I couldna say what had caused it; but I heard it, just as if some person was in great distress. It was by in a minute.'

'Why did you not go down?'

'It was all quiet afterhind and I didna think of going doon.' If the noise had continued any time, he added, it would have been alarming and 'we' would have had to call in the police. But a couple of 'lood squeals' apparently seemed to him too trivial to worry about. Nobody seems to have observed the plural 'we'.

'When you found in the morning that Jessie was not there and her door locked, why did you not send for the police?'

It had never occurred to him to send for them, said the old man; he was aye thinkin' she was awa' wi' some o' her freens; it had not entered his head that there was murder or anything else o' that kind gaun on in the hoose.

'In the course of the night you had heard squeals indicating that some person was in great distress, and you did not see your servant in the morning. Can you tell me why you didn't in these circumstances give information to the police?'

'I didna think aboot anything at the time. I was aye lookin' for her coming back, and if any drink or anything had been gaun she might have been induced to go out and would be back and I never thocht of calling for the police. I was looking for her back every other minutes,' rambled the old man, 'I thocht she would be back and it never occurred to me—trouble or murder or any such thing.'

'Her going away was a very unexpected thing to you, was it not?'

Yes, it was, he said; so, *pace* Lord Deas, evidently young Fleming was not the only person who had heard nothing of any such plan.

'When she didn't come back all Saturday,' insisted Mr Clark, 'why didn't you send for the police?'

'I didn't think of sending for them.'

'And when she did not come back all Sunday—why didn't you send for the police?'

'I kent Mr Fleming would be home on Monday,' said the old gentleman happily, 'and would put a' things richt.'

They passed on to the basement where he had admittedly spent a good part of the three lonely days. 'Was there anything in the kitchen that attracted your attention on the Saturday?'

'There was naething.'

'Nor upon the Sunday?'

'Nae, nor upon the Sunday.'

'Nor upon the Monday?'

'Nor upon the Monday.'

'You were a great deal in the kitchen during these three days?'

'It was gey wat they days' (so much for the promise of that fair Saturday morning!), 'and I was glad to go doon to heat ma cauld feet. I mended the fire in the morning. But it was in, so I just had to put on some coals.'

'You kept the fire burning?'

'Ay, and I put on a gathering coal at night.' A gathering coal was a large lump of coal for keeping in the kitchen fire overnight; we may recollect that Elizabeth Brownlie, sleeping in the basement next door, could sometimes hear the big coal being broken in the grate.

'Did you see any blood in the kitchen?'

'None.'

'Did you see any blood on your shirts?'

'When I was laying them by, there were two which were marked.'

'Did you not think that queer?' said Mr Clark.

'I never thocht of blood, or murder or ony trouble of that kind. It never struck me there would be anything which would cause blood.'

'How do you account, Mr Fleming, for the blood on your shirts?'

Mr Fleming did not answer directly. 'I know I mentioned to the Fiscal and them, him who was examining me, that I saw on one of the shirts something like paint or iron ore.' The two shirts were shown to him. 'I see two of them marked red.'

'That is what you saw?'

'That is what I seed.'

'Did you not think at the time that it might be blood?'

'I thought at the time,' the old man admitted, 'that it might be blood.'

'When did you notice this blood on your shirts?'

'On Saturday night, when I was laying them by.'

'But then, Mr Fleming, when you saw the blood upon your shirts, how did you account for it being there?'

The old gentleman gave up the uneven struggle. 'I can't say.'

'Did you not think something was wrong?'

'No, I didna,' he insisted. 'It never entered ma heid.'

'When you heard squeals of great distress and could not see Jessie, had not even seen her for a day, and also found her door locked as well as blood on your shirts—did you not, Mr Fleming, think that something was wrong?'

But no, said Mr Fleming; he had never thocht that anything was wrong.

'It never occurred to you that anything was wrong?'

'The squeals were only for a minute and I did not give heed to them. I never thocht on the matter.'

Mr Clark left it there and turned to more practical matters. 'Why didn't you get Jessie's door opened?'

'Mr Fleming opened it,' pointed out the old man, reasonably.

'Why didn't *you* get it opened?' insisted Mr Clark, unimpressed by this argument.

'I never had the recollection to take that key off the ither door. If I had thocht of it, I would have done it.'

'Why didn't you send for someone to open it—you who are

accustomed to this sort of thing: to get doors opened and locks repaired . . .?'

This was a shrewd one. 'All I can say is,' said Mr Fleming lamely, 'that I didn't.'

'When Darnley came upon Saturday, did you know he was a friend of Jessie's, and did he tell you that he was from Falkirk for the purpose of seeing her?'

'He had been in toon along wi' ither twa young gentlemen who were waiting upon him when he came to the door'—this in fact was true; Mr Clark was not quite correct here, Darnley had not come specially to Glasgow to see Jessie—'and he said he had to go away in the train at half-past eight o'clock. He, however, called again upon the Sunday, as I told you.'

'Why didn't you tell Darnley Jessie was a-missing for so long a time?'

'I did not tell him. I had no business to tell him.'

'Weren't you anxious about Jessie?'

'I was looking for her every minute to come back.'

'Did he say he had stopped overnight to see Jessie?'

'No, he never mentioned that.' And it had not in fact been the case; he said himself he had simply changed his mind and stayed the night with a friend. Mr Clark seems to have been in a slight muddle about Darnley.

'Why didn't you tell him on Sunday night that she'd been away for two days?'

'He only stopped a minute and I had no occasion to tell him.' (He stopped long enough, however, to ask where Jess was, whether she had gone to church, and if so, which way she was likely to come home: Mr Fleming himself had said so in answer to Mr Gifford.)

'Was she ever out such a length of time before?'

'She had often been out to see her friends; been out for the day.'

'But she told you where she was going?'

'Yes.'

'Did you make enquiry at the shops about her?'

But Mr Fleming had not; nor had he mentioned her to Mr M'Allister whom he had met on Sunday on the way to church, nor had he said a word during his visits to the office to anyone, not even to his son's confidential clerk. 'I was expecting her every hour and every minute.' But he had shared his hopes of her return with no one.

'When did you see your son first?'
'Upon Monday after he came to his dinner, about four o'clock. I saw ma grandson at the same time—they both cam' hame togither.'
'Yes. Now, Mr Fleming—did you look for silver spoons when you wanted to take your meals?'
'No, I did not. I did not require them. I had a teaspoon; it was enough for me.'
'What sort of a teaspoon was it?'
'A silver teaspoon.'
'Was that the teaspoon left in the house afterwards?'
'I ken naething aboot it. I had no charge of the silver at a'— Jessie had the whole charge.'
'Where did you get that silver teaspoon?'
'There was always a silver teaspoon in the kitchen. I sometimes have seen tablespoons there too.'
'Do you know what has become of that silver teaspoon?'
'I tell you, I ken naething aboot it. I took nae charge.'
'What had you to your dinner on Saturday?'
'I was not verra particular for ma dinner. I had a dish of ling fish that I had steeped. It served me baith Saturday and Sabbath.'
'Had you no other teaspoon than the silver teaspoon?'
'I had none.'
'You didn't look for any?'
'I did not need them.'
'Or fork?'
'I used a fork.'
'What kind of fork?'
'Just a table fork. It served the table many a time.'
In fact there was nowhere much to be got with the silver. He had not gone up to the dining-room to get some—that was the burden of his answers, and it was sufficiently consistent with his innocence. An old man, used to sitting over bowls of porridge and cups of tea in the kitchen with the servants, would probably not fuss much about his utensils. But to have acknowledged going to the dining-room—of course that would have been fatal. Even old Mr Fleming could hardly have missed the open side-

board and all those spaces where the familiar pieces of silver should have been. (But who, if he never visited the dining-room, put out the lighted gasolier the M'Lean girls saw?)

They were coming to the end. Mr Clark ran over one or two small points. 'What sort of dress had you on that Friday? Had you a brown dress at that time at all? And the coat?' The old man had worn his everyday clothes, he said: a pair of 'mixed' trousers, black waistcoat and black coat. The trousers were brownish. He had had a brown coat but he had sold it to an old-clothes man.

'When was it sold?'

'It might have been twa-three weeks afore this took place.'

'To whom did you sell it?'

'I sold it to a person named Paton, one of the tenants; along wi' some ither clothes.'

'Is that Daniel Paton, of the Bridgegate?'

'Yes.'

'Did you never have a brown coat after that?'

'No.' It had presumably never been brought to anybody's notice that Daniel Paton, the old-clothes man, had long ago declared before Jno. Gemmel that Mr Fleming had sold him his brown coat two or three years ago and at the time of the murder was in the habit of wearing a blue coat. He was subsequently to declare that what the old man now said in court was absolutely untrue. But the whole subject of Mr Fleming's wearing apparel at this time was to be allowed to fall into a curious pool of silence. No investigation as to bloodstains was ever brought forward— a solitary button in the grate, a pair of (innocent) old socks in a corner, and a description by one or two witnesses of what he had on at this time or that—and that was all. Whether or not any of his wardrobe was missing, no one seems to have enquired, or if they had, the answers did not appear.

So Mr Clark changed tack. 'Are you quite certain that you never saw the prisoner within twelve months?'

'Unless at the examination in the County Buildings,' said the old man, 'yes, I am.'

'Had you any quarrel or dispute with Jess M'Pherson?'

'Never.'

'Of any kind?'

'No.'

And again. 'You read the newspapers regularly?'

'Yes.'

'Do you use your spectacles when you read?'

'I have got a pair of new ones,' said the old man.

He had got the new spectacles—yesterday.

'Did you ever use them before?'

'I got a present of them and have got a pair of new glasses put in.'

'When you read, did you use spectacles—till yesterday?'

'No. I could see weel eneuch tae read without them—at least gey weel,' admitted Mr Fleming. Was he conscious that a claim to need spectacles would have been convenient in respect of all the blood-stains he had missed seeing, during those three days spent largely in the basement?

And so once more back to Mr Rutherfurd Clark's trump card— the milk-boy. 'Was no milk taken in till the Tuesday?'

Mr Fleming's last words in the witness box are variously reported; he said either that on the Sunday he had opened the door for milk but that none was taken on Monday; or 'There was nae milk taken on Sunday, Monday or Tuesday. Sometimes I did not even open the door when the milk came.' (The milkman later gave evidence that he delivered milk twice daily except on Sundays; but no mention is anywhere made of a second visit on the Saturday.)

Mr Clark sat down. The Judge would look enquiringly at Mr Gifford, but Mr Gifford too had had enough of old Fleming and did not rise to re-examine. 'Have you any question to ask?' asked his lordship of the jury; but they hadn't, either. And even Lord Deas had nothing to add, so 'Now,' he said to Mr Fleming, 'you may go.'

One wonders whether the old gentleman was quite so nimble as he made his way down from the box; but 'Lord Death' doubtless beamed after him benignly as he went. Whatever we may think of Mr Fleming's showing, one thing is a matter of fact and not opinion: his lordship had made up his mind in favour of old Mr Fleming before ever he entered the court, and through thick and thin, stood by him to the end.

But it was not James Fleming who was being tried.

CHAPTER FOURTEEN

The Court having adjourned for a fifteen-minute breather, Dr Ebenezer Watson followed James Fleming in the witness box. He described how John Fleming had called him in and the condition of the body as he saw it—the first expert witness to do so—lying on the bedroom floor. He had, with Dr Fleming, the police surgeon, examined the rest of the basement and noted the marks of blood in the kitchen and the trail where the body had been dragged through the lobby.

Under cross-examination, with a good deal of interruption from the judge, he was taken through the business of the key on the inside of the bedroom door; John Fleming had told him about it as they hurried back to the house. He was the only one of the doctors to have observed the 'remarkable' bruise on the lower part of the back, and obliged by a physical demonstration on himself as to where precisely it was located. Lord Deas remarked that he couldn't very well write it down but would 'require to draw it.' It is perhaps carping to suggest that from the description 'the small of the back—the lower part of the backbone, near the spine' we can really pretty well place the bruise for ourselves, without any need for a picture. In Dr Watson's opinion, the bruise could have been caused by a blow from a blunt instrument or from a fall: he agreed that 'a knock from a heavy shoe' could account for it. If a blow had caused the bruise, it must have been a violent blow, and forcibly given. . . .

'Must it have been given by a person with great force?'

'Yes.'

Lord Deas: 'If it was given by a person at all?'

'Surely, my lord.' ('Surely' was a great word of Dr Watson's.)

Mr Rutherfurd Clark: 'Were any of the wounds in the head inflicted by a flat instrument?'

Lord Deas: 'You mean by the flat surface of an instrument?'

Mr Clark: 'I understand that the doctor has been speaking of the wounds on the head being inflicted by the cleaver?'

Dr Watson: 'One of the wounds on the head might be inflicted by that instrument, used laterally.'

'Is a hammer not the more likely instrument?'

'Quite as likely.'

'To produce that wound?'

'What wound?'

'The wound behind the ear?'

'If the wound behind the right ear, yes.'

'Was the wound across the nose fitted to produce stupor?'

'Not necessarily.'

'Was it likely?'

'I should say it was rather likely but not necessarily.'

'Is it the wound across the bridge of the nose you speak of?'

'Both wounds. They might not necessarily lead to stupor.'

Death, he thought, was the collective result of the wounds; none of which would have proved immediately fatal.

Dr Fleming, surgeon of police, described how he had been called to Sandyford Place and there with Dr Watson examined the body. He read out the report agreed on between himself and Dr Macleod, after their post-mortem conducted the following day (apparently on the spot; the body remained in the house for some days) on 'the body of Jessie M'Pherson which had been found under circumstances of great suspicion in a front room in the ground floor of the above house.' Lord Deas here interjected that it was proper to state to Dr Fleming as a police surgeon that there was matter here not suitable to a medical report. Dr Fleming persevered with his reading, winding up with the eight inferences drawn by himself and Dr MacLeod, reproduced on page 72. Of these, numbers 3, 6, and 8 were to prove of particular interest: to wit, that a severe struggle had taken place before death, that all the wounds except the three on the nose and forehead had apparently been inflicted by a person standing over the victim as she lay on the ground, and that the body had been drawn by the head, with the face downwards, along the lobby from the kitchen to the bedroom.

The report was signed by Drs Fleming and Macleod, after the customary phrase, 'This is the truth on soul and conscience.' So it doubtless was; but as it transpires on not a great deal of sense.

Mr Gifford resumed his examination. Had Dr Fleming formed any opinion as to whether the bed had been slept in?

Dr Fleming said that it would be difficult to form an opinion but he thought it highly probable that it had been slept in.

The sheet referred to in his original report—the sheet that was found rolled up under the wash-stand—appeared to have been washed but it had, notwithstanding, a large quantity of blood in the centre.

'Did you draw any inference from that?'

'The inference which I drew was that the sheet belonged to the bed and that it had been taken from it. I don't know whether there was any sheet on the bed or not. The impression upon my mind is that there was no sheet on the bed.'

The witness had noticed the two pillows which were 'scattered about the bed along with the bedclothes'. There were large marks of blood on them. There seemed to be large spots of blood on the floor; and all round the table in the middle of the room—a mahogany table, four or five feet square—there were marks of blood. The body was lying between the table and the bed. There was a track, about the breadth of a body, partly blood, partly 'just marks of streaking', between the bedroom and the kitchen. It became apparent in the course of their examination, said the witness, that the body had been dragged through from the kitchen (where evidence of a severe conflict was obtained) along the lobby to the apartment where it was found, and also that imperfect attempts had been made to obliterate traces of this removal.

Mr Gifford, for the prosecution: 'You say that in the kitchen there was evidence of a severe conflict having taken place. What was the nature of that evidence?'

'There were blood-stains upon the end of the jaw-box at the inner side of the kitchen door.'

'But what led you to say that there had been a severe conflict?'

'These marks were principally upon the flags.'

'How did that show there had been a severe conflict?—the dragging of the body was not a sign of severe conflict; I therefore want to know what marks of a severe conflict were apparent to you, before the dragging commenced.'

'My conclusion that there was a severe conflict was founded upon the streaks upon the kitchen floor.'

'I again ask, what were the marks of a severe conflict before the dragging took place?'

'There were regular marks as if caused by some rough substance.'

Lord Deas put an end to this curious exchange—in which the answers certainly appear to have had very little connection with the questions—by observing that the remark in Dr Fleming's report about 'evidence of a severe conflict' just confirmed what he had already said as to the introduction of matter not proper to a medical report.

So that was one up to Lord Deas.

Cross-examined by Mr Clark, the police surgeon said that the blood on the mattress was on 'the upper part of the bed'; this, if he meant the pillow end which he presumably did, might well be significant but it wasn't quite clear. The sheet was quite damp and appeared to have been washed—the sheet that was found rolled up under the wash-stand, that is—but was very much blood-stained.

'Was there any appearance of the deceased's person having been washed?'

'The face, neck and upper part of the chest appeared to have been washed.'

The kitchen floor had the appearance of having been washed between the sink and the lobby; and between the kitchen and the bedroom, but stopping at the bedroom door, there was a distinct appearance of the 'pavement' having been washed.

'When you saw these places in the kitchen and the lobby washed—were they dry or moist?'

'The lobby was perfectly moist; it was very damp as if it had been washed recently. The kitchen was drier, but still there was a damp appearance.' (This was at half-past five on the Monday afternoon, fifty or sixty hours after the murder.)

'When you say washed recently, what do you mean? What time do you mean?'

'It had a damp appearance as if it had been recent.'

Lord Deas: 'You are asked how recently. Was it an hour or a day before?'

'It might have been a day before from appearance.'

'Did the lobby and kitchen seem to have been done together?'

'They had the appearance of not having been done the same day but that would depend much on the stone.'

'Was the appearance of the two stones different?'

163

'They might be.' (In fact they were the same.)

As to whether or not the washing could have been done on the same day, he said, that would depend a good deal on the state of the kitchen fire. When he saw it, it was burning. The moist part in the kitchen would be seven or eight feet distant from the fire, the part he had looked at particularly would be ten or twelve feet distant. There was only one moist patch.

And there was blood on the door. 'It was a mark of blood of such a description as if a brush had been steeped in blood and drawn across the back and post of the door.' Another way of accounting for the mark could be that a bloody dress might have come across it. Any part of a woman's dress.

Mr Clark: 'Any bloody cloth would do it?'

'Yes.'

'Was it a very obvious mark?'

'It was a very obvious mark.'

'Was the door opposite to the window?'

'No, it was on the right-hand side.'

'But there was plenty of light showered from the window upon it?'

'There was a large kitchen table between the window and the door, which somewhat darkened it.'

'But there was plenty of light to see the marks?'

'If your eye had been turned in that direction they might have been seen at once.'

'You say that it was an obvious mark?'

'Yes.'

'And that there was plenty of light to see it?'

'Yes.'

And there were marks upon the 'jaw-box', the end of which faced the window; which marks were 'quite distinct and obvious'.

But as to the remarkable bruise on the dead woman's back reported by Dr Ebenezer Watson, this was not so distinct and obvious, in fact Dr Fleming couldn't recall having seen a bruise there; and from the fact that he had not made a note of it, he 'rather thought' it could not have been there at all.

It may be convenient to take the evidence of Dr Macleod at this point, though in fact it was given considerably later—presumably only for some outside reason, for it naturally reflects upon the foregoing. Dr Macleod had been called in late on the Monday evening and did not get to the Sandyford Place till after eleven; he had had a look round and then left, returning the following day to make the post mortem examination with Dr Fleming and compile the report with him.

Counsel for the Crown took him through the report. 'You say, "The neck and chest appear to have been partially washed." Well, can you explain more minutely what that means?'

'Yes. The neck and chest had apparently been cleaned to a certain extent; still there was the appearance of blood round the circumference of the washed part and it had not been entirely cleared of its bloody appearance. I cannot very well explain it in any other way than that.'

'What I want to know is, whether did water appear to be used or did it appear as if it had been with a cloth?'

'My impression was that water had been used.'

'I wish to draw your attention to this statement in the report: "On further examination it became apparent that the body had been dragged from the kitchen (which lies at the back of the house) and where evidence of a severe struggle was obtained." Does this statement mean that the struggle took place in the kitchen?'

'Yes, in or about the kitchen.'

'And in what consists the evidence?'

The witness went off into a long description of the condition of the kitchen and of the lobby, stairs, etc. Lord Deas started to ask him about the blood-stains on the lower part of the stairs, and when he answered, pulled him up and told him to confine himself to a description of what he had seen in the kitchen. What the witness had seen in the kitchen, apart from the blood on the sink and inside the door post, he described as follows: 'Upon the washed portion of the floor there were considerable stains; it was quite apparent to me (he went down on his knees and "let a light fall upon them") that they were the marks of blood. They were greasy and had the reddish look of imperfectly effaced blood. Around the circumference of the part of the floor that had been washed, there were impressions on the floor which I was then convinced and am now convinced had been foot-marks—confused footmarks. If I might be allowed to explain exactly what I mean by footmarks, they were the marks of a sort of twist or turn of the heels on the floor; and the ball of a foot had also left its mark on the stones.'

And there were wounds upon the hands and wrists of the deceased, he said, which he thought could only be accounted for by the deceased having endeavoured to protect herself in a struggle with another person.

'And that tended to confirm your opinion?'

'Yes.'

Dr Macleod was more positive than Dr Fleming about the 'remarkable bruise'. He had twice examined the body and had taken careful notes. There was no such mark.

They came to the footsteps in the bedroom. Dr Macleod had advised that the pieces of flooring containing the two best marked, should be cut out and they were now produced in court. He described his comparisons of the prints with those of the dead woman and old Fleming: but the dead woman's foot was longer and broader, larger in every way, and the old man's feet were 'so perfectly different that I did not think it necessary to compare them minutely.'

'Is there any peculiarity about old James Fleming's feet?'

'Yes; his is a flat foot.'

Lord Deas: 'In contradistinction to what?'

'A high sole.'

A slight breeze arose when counsel asked if the witness had compared the prisoner's feet with the footprints on the flooring. The witness was withdrawn while Mr Clark asked what Mr Gifford meant by that question. But Mr Gifford said he had put the question only to see if the witness had, from the examination, formed any opinion as to whether the footprints could have been made by the feet of the prisoner; and Mr Clark said that if that was all, he had no objection. The answer was that comparison showed that the footprints on the floor could have been made by the accused.

Cross-examined, Dr Macleod said that the marks of dragging in the lobby appeared to have been rubbed over, whether with or without water he could not say. In the kitchen, the floor had been washed.

'I forget, Doctor, did you take the hour at which you reached the house?' (i.e., on the Monday night).

'We have that already,' said the judge. 'It was eleven o'clock.'

166

But the witness had not examined the floor of the kitchen until Tuesday morning. It had then been dry—'dry and glazed as if it had been washed.'

Mr Clark took the witness back to the footprints again. Yes, the footprint of the deceased was larger than the marks, 'and I might add that there was a decided bunion on the left foot of the deceased which would have left its mark.'

'Look at the impression on the board. I have to ask whether the fact of the impression being smaller than the deceased's foot may be accounted for by the impression being imperfect?'

'I think not, because the person by whom these impressions have been made has been leaning upon the foot and standing. In taking the measure of the foot of the deceased, it could only be done by pressing paper against the foot without there being the weight of the body upon it, and if the foot was so much larger without the pressure of the body, if pressed this way on wood, I would argue *a fortiori* that it would have been still greater.'

'Is there no defect in that impression as to the size of the foot from the whole of the impression not being left?'

'This footprint was cut out of part of the floor so close to the window that the person who left the impression must have been standing. It is not the impression of a person walking, which is a more imperfect impression than that made when standing.'

'You don't understand my meaning. May the foot that made the impression not have been longer than the impression now left?'

'Not very much.'

'Why?'

'Because it was clear when I examined it first.'

'Was it perfect at the toes and heels?'

'It was very perfect, considering all things.'

Finally Dr Macleod conceded that though all the vital injuries must have been caused by a heavy, edged instrument such as the cleaver, this was true only of the vital ones—those on the right side of the head and below the right ear.

The bite marks on the prisoner's hand, this prosecution witness most frankly said were not the marks of human teeth—he had compared them with the teeth of the deceased—and were consistent with her own story of having been nipped by her dog.

*　　　*　　　*

Alexander M'Call, Assistant Superintendent of Police in Glasgow, had arrived at the house at about half-past nine in the evening bringing with him two assistants. In the bedroom, he said, the part of the floor in front of the cupboard opposite the door, seemed to have been washed, though it was then dry. It was white and clean, whereas if it had been washed a considerable time before, it would have been like the rest of the flooring. The blood on the kitchen door was quite obvious to him. He had noted the bloody footmarks in the bedroom and had had the pieces of flooring cut out. He described his famous experiment with the piece of stick. He could not tell the learned judge what were the comparative lengths of the dead woman's foot and that of the footprints, but by keeping his 'finger and thumb in the place' he had satisfied himself and presumably hoped to satisfy the court, that the feet of the deceased could not have made the prints—they were half an inch longer. 'I did it with a piece of stick. I laid it upon the impression.'

'Was that all the material upon which you formed your judgement?'

'Yes.'

'You hadn't even a footrule?' said Mr Clark.

'No,' said Assistant Superintendent Alexander M'Call.

Detective Officer Donald Campbell had also compared the prints with the assistance of his little 'spale'. He was all for producing this in court, but counsel for the defence seemed to have some fussy notion about the inadmissibility of exhibits of which no one had ever heard, being produced without warning from the witness's pocket. Anyway, he agreed with the earlier witnesses that 'by the length of the foot-mark' the print could not have been made by the deceased.

Detective Officer Campbell, in fact, was a really splendid witness. In the full light of the Monday afternoon, at half-past five, he had examined the kitchen floor and where all the other witnesses had seen the large damp patch, had found it 'quite dry at the time and it appeared as if it might have been done a couple of days previously.' It did not appear (despite Doctors Fleming and Macleod and their evidence of 'a severe struggle') to have been much trodden upon since it had been washed.

Mr Clark: 'Did you notice any blood on the kitchen floor?'

'Well, I did not.' But, he acknowledged, the floor had a greasy appearance in parts where it had been washed up, and had a reddish tinge upon it as from a greasy substance.

'Did it appear as if blood had been washed from off the floor?'

'That was my impression at the time.'

The lobby, however, he said, did not appear to have been washed.

He was left in the house that night, and had searched the house. So it was he, presumably, who kept the kitchen fire so merrily burning and with it all evidence that might have been in process of incineration there; and who missed the blood-stained hammer on the kitchen dresser. It was not till the following Saturday that the Sheriff's Officer, M'Laughlin, turned up to make further investigations, and so discovered the hammer, and sifted the—now meaningless—ashes in the grate.

This ended, to all intents and purposes, the prosecution's evidence as to the condition of the body and of the scene where it was discovered; except for confirmation about the key of the pantry which was duly proved to have fitted the bedroom lock. Superintendent M'Call described the chest in the bedroom which he had found closed but—the catch being broken—unlocked; and which had been raked through by 'a bloody hand' and left almost empty. There was a small bandbox, broken open, blood-stained and also empty, inside the chest. And Detective Officer Campbell had found blood spots in the middle of old Mr Fleming's 'wardrobe room' across the passage from the kitchen.

'Did you find anything in the room where old Mr Fleming kept his clothes?'

'Yes, I found some shirts in a chest of drawers with spots of blood on them.'

Lord Deas: 'With spots of blood on them, you say?'

'Yes.'

Lord Deas: 'Do you say that these were found in a drawer pointed out by old Mr Fleming?'

The detective had said absolutely nothing of the kind; he said, in fact, no more than the above sentence, 'I found some shirts in a chest of drawers with spots of blood on them'; so this attempt to give the old innocent a gratuitous pat on the back for speaking up did not come off. One drawer of the chest had been locked and Mr Fleming on request had handed over a bunch of keys, one of which opened the drawer. It was the only thing in the room that was locked.

And the officer had found in a cellar, or cellars, a number of cloths which could have been used to clean up the blood, though they showed no marks of blood. On the other hand, they were still wet.

The Superintendent had had a word with old Mr Fleming that Monday evening. 'He made a statement to me.'

Mr Clark: 'What did he say?'

Lord Deas: 'Do you want to hear anything he said?'

Mr Clark: 'I want to hear everything he said.'

Lord Deas: 'You had better ask your questions in detail.'

Mr Clark: 'Did he say anything about the noise he heard?'

M'Call: 'He said he had been wakened by the screams and he thought he heard another scream. He said he thought they came from the outside.'

'Did he say what kind of screams they were?'

Lord Deas: 'These are questions to be put to the man himself.'

Mr Clark: 'The position I wish to occupy is to lay before the jury the same evidence which would have been laid before the jury if Mr Fleming had been the party at the bar; because one of my defences is that Mr Fleming was the person who committed this murder. Surely I am entitled to go into that evidence for my own justification, which the Crown would be entitled to go into for the purpose of proving an accusation? If Mr Fleming gave to this witness a different account regarding what he had seen and heard, I am entitled to bring it out.'

Lord Deas: 'I don't object to your putting questions to the witness with the view of contradicting anything that James Fleming said in the box, but I question the correctness of a course which might lead to the contradiction of what has been said out of the box. What I have down is that James Fleming said to the witness that the screams he had heard came from the outside.' (Actually what he said at the time he was examined was that he had first thought they came from outside, and then that they came from 'down below'.)

Mr Clark, resuming cross-examination: 'Did he say from what kind of person those screams came?'

'No.'

'Did he not say anything like "the screams of loose women"?'

'That was the explanation he gave me.

'Did he say he had got out of bed?'

'No, he did not.'

'Did he say what he had done *in* bed?'

'Yes. He said he raised himself upon his elbow and looked at his watch which he said he kept beneath his pillow.'

'Did he say that he jumped out of bed?'

'No.'

So the judge's permission for contradiction of anything Mr Fleming had said 'in the box' was most handsomely justified: for he had said in the box that very morning that when he heard the odd kind o' squeal, he had jumped oot o' bed but, a' being quate in the coorse o' a minute's time, he had gaed awa' tae his bed again. Even Lord Deas had nothing to say about that.

And then M'Call had got information about the plate that was pledged and he had gone off to the prisoner's house in the Broomielaw that same day, and told her that he was making enquiries about Jess M'Pherson's murder. . . .

'What did she say?' asked Mr Gifford; but Mr Clark objected. It was agreed that the witness should confine his answer to the one question, without entering into the details of the conversation. This all fell rather flat, however, for in fact Jessie had made no reply.

And so witness had taken her into custody.

In the house had been found a sleeve or part of a sleeve, Exhibit number 23 in court. It was picked up by Mary Adams, the washer-woman, and handed over to the police by her.

And in a cupboard in the basement of the house at Sandyford Place, there was a bottle, uncorked, containing a little rum.

The hours passed. Evidence was taken about keys—which amounted to this, that the defence could produce no key which would have admitted the prisoner to her own home on that Friday night; the door could be opened only from the inside. Mrs Fraser testified to having called, had a glass of rum, and set off with Mrs M'Lachlan, parting from her at the corner of Stobcross Street. Mrs Campbell, the lodger, described Jessie's movements before she left the house that evening, borrowing a bottle from the cupboard and going out for rum and biscuits—the bottle was a common bottle; Exhibit number 5 was about the size, shape and colour of the one borrowed, but she could not say that it was the same one. She had heard Mrs M'Lachlan go off with Mrs Fraser but didn't see her leave. She was awakened in the morning by the crying of the child and saw by the Broomie-law clock that it was then about half-past five. (At this mention of her little boy, for the first time Jessie's courage failed her, and she hung her head and wept a little tear. She was by this time very pale and appeared exhausted by the interminable day.) She did not go back to bed, continued Mrs Campbell, but remained up, in her room; sometime after eight she took in the milk from the milk-girl. Mrs M'Lachlan returned at nine o'clock and was carrying a large bundle. A short time afterwards she reappeared from her own room and went down to the cellar, wearing a dress the witness had never before seen, 'a merino dress of reddish-brown colour and the back of it pleated, and I think it was trimmed with blue velvet.' Shown Exhibit number 32, the dress sent by Jessie to the dyer's to be dyed black, 'That might be the same gown, but I cannot say. The colour is changed and it looks as if it had been dyed. The trimmings on it do not appear to be like the way it was trimmed before.'

She was shown thirteen pieces of a torn-up flannel petti-coat; it was 'very like' one Mrs M'Lachlan had had, which she had said was made out of a piece of blanket. And twenty pieces of coburg were 'very like the dress Mrs M'Lachlan wore on the Friday. They look like the colour of the dress. That was a dress I knew very well.' Mrs M'Lachlan's dress had had three flounces and here were the remains of flounces. And shown three pieces of a wincey petticoat: 'That is not like the colour of the dress (*sic*) I examined before. It may be the gaslight.' When she had seen it before at the Fiscal's office, she agreed, she had thought it was something like the wincey petticoat that Mrs M'Lachlan used to wear. But, shown a flannel petticoat, Exhibit 24, she had never seen that before, except at the Fiscal's office. (This would pre-sumably be Jess M'Pherson's petticoat.)

She had been at home all the Friday, over the weekend and on the Monday, except that she might have been out for a few minutes on Friday. She had not seen any strange man call on Mrs M'Lachlan on the Friday, nor had anyone called on the Saturday. She had never seen any old man call on Mrs M'Lachlan.

Mrs M'Lachlan seemed very unwell on the Saturday and Sunday. On the Monday, she was going out and in all day.

It being now nearly nine o'clock and Lord Deas despairing of 'bringing this trial to a conclusion in the course of the present sederunt'—not unnaturally, since in fact it took another three days—he decided that the Court should rise till the following morning at a quarter to ten, and 'ordained all concerned then to attend under the pains of law and the baill fifteen jurors now in the box being hereby ordained to repair under the charge of the macers of Court, and of John Murray, Sheriff-Officer, Glasgow, as their assistant (who, being present, was duly sworn *de fideli*) to Carrick's Hotel, George Street, Glasgow, to remain under their charge till brought here tomorrow morning, in the hour of cause above mentioned, being kept strictly secluded during the period of adjournment from all communication with any person whatsoever on the subject of the trial, the Clerk of the Court having liberty to communicate with them in relation to their private affairs. . . .'

It was pretty tough going a hundred years ago, for those who got mixed up in legal affairs, on whichever side of the bars they might be.

CHAPTER FIFTEEN

The second day of the trial opened with the evidence of Mary Adams, who had 'washed for' Mrs M'Lachlan at the Broomielaw. She described her various errands to the pawnshops, and the forgotten message to the locksmith about the key to the outer door; and Mrs M'Lachlan's having given her the burnt crinoline wires for Sarah. Faced with the various petticoats she was indefinite, but the brown coburg dress from the Hamilton fields she identified positively as the prisoner's—the missing sleeve she herself had found at the Broomielaw and handed over to the police. She and defence counsel got into a fine old tangle over the cinnamon merino which Jessie was alleged to have dyed black. She had said in her examination-in-chief that she had never seen Mrs M'Lachlan with it, or seen it at all till it was shown to her at the Fiscal's office. Mr Clark for the defence asked her: 'You said that it appears to you to be dyed?'

'Yes.'

'Why do you think that?'

'Because I see it's dyed.'

'You mean that it is coloured?'

'Yes, from the colour it was.'

'How do you know that?'

'I see that it's dyed.'

'How do you know that it was not coloured before?'

'Just because I see it's dyed. It's not its first colour.'

The Judge: 'You say you think it is not the original colour?'

'It has been dyed, whether it's the original colour or not. It's new.'

Mr Clark: 'How do you know that is dyed new?'

'Any person can see that it's dyed.'

'Can you give me any reason how you know it has been dyed?'

'I can see it.'

'New dyed?'

'I don't know whether it has been dyed new or not, but I think the dye is new.'

'How can you tell that it has been newly dyed?'

'Anybody could by the smell.'

On about July 4, the day of the murder, or a little earlier—she couldn't be sure of the date—the prisoner had said to her that she 'would have to get money somewhere or another.' 'I don't know what for. She would be needing it, I suppose. She did not give any reason.' She had thought, said Mrs Adams, that Mrs M'Lachlan's husband must have a few pounds by him that she was going to lift, or that she herself must have a little money put by and was going to break into it. (James M'Lachlan was subsequently to say that he had no money put by.) Her impression was that Mrs M'Lachlan wanted to get her clothes out of pawn and must have some money for that purpose. Most of this information was elicited from her by Lord Deas.

Her daughter, Sarah, followed. She described the episode of the trunk which she eventually took for the prisoner to the Hamilton station, and an errand to Sandyford Place four or five months before the murder, with instructions to ask Jess M'Pherson for the loan of £2. She positively identified the torn-up woollen petticoat; 'I know it by the stitching.'

Lord Deas: 'Did you say you know the stitching?'

'It is my own stitching.' The prisoner being in a hurry one day, she explained, had given it to her to finish off the sewing. She very positively recognised Jessie's brown coburg dress and the separate sleeve; but as positively denied any knowledge of the crinoline wires—evidently Mama did not hand them on to her little daughter as Mrs M'Lachlan had suggested.

Mr Rutherfurd Clark contented himself largely with the destruction of Miss Adams' character for reliability. Sarah admitted that two years ago—she being then ten years old—she had given evidence in a case between Jessie Mackay, who was a friend of her mother's, and Edward M'Geachie. Her mother and Miss Mackay had later quarrelled and Sarah had been re-examined 'for the defender'—Mr M'Geachie. 'And did you then say that all you had said in your first examination was quite untrue?'

'I told them that Jess Mackay had told me to tell lies. She said she would give me a dress and a bonnet.'

Cross-examined about the coburg dress, she said she knew the prisoner had had a dress of that colour and material, the bodice trimmed with narrow velvet; but she agreed that she could not say more than that. Lord Deas was having no such convenient equivocations, however, when they were favourable to the accused. He ordered that the child be confronted again with the pieces of coburg and asked her if she had any doubt that these were part of the prisoner's dress. He then distinctly heard her reply. 'They are part of the prisoner's dress,' whereas the reporters (an unprejudiced body) had as distinctly heard her say, 'I *think* they are part of the prisoner's dress.' The jury, appealed to, knew better than to hear otherwise than as his lordship heard—thus qualifying for the first flower in the large bouquet of praise which he was to bestow upon them at the end of the trial. Having established the reply firmly in their minds, he invited counsel to put the question again. But Mr Clark didn't bother. What was the use?

Mrs M'Gregor, a dressmaker, somewhat revenged Mr Clark, though she had been brought there by the prosecution. An eminently fair witness, she refused to commit herself regarding the pieces of the brown coburg dress, though if in fact it was the prisoner's, she herself had made it. It seemed to be the same kind of colour and cloth, and she had had a similar trimming in the shop. She thought the sleeve and the dress belonged together but under cross examination she agreed readily that she could not say more than that they were of the same cloth and the same colour, and the lining was the same—but it was a very common cloth and a very common lining. Unfortunately Mr Clark, perhaps a little over-elated, now pressed her too hard. She agreed that there was no real reason that the sleeve shouldn't belong to another, similar, dress; but then she added, 'it would scarcely correspond with the dress as to the exact shade.' Mr Clark sat down, doubtless wishing he had done so just two questions earlier.

Thomas Millar gave evidence as to articles pawned for Mrs M'Lachlan by the Adams's, *mère et fille*; pawned over many months usually in the name of Mary Fraser and with a false address. Thomas Robb, superintendent of police, had found forty-one tickets in the prisoner's home, all under the name of Fraser with varying Christian names. A clerk of the Caledonian railway described the trunk brought by Sarah Adams—it weighed twenty-one pounds: empty, it weighed twelve pounds, the deduction being that it contained nine pounds weight of—something. Three days later, the prisoner, after walking three or four times past his office door, came in and asked him if the trunk had been sent off. Aaron Wharton told of the arrival of the trunk at Hamilton. Several days later a boy had come in and asked if it was there; on hearing that it was he went out and came back with a woman, who, signing herself 'Mrs M'Lachlan', collected the trunk and helped the boy carry it away. The Chassels family told of Jessie's visit to their house, of twelve-year-old James going back with her for the trunk, and afterwards taking it, empty now, to the saddler's for repair. She had gone off, carrying the big bundle, tied in a kerchief. Mrs Chassels had seen part of a brown wool flounce, sticking out of the bundle, and the lady had said it was a merino wrapper. Later she had met Mirrilees and given him the kerchief, which she said she had found; and told him to take it home and get it hemmed. And Elizabeth Gibson described the frail, weary creature coming to her public house a mile out of Hamilton, and asking for a glass of spirits: and creeping off again, carrying her heavy bundle. The two small girls identified her as the lady they had met near the Tommy Linn Park who had asked them if there was not a burn or sheugh whaur a person micht wat their lips; and told how they had subsequently found the torn and blood-stained clothing hidden in the fields a little further on. Various members of the Hamilton police confirmed these discoveries.

Mr Rutherfurd Clark let it all go by with hardly any cross-examination at all.

And Miss M'Crone described how on the morning after the murder, a woman—she could not identify her as the prisoner—had brought in the cinnamon merino dress to be dyed black and the grey cloak to be cleaned, giving the name of M'Donald. And Mrs Rainny told how she had first redeemed the blue and black poplin and how Mrs M'Lachlan had changed into it before taking the cinnamon merino to be dyed. Shown the merino she would not swear to it as the same dress, but 'by the shape and the make' she thought it was. 'This is dyed, ye ken. It was a brown one then.'

Robert Lundie gave evidence of the pawning of the silver from the house in Sandyford Place on the morning after the murder.

He agreed with counsel for the defence that when confronted with the prisoner, he had had some difficulty before he finally identified her. She had given the name of Mary M'Donald and said she had been sent by her mistress—she was alone, she had no child with her. She came in some time between twelve and one. On the following Tuesday he saw an account of the murder in the papers (he had meanwhile been out of town) with a description of the missing plate. He examined the silver, found it was marked with an 'F', and immediately handed it over to the police. His assistant confirmed very positively that the plate had been pawned after midday.

And William Smith Dunlop recognised the black japanned box as having come from his shop—it had their private mark on it. It was sold on the morning after the murder by an assistant called Nish who had since gone off to Antigua. He did not see the woman at the time the box was sold, but recognised the prisoner as having come in several days later; she either took the box away with her or it was 'by her orders sent after her to some station'. She said she was sending the box by some railway—not going with it herself.

Mr Rutherfurd Clark embarked upon another of his adventures —he appears to have specialised somewhat in mixed-up witnesses. 'You say that this is a common box of which you sell numbers?'

'Yes.'

'Now, how can you tell us that that (Exhibit 28) is the box that the prisoner spoke about on the Tuesday or Wednesday when you saw her?'

'I beg your pardon? I don't understand the question.'

'How is it that you know that it is the box to which the address was affixed of which you spoke?'

Had Sir Winston Churchill been present he would doubtless have muttered that this was sheer pedantry up with which he would not put. William Smith Dunlop simply looked blank and said nothing.

'How is it that you know that this is the box that left the shop on Wednesday?'

Mr Dunlop took refuge in an alibi and said that James Fullerton had been beside him and seen the whole.

'No, no, never mind what James Fullerton saw. You have

said that this is the box which was sent out of your shop on Wednesday. How do you know that it is?'

'I know it because it has our private mark on it.'

'Have the other boxes that you sell not the same private mark?'

'No, they have not,' said Mr Dunlop, vaguely triumphant.

The judge interposed to try to straighten things out. 'Is there a private mark on the other boxes that you sell?'

'Yes.'

'Well, is the mark on that box different from the private mark on the other boxes?'

'No.'

'Do you put the same private mark on other boxes of that description?'

'We do on boxes of that size.'

'Then what the gentleman is saying now is this—if you put the same private mark on the other boxes of the same size that you make, how do you know that that is the very box you sent out that Wednesday afternoon, and not some other box made in your shop?'

It was all too much for poor Mr Dunlop. 'I don't think I can answer that question.'

Mr Clark came back into the fray. 'Do you say anything more than that this box was made in your shop?'

'I can say nothing more than that, and that the prisoner at the bar is the person who came in that day.'

'And that she took away a box of that description?'

'Yes.'

'That, surely, is not sufficient to warrant you in saying that it is the box which she took away?'

'It has our private mark,' insisted Mr Dunlop.

'I suppose all your boxes are marked in the same way?'

'In just the same way.'

'Dear me,' exclaimed Mr Clark, by now so exasperated that he began to double back on himself. 'Can you say nothing more than that it was made in your shop?'

'I can say that it was made in our shop.'

'And that the prisoner took a box *of that description* away; or that it was sent after her?'

'Yes.'

'And even of that you are doubtful?'

'I have no doubt the box was taken or sent away.'

'Then don't say that that box is the box that the prisoner took away,' said Mr Clark, angrily; and angrily sat down. Poor Mr Dunlop was doubtless a sadly puzzled man as he made his way thankfully back to his place. Whatever had he done to offend? After all, all their boxes did have that private mark. . . .

Mr Fullerton, his assistant, identified the prisoner as the woman who had bought a box on the Saturday morning; as to the rest he was uncertain, having left the matter with Nish, but he thought she had altered the address first put on the box, and he thought she had arranged for them to send it to the station for her, and he thought it had now been addressed to Ayr.

John Roke, railway clerk at Bridge Street Station, had 'a faint recollection' of the black tin box—if he looked up his entry of any article that passed through his hands it conjured up a faint recollection of that article. Somewhat roughly handled, he stuck by this very credible trick of memory; he could not recall and had never pretended to be able to recall the size, shape or colour of the box—but he did have a faint recollection that the entry on the relevant way bill referred to some sort of japanned tin box. He could not add, poor chap, that really it all couldn't matter less anyway—all he was saying was that he had a faint idea that the way bill referred to a tin box, and this could be amply proved by half a dozen different witnesses yet to be heard.

Messrs M'Millan, Craig, Blair and Young, railway employees, gave evidence of the pleasantly human arrangement by which they had obliged a fellow—now identified as James M'Lachlan—who had turned up at the Bridge Street Station on July 10 and asked them to get back a box for him which was lying at Ayr Station, addressed to 'Mrs Darnley'. A porter wrote a note to the clerk in the office at Ayr and a guard delivered it for him, the box was handed over and brought back to Glasgow—and there was no charge. It was finally taken away by the fellow—who of course was James M'Lachlan.

There was difficulty over the evidence of James' sister, Elizabeth Reid, regarding his movements, since he himself was not to be called. Mr Clark fought every step of the way, but Lord Deas was as usual on the other side. Even when the prosecution offered to withdraw a question, he replied querulously: 'You can do as you please,' but continued to insist: 'I consider the question competent.' Thus encouraged, Mr Gifford at last repeated the question: 'Well, who brought the box?'—to Mrs Reid's house at Greenock.

Mrs Reid, distressed and weeping, acknowledged that her brother had brought the box, and it had been unpacked and the contents laid out on a bed—a velvet cloak, a cloth cloak, a black silk dress, a brown silk dress, a silk polka and a black plaid. 'You saw the dresses less or more?' asked Lord Deas—it is difficult to see why, since she had just admitted seeing them all, as listed. That was on the Saturday, July 12, the day after the box was brought from the railway station.

Mr Gifford, for the prosecution: 'Where did you see these things on the Saturday morning?'

'I saw them lying on a bed in my house.'

'Did you put them anywhere?'

'Yes, I put them into a drawer.'

'You did not put them into the bed?' enquired Lord Deas: no doubt the jury added a second blossom to their bouquet by conjuring up a hinney of respectful laughter. Mrs Reid simply said, 'No.'

Mr Gifford: 'Did you see anything done with them on Wednesday?'

Mr Clark interrupted. Would not this be the day after James M'Lachlan had been arrested with his wife, examined and released?

'I don't think it matters,' said Mr Gifford.

'I think it matters a good deal,' said Mr Clark. Lord Deas, however, could be relied upon to be satisfied that Mr Gifford's question had been perfectly competent and it was asked again.

Yes, Mrs Reid had seen the things put back into the box and an addressed label tied to the box. A porter called Laurie called for it and took it away.

Donald Laurie agreed that he had collected a box from that address on the date suggested—a box very much like the one shown to him in court. But he couldn't be sure for his eye-sight was not so good now—a rapid deterioration, for this had all happened only eight or nine weeks ago.

James Hughes, parcel deliverer at Greenock Station had

handled the box and there was another sharp tussle over a 'faint recollection' of what it looked like; but Hughes, like John Roke at Bridge Street, stoutly defended his ability to recall, when he saw an entry in his own handwriting, a vague picture of the article it referred to. He had taken no particular notice of the box at the time, but he could be sure that it was about the same colour, size and shape as the one he saw in court, and his entry was 'T. Box' which stood for 'tin box'—and *not* for 'tea box' as defence counsel suggested. John M'Intyre, also of Bridge Street, identified the box quite positively—he had handed it over when it was asked for by Superintendent M'Call; and what was more, the lock being then broken and the lid a little open, he had caught a glimpse of the clothes inside.

Margaret M'Lachlan (no relation) identified the contents of the black box as having belonged to Jess M'Pherson and was particularly positive about the black plaid—she had had it often in her hands, having been a servant at Sandyford Place for several months earlier that year. Mary Downie who had been in service together with Jess for many years and who was the friend with whom she set up her little grocery shop, was also positive in her identification—most of the things had been bought in her company. Margaret Fleming, John Fleming's sister who ran the house for him, also knew Jess well, of course, and 'had often occasion to see her dresses'; but Lord Deas was evidently fed up with all this vain repetition for he 'discouraged the re-opening of this line of evidence.' And anyway it was nearly nine o'clock. The Court adjourned again until ten the next morning. This was their second consecutive eleven-hour day.

The third day opened with the evidence of Andrew Sloan, clerk and cashier in John Fleming's office. He agreed that he knew old Mr Fleming—he didn't know his age but had heard him refer to it some time before this case as about eighty-five. He described the old gentleman's little job, collecting the rents of a small estate of about twenty tenants. Mr Gifford asked him: 'What sort of man is he mentally?'

Lord Deas interrupted. He thought that the Court had as good an opportunity of judging as the witness, who was not a medical man. (The witness had observed the old man over a period of years and the Court for perhaps as many hours; but that apparently didn't count.) 'You may ask him this.' He put the question to the witness: 'There is nothing wrong with his mind that you ever heard of?'

'No,' said Mr Sloan, briefly.

'And he has faculties as entire as you could expect at his age?'

'Yes,' said Mr Sloan, briefly again. His not to make reply that in fact for a man of allegedly eighty-seven Mr Fleming's faculties were not 'what you would expect' at all, but quite outstanding— sight and hearing practically unimpaired, health and agility excellent, and only some slight tendency to winter colds. . . .

Examination continued: 'Yes, I remember the Monday when the murder was discovered.'

'That is the day when Jessie M'Pherson was found dead in the house in Sandyford Place', explained Lord Deas kindly. It seems a little unlikely that anyone present let alone John Fleming's own clerk, should have confused it with any other. 'I recollect that,' said he.

The old gentleman had been in the office on the Saturday and also on the Monday, but appeared just as usual and had mentioned nothing about the maid's being missing.

John M'Allister who had known old James Fleming for forty years had met him on the Sunday following the murder and exchanged a few words; nothing being said, however, of the missing servant. Yes, as far as he knew, Mr Fleming had always had a respectable character.

Mr Clark rose to cross-examine. Here was his opportunity to bring out the fact that old Fleming had, about ten years ago, confessed to the elders of his kirk—to which same church the witness belonged—that he had recently committed the sin of fornication and had a child by a servant maid. 'At least you never *heard* anything against him?'

'No; never till this case happened.'

'Do you not know that he was before the kirk session?'

'I did not know till this affair.'

'Then you *have* heard something against him?'

'Yes, in the newspapers I have.'

Lord Deas intervened once more. 'Now, Mr Clark—this need not be opened up just now with the witness.'

Mr Clark appears not to have protested at all. He sat down meekly: and that was the last the Court ever heard of 'the old innocent's' confessed fornication and Indian summer of parenthood.

Evidence from the National Security Savings Bank of old Mr Fleming's little nest egg of a hundred and fifty pounds; evidence of a further thirty pounds in the Royal Bank of Scotland. Evidence of Elizabeth Brownlie, the maid next door, who had tried to borrow the spade on the Saturday afternoon and been sent away empty-handed because 'the girl was out' and Mr Fleming didn't know where to find the key of the garden shed. She had seen Mr Fleming at ten o'clock on the morning after the murder, going down to the end of the garden for coals and had been struck at the time by the fact that he looked round to see if anyone were watching him. She had something to offer on the character of the old man—Jess had told her that he watched everything that went on in his own home, and next door. One night about a fortnight before the murder, she had had a word with Jess who was down at the garden door, admitting a man and a woman—presumed to be Mrs M'Lachlan who admitted such a visit, though she had no man with her. It was ten o'clock and Jess had remarked to Elizabeth that that auld deevil was only jist new awa' tae his bed. Lord Deas interrupted at this stage with a remark to the general effect that what the soldier said was not evidence but did not disallow the answer: and Mr Clark asked, 'Did you understand the "old devil" to refer to old Mr Fleming?' It was at this point that Lord Deas admitted, 'I suppose we all understand that.'

A juror now rose to ask—with odd irrelevance—if he and his companions might have the plans of the house in Sandyford Place laid before them, and Mr Gifford said he was most willing to oblige. But the next witness was Andrew Darnley, whose evidence would seem to necessitate blueprints as little as Elizabeth Brownlie's. He described his visits to Sandyford Place on the Saturday and Sunday following the murder, when the old man had simply told him that Jess was 'out'. He had commented sarcastically on the second occasion that she was often out just now. Mr Fleming had made no reply.

However, perhaps the juror had after all been possessed of some second sight, for the next witness was the architect who had made plans of the house in Sandyford Place—a dismal job for a layman, for the body still lay on the floor in the bedroom and had now lain there for several days. And all in vain; for, Mr Gifford requesting permission for copies of the plans to be passed to the jury, His Lordship expressed the opinion that according to his experience the less they confused themselves with plans the better. The jury finally decided not to benefit by this remarkable advice and plan number 1 was handed over to them. Mr O'Neill gave evidence of the blood-stained trail leading from near to the kitchen cupboard, through the passage outside and into the bedroom. Part of the kitchen floor and part of the bedroom floor appeared to have been washed. All the floors were dry when he saw them.

The quartermaster aboard the steamer *Pladda* swore to James M'Lachlan having been with his ship for a week from the Thursday before the murder.

Thomas Railton, clerk and cashier in charge of the rent collecting for the property in the Broomielaw, gave evidence that on Friday, July 4, Mrs M'Lachlan was in arrears to the tune of £4 19s. On the following morning she had come into his office and paid £4. She came in between eleven and twelve o'clock; he was sure it was not later, for they had to bank their takings on Saturdays by twelve. (It will be recalled that the silver was not pawned till after twelve.)

It would take a quarter of an hour to walk between their office and Lundie's pawn, where the silver was pledged.

And another clerk described how the prisoner, always in arrears, had still been given a month or more to pay—had not been pressed in any way, had been told that she wouldn't be pressed.

And finally—in the case for the prosecution—expert evidence was given of the presence of blood-stains on the cleaver found in the kitchen at Sandyford Place, on the crinoline wires, on the articles of clothing found in the fields outside Hamilton; the brown coburg dress was in several pieces and much torn, and in certain parts appeared to have been washed with some strong chemical agent (such as soda), for the colour was sensibly changed and the fibre of both cloth and lining very tender and rotten. In no case was it possible to identify the blood as human but it was all definitely mammalian blood.

That ended the evidence for the prosecution. The Court settled back to listen to the reading of the three Declarations made by the accused—the first upon her apprehension on July 14, the second and third from prison in the course of the following week.

Counsel for the defence leapt up to object.

Mr Clark's submission was that these three declarations were inadmissible, and he based his argument upon the case of *Agnes Kelly*, tried twenty years earlier before Lord Justice Clerk Hope, 'than whom I am sure no greater criminal lawyer ever sat upon the bench.' That case was one of wilful fire-raising on a farm, and the accused a 'common farm servant'. As in the case of *M'Lachlan*, three long declarations were extracted from the prisoner; nor were these simple statements, but were obtained by skilful questioning based, in the case of the second and third declarations, upon additional evidence which emerged when the first was being checked. Lord Justice Clerk Hope considered this procedure most unsatisfactory and an abuse of the objects for which the party accused was brought before a magistrate for a declaration. It was pretty plain, said the judge, that the declarations had been taken, not with the purpose of allowing the party to give any explanation but with the direct object of rearing up evidence against her: of tricking her in fact—though he did not use so positive a word—into giving incriminating answers over matters which she might think unimportant, and upon which the authorities had obtained information between the declarations. There was no equality, he suggested, between a procurator-fiscal, 'with all the alarm of imprisonment and the authority of a magistrate and the terrors of an accusation to back him—and a poor countrywoman of fifty-five years of age, uneducated and illiterate; if such an encounter of wits was to be permitted, he thought the whole purposes and objects of taking a declaration from the accused had been overlooked. . . .

And so had they been, insisted Mr Clark, in the case of the prisoner Jessie M'Lachlan: and with this aggravation, that she had been catechised like a witness by the Prosecutor-Fiscal upon information elicited from her husband. But her husband could not have been precognosced as a witness nor examined in court, and it was Mr Clark's submission that this information had been got from him under what amounted to false pretences—by the simple expedient of charging and apprehending him when the authorities knew perfectly well that he had been far away from the scene of the crime when it was committed and could be in no way involved

186

in it. Having got what they needed from him, they had discharged him, and then used the information to trick—once again this was not the actual word used—incriminating admissions from his wife. Taken under such circumstances, her declarations did not serve their proper purpose as declarations, and statements had been taken from her which should not have been taken and which therefore should not be used as evidence against her.

Even to the layman the submission—whether justified or not—seems sufficiently clear. Lord Deas, however, professed to be as muddled as poor Mr Dunlop with his marked boxes. 'As far as I can follow the eloquent speech which has just now been made, it rests upon three grounds. . . .' He enumerated them, all three. If there were any others involved in the speech of his friend, Mr Clark, he would be glad to be informed of them.

Mr Clark immediately obliged. 'Then there is a fourth reason,' said Lord Deas placidly. These objections, he continued, he could only dispose of upon the evidence before him, which had been recorded in cross-examination of the Sheriff-Substitute and Fiscal——

'The declarations themselves?' suggested Mr Clark.

But Lord Deas would have nothing to say to the declarations themselves.

'The evidence, I say, consists of the cross-examination of those two gentlemen, for Mr Hart was not asked questions in regard to this point.' (Mr Hart was joint Procurator-Fiscal—with Jno. Gemmel—and had merely given evidence that the third statement had been taken in his presence, the prisoner making it freely and voluntarily and having been in her sound and sober senses at the time.) And, looking to that evidence and taking all the declarations, said the Judge, he could find no ground for holding that when the prisoner's husband was examined and his declarations taken he was known to be innocent and that his declaration was taken from him as a precognition. Both the gentlemen (Jno. Gemmel, the Procurator-Fiscal, and Mr Strathern, Sheriff-Substitute) had sworn expressly, had sworn distinctly, that they did not know at the time that James M'Lachlan had been absent from town and could not have been implicated in the crime.

Mr Clark: 'My lord, the Procurator——'

Lord Deas: 'Will you wait till I have done?'

Mr Clark: 'The Procurator-Fiscal said he had no reason to doubt——'

Jno. Gemmel's evidence may be found in the very early stages of the trial, immediately preceding old Fleming's appearance in the witness-box—page 128. The reader may care to glance back and judge for himself how positive had been his denial that he could have known before James M'Lachlan was questioned that he almost certainly was innocent of the crime. Lord Deas, however, would have none of it. He thought the authorities had been perfectly right to apprehend M'Lachlan at that stage and to take a statement from him. So that finished that.

And the second ground of complaint, he said, was that a great many questions had been put to the prisoner in the course of her declarations. Well, that was nothing more than was done in every declaration. And as to the length of the statements, their length must depend on the nature of the case: in fact it was quite right that she should have the fullest opportunity of explaining everything that she could explain—and he thought they would find the declarations full of explanations which his friend Mr Clark would not willingly throw aside when he came to address the Court. (His friend Mr Clark must have rolled up his eyes to high heaven.) The fourth objection was that the prisoner was asked about certain articles before the articles were shown to her. But the Sheriff had said that, though there were some preliminary questions before the articles were produced, these did not occupy above two minutes. . . . How true this was, at any rate in the spirit, may be judged by a reference to Jessie's second declaration, (commencing on page 96.) Lord Deas, at any rate, was satisfied with it, Lord Justice Clerk Hope and poor fire-raising Agnes Kelly notwithstanding. 'Gentlemen of the jury, you will now hear the declarations read.'

Taken straight through in the monotonous drone of some court official—how quick and glib they must have sounded, how compact, considered, specious and deliberate: those poor muddled, desperate wrigglings on the hook of provocative interrogation, of a woman alone and abandoned and sick with dread. Well indeed for Jessie if the County Buildings could have burned up, as she had said to her fellow-prisoners she wished they would—before ever those foolish, frantic 'explanations' were published to the incredulous ears of the listening Court.

Mr Clark called the first witness for the defence.

The first witness for the defence was George Paton, the milk-man, to be followed by Donald M'Quarrie, his boy. A comparison between their evidence and that given under cross-examination by old Mr Fleming at the beginning of the trial (pages 144 onward) may well prove a rewarding, not to say a convincing, study. George Paton appears to have been an alert young man of twenty-five. He was in the habit, he said, of supplying milk to the houses in Sandyford Place. He had heard of the death of the servant at No. 17 on Tuesday the 8th, the day following its discovery. He then remembered having been at the house on the previous Saturday morning, arriving there between half-past seven and twenty minutes to eight. He was quite sure of the time. He came off the cart but did not go up to the house—the boy Donald went up, and he rang the bell. 'It was answered immediately.'

Mr Clark, for the defence: 'Did you see who answered it?'

'No.'

'But you saw the door opened?'

'I saw the door opened a small bit but I did not see who was at it.'

'How much delay was there in opening the door?'

'Very little delay. I could not pay much attention, in serving other people, but there was not much delay.'

'Was the bell rung a second time?'

'I couldn't say.'

'Was any milk taken on that occasion?'

'No, none was taken.'

'Were you there on the following day, Sunday; and the Monday? Was milk taken then?'

'I was there both days and no milk was taken.'

The only time he had actually seen old Mr Fleming was on the afternoon of Monday.

Cross-examined by Mr Gifford, he agreed that he served fifteen or sixteen families in Sandyford Place. He called upon them every morning and had called on that Saturday morning. At that time of the year, however, a great many families were out of town.

'Does it frequently happen at that time of the year that milk is not required?'

'They all get milk that are at home. Some of them do not get it.'

The judge: 'Do some of the houses which remain inhabited not take in milk at that season?'

Paton evidently understood this question; at any rate he answered yes.

Mr Clark, re-examining: 'Did the Flemings always take milk?'
'Yes.'

'Do you remember any instances, except Saturday, Sunday and Monday, when the milk was not taken in at their house?'

'Never to my knowledge,' said George Paton.

And so to M'Quarrie, Mr Roughead's 'historic milk-boy', witness, star witness—for the defence—in this historic case; unless you count the old gentleman himself, whose evidence was, however, supposed at any rate to have contributed to the other side. Short, sharp and very much to the point. Yes, last July he had been with George Paton as usual helping to take round the milk, calling as usual at Sandyford Place. 'I know old Mr Fleming, who lives there. I mind of hearing of the death of the servant in that house. I heard of it on the Tuesday morning. I mind the Saturday before that Tuesday morning. . . .'

'What happened on that morning?'
'I went up and rang the bell. Old Mr Fleming answered it.'
'Did you ring more than once?'
'No, I only rang once. I hadn't to wait any time before it was answered.'
'Was the door shut?'
'Yes.'
'Did you hear anything before Mr Fleming opened the door?'
'The first thing I heard after ringing the bell was the chain coming off the door.'
'Are you quite sure of that?'
'Yes.'
'And after the chain came off the door, the door was opened?'
'Yes; by old Mr Fleming.'
'You saw him?'
'Yes.'
'Was he dressed?'
'Yes, he was dressed. He had on black clothes.'
'Did he say anything?'
'He said he was for nae milk.'
'Did he say anything more?'

'No, nothing more.'

'And this would be—what time?'

'This would be about twenty minutes to eight.'

'Is that the usual time of getting to Sandyford Place?'

'That's the ordinary time of getting to Sandyford Place.'

And—'Are you sure, quite sure, of everything you have said?'

Yes, Donald was quite sure of everything he had said.

Cross-examined by Mr Gifford, he replied there was no day on which the door was not opened at all at No. 17.

And to one final question from Mr Clark: No—he had never before known old Mr Fleming to answer the door.

Mrs Mary Smith followed. She had known the dead woman over five or six years, and knew the prisoner also. She had heard Jess M'Pherson speak of Mrs M'Lachlan many times, and always 'in a very friendly way'. She had last seen Jess about a week before her death; they met on Sauchiehall Street, and Mrs Smith, who had not then seen her for a couple of years, was astonished at how wretched she was looking. 'She was looking real ill and I asked her, "How are you liking Mr Fleming's family?" She said, "I do not feel very happy or very comfortable with old Mr Fleming, for he is actually an old wretch and an old devil." '

'Is that what she said?'

'Those are the words she said.'

'Speaking quite seriously?'

'She said that very seriously.'

'And then?'

'I then asked her if she was not comfortable with him, as I never heard her saying anything bad of him before. She said she was very unhappy and uncomfortable, and stated that she would come and see me on that day fortnight, as it was her Sunday out, and stay to tea. There was something, she said, she would like to tell me, but as Sandy [the witness's husband] was walking beside me she would tell me when he was not there.'

'I understand she was to come to your house on Sunday fortnight to tell you something? What did you understand that something to refer to?'

'I could not tell what it was about for she never lived to come and tell me. I said to her, "You are looking ill," and she said, "I cannot tell you what is the cause because Sandy is with you." '

She had seen Jess M'Pherson and the prisoner many a time together in Jess's little grocery shop, and they always seemed fond
and affectionate. They were great friends.

Lord Deas: 'Did you ever understand that Jess M'Pherson was
thinking of going abroad?'

Mrs Smith had not.

And Mary M'Kinnon, foster-sister of Jess, had reproached her
for not coming more often to see her; and Jess had replied that it
was 'easy for me to speak; she had got so much to do by some servant going away [probably meaning the second servant, who
went, by custom, with the family to the summer house at Dunoon],
and that her heart was broken by the old man, who was so inquisitive that the door-bell never rang but he must see who was there
and know all about them.' And Martha M'Intyre, who had been in
service there, confirmed that the old man was tirelessly inquisitive
as to who was in the house and what the maids did with their time
when they went out; and specially so in his enquiries about Jess.

Lord Deas: 'What do you mean by "specially"? I thought he
enquired about all?'

Counsel: 'Did he enquire more particularly after her than the
others?'

'He always enquired after her.'

Counsel asked her, lastly: 'Was Jess M'Pherson a strong
woman?'

'She was a wiry woman,' said Martha M'Intyre.

P.C. Cameron was called next, and there was a slight scramble
as he was found to be in the dock, guarding the prisoner. His evidence related largely to the odd little episode of Mr John Fleming
having said to all and sundry that he had heard the key fall from
the lock inside the room where the woman lay dead; but as has
been said, this business was almost certainly some muddle made in
over-excitement and is of no importance.

Jessie's sister gave evidence that James M'Lachlan always gave
his wages—thirty shillings a week—to his wife (though we know
he was obliged to take back twelve for his own use). Their brother
was very generous to her; after every voyage he gave her money,
and had once given her as much as twenty-five sovereigns: that
was last November.

Her sister's health was very bad; she had known her bedridden
for as long as four months—following the birth of her child—and

since she had been at the Broomielaw she had had at least one spell lasting six weeks.

Robert Jeffrey, a police officer, said he had found a bag in old Mr Fleming's bedroom upstairs, a large grey canvas bag for keeping dirty linen in. A bag was confidently produced in court, and he threw them all into something of a tizzy by saying that it was not the one he had found. But anyway, the mark was about the size of a shilling, in the centre of one side of the bag. It was dry and appeared to be 'not new'. It had the appearance of blood. ('Might it not be something else?' prompted Lord Deas: he had never suggested that the marks on the rags up at Hamilton 'might be something else'. But tiresome Jeffreys stuck to his opinion. He thought it had been blood.)

He had found the bag on either the Tuesday or the Wednesday after the murder. He further found a narrow strip of cotton on it 'under the covering of a chair' in the bedroom; which, however, as we have said, seems likely to have been only some old piece of bandage and not worth troubling about. Under cross-examination by Mr Gifford, ably supported by the judge, he agreed that with this exception there were no marks of blood on any article in the old man's room upstairs, nor upon his clothes. With Donald Campbell and another detective he had made a search in the house in order to find evidence against Mr Fleming, if such existed, and the witness thought he could say he was sure that nothing could have escaped their notice of that kind which might have been evidence of Mr Fleming's guilt. Mr Fleming was in custody at that time.

(Donald Campbell had, in fact, found spots of blood on the two shirts in a drawer in Mr Fleming's basement wardrobe-room; and as Jeffrey was in some sort speaking for all three searchers his answer does not in fact convey a true impression. However, as no one in court, including the defence, chose to remark upon it, perhaps it is not the author's business to do so.)

Alexander M'Call, superintendent of police, who had given evidence at the beginning of the trial, was now recalled by Mr Clark. He remembered finding or being shown the bag and seeing the blood-stain; unlike Jeffreys, however, who had seen it as the size of a half-crown and on the side of the bag, M'Call had seen it as extending across the whole bottom of the bag—the bag being about three feet long by two feet broad. There was some soiled linen in the bag, which was free from blood-stains; the bag looked as though it had been washed since the stain appeared there, though whether recently or not he could not say. Both bag and stain were quite dry when he saw them.

On the Monday night, when he first came to the house, he had found the little wicket or window into the area fastened; but the old man had told him that on the Saturday morning it was not 'snibbed'. There were no marks of footsteps on the sill or in the area.

And finally—P.C. Campbell, who had been on his beat, including Sandyford Place, from eight o'clock on the Friday night till six next morning. He had that night seen nothing, but on the following evening, some time between half-past eight and nine, he had seen two women come to the door of No. 17 and stand talking a minute; had seen one woman go back into the house and the other come away. He knew it was that night, for he had just turned back to post a letter to his father in Oban. . . .

Asked to look at the prisoner—who 'stood up and confronted him deliberately'—he said she was not either of the women he had seen. He was quite sure of that. It was clear daylight. Well, yes, it was evening, but it was perfectly clear.

A bonny evening in early July: and everything perfectly clear.

In accordance with Scottish law, in which defence counsel always has the last word, Mr Gifford, for the prosecution, rose to address the Court.

CHAPTER SIXTEEN

It was five o'clock—an hour when any present-day court would certainly have adjourned, to take the speeches of counsel and the summing-up on the following day, when both speakers and jury would have been fresh and unwearied. But it was once again to be nine o'clock when the judge rose—having even at that hour expressed himself as willing to address his 'few observations' to the jury—an offer which they found themselves unable to accept. (They must have been thankful later: the few observations occupied four hours.) It was the third day that they had sat there listening, for eleven hours each day; the third day that counsel had laboured under deep concentration, in one case at least in deep anxiety, for eleven hours; the third day that for eleven hours the frail, anxious, lonely figure had sat silent in the dock—a woman whose doctors were said to have declared that she might die at any moment if too much strain were put upon her unsound heart.

Mr Gifford's speech lasted till half-past seven.

It was a very fair speech—a fair and honourable speech, whose burden came in its second paragraph: 'While our hearts may bleed, our hands must do justice.' But it left unaccounted for some astonishing facts that had emerged from the evidence.

Mr Gifford took first the charge of theft. The silver articles from the dining-room at Sandyford Place had been proved (by old Mr Fleming) to have been in the house on Friday, July 4. They had been pawned next morning and the woman who pawned them was identified positively as the prisoner. The jury had heard her declaration admitting that she had pawned them and giving her story of how she came by them—old Fleming having brought them to her house. He postponed comment on the dresses missing from the dead woman's room because their theft was so intimately mixed up with the charge of murder.

The special defence against this charge was that the crime had been committed by James Fleming.

But this was not a trial of the guilt or innocence of old Mr

Fleming. It was not even relevant, said counsel in substance, that in any crime there might be more than one person concerned. 'For the question always is, and the only question is: Is the prisoner guilty or is she not guilty?' It was no part of their verdict to say that anyone else might be concerned. All they could find was that the prisoner was concerned.

He took them over the scene of the crime, over the post-mortem findings. The conclusion was that the deceased had certainly been murdered, and in conditions of extreme ferocity. He ran over the evidence and from it suggested the conclusion that it was not very clear whether the woman had been murdered in the kitchen or the bedroom—and that it was not, anyway, of much consequence. He directed their attention to the slightly differing evidence about the marks of washing on the floors, and the trail, 'or wipe rather', that existed in the lobby, which he deduced from Dr Macleod's evidence was not a mark of washing, though the thing that was trailed might have been wet with blood.

And then: 'Who was in the house that night?' The circumstances of old Mr Fleming's conduct during the three days that the maid was missing—was in fact lying dead in her room—he acknowledged to be extraordinary; but the discrepancy in his statements and those of the milk-boy he thought not very surprising. After all, said counsel, he was a very odd old man, a man of peculiar habits, great curiosity, inquisitive—'to the annoyance and distress, apparently, of his family, who got out of all patience with him.' (Where Mr Gifford got this bit of comment from it is difficult to see. It emerged nowhere from the evidence.) You could not found the same observations on his actions as you might on those of a more ordinary man. But, anyway, all that sank into insignificance compared with the evidence against the prisoner.

As to this, he drew attention first to the acknowledged intimacy of the prisoner with the dead woman, to her intimate knowledge of her ways and her habits and of the place where she lived. She knew, for example, of the back garden door into the lane running behind Sandyford Place. Having regard to old Mr Fleming's tiresome curiosity, it was probable that this door was frequently used.

He then came to the prisoner herself: to her movements on the evening of the murder and the fact that she was certainly out all night. As to her starting out so late in order to avoid the old man, 'the reason is a very justifiable one and, so far as we have gone, not an unnatural reason, and it is an evidence of innocence—frankly, I admit—that she asks Mrs Adams to keep her child and says where she is going. That goes against premeditation of murder certainly. But it does not go much further, for it leads you to suppose—naturally to suppose—that the person does do what she says she intended to do: go and visit Jess.'

And she had returned home next morning with a bundle, and later pawned the plate—'the first flash of lurid light that is thrown upon the murder'—and handed in her own cloak for cleaning and a dress to be dyed: a cinnamon-brown merino which she herself had worn that morning, but which was proved to have belonged to the dead woman. And then there came the purchase of the japanned tin box, the adventures of that box and the identification of the clothes it contained as having belonged also to deceased. The prisoner had made statements as to how she came into possession of the dresses—conflicting statements in some parts.

And then the trunk and the adventures of the trunk, the discovery of the torn and blood-stained garments up at Hamilton. One petticoat had belonged not to the prisoner but to the dead woman. 'We thus have the blood-stained clothing of the prisoner and of the murdered woman. You will judge by the evidence if they had been placed there by the prisoner. Why? She was with the deceased that night. Jessie M'Pherson lay upon her face when found, and while she was in that position the iron chopper, or an instrument like that, was wielded upon her body with fearful effect by a person standing over her, so that blood flowed in torrents— clothes were blood-stained and it was necessary to dispose of the bloody clothes.' As to the blood-stained crinoline wires, she had thought 'the fire would purify them. But, gentlemen of the jury, it takes a hot fire to purge a crime. The wires told what they saw of this deed.'

So much for the stolen things. 'Was there a louder, shriller, more dreadful tale ever told by clothes?' But then, said counsel, all our actions did tell a tale. It was no poetical fancy, it was a wonderful fact that the neighbourhood of a murdered body did retain the impress of the murderer. Crimes had always left their footprints—and in Jessie M'Pherson's bedroom there were indeed footprints: bloody footprints. They were not those of the deceased, nor were they James Fleming's. 'The prisoner—the party who had all the bloody clothes in her possession—the party who had the plate in her possession—the party who came away that Saturday morning wearing Jessie M'Pherson's gown—it must have been her foot that made these impressions. It is circumstantial evidence, gentlemen, but strong, you see, when you put the several circumstances together.'

And then it might be only a detail, but it was a fact that the prisoner bought some rum on the Friday night, and a bottle was missing from her home in the Broomielaw. A bottle smelling of rum was found in the basement at Sandyford Place.

Then as to the motive for the murder. On July 4 she must have had no money; she had to pawn a mirror to redeem her cloak before she could go out. All her things and many of her husband's had been pledged—to the tune of forty-one pawn tickets. But the day after the murder—she had money. 'She had money before she was in Lundie's pawn—she paid £4 of rent before twelve o'clock. What I have to say is—is it not likely that Jessie M'Pherson, a saving, industrious woman, had money in her trunk? I do not charge the pannel with having stolen money——'

Mr Clark: 'She is not charged with stealing money.'

'—I do not charge her with it, but I say this is an element which you must take into account if you found there was any probability that Jessie M'Pherson had money besides dresses.'

So he came to his peroration. 'I will not dwell upon the contradictions of the prisoner's declarations. I do not ask you to convict upon lying declarations. You have the story told by the facts, by the articles produced, which need not the lies of the prisoner to enforce belief upon you. . . . I say nothing of the peculiar manner in which this murder has been attempted to be explained. You will weigh everything upon the evidence and leave nothing to be determined without proof. I make no appeal to your feelings. May the Omniscient and Almighty God give you grace and wisdom to return according to your oaths a true verdict upon the evidence.'

Mr Gifford sat down.

Andrew Rutherfurd Clark rose to open his speech for the defence.

It was half-past seven in the evening—the end of the third eleven-hour day. It seems inconceivable that with this natural break the court should not have adjourned; they sat on, however, except for a ten-minute interval, and indeed, as has been related, when an hour and a half later counsel closed his address the judge went so far as to offer to begin his summing-up. Mr Clark must already by this time have been both physically and mentally exhausted: that he was terribly anxious, weighed down by a sense of responsibility, he freely confessed to the jury. They could not then know of the doubly heavy burden he laboured under—the secret knowledge of the prisoner's statement whose suppression, against her own wishes, was ultimately his own responsibility. It had hampered him greatly in cross-examination; now it must hamper him equally in his address. If the verdict proved to be in her favour—well and good and she would go totally free. If not, then a new story altogether must be put before the Court, and it had been important throughout, was doubly important now that he came to address the jury, that nothing should be brought out that would prejudice that story. That the prisoner had in fact been in the house some time that night the jury might sufficiently suspect by now: that it could not be *proved* that she had been there was the burden of his defence. Yet his defence must not be inconsistent with that other story when, or if, it ultimately came to be told.

He began with what the reader may agree was the likeliest argument of all. Here was not an ordinary murder—not a murder caused by a blow given in the heat of passion, not a murder committed in a struggle between two people who had been hostile to one another before. No. The charge was that poor dead Jess M'Pherson had been murdered by 'her own most intimate, most kind, most dear friend', that upon that night this weak and delicate woman, who for long years had been ailing, had stood over her friend and wielded against her the instrument by which she met her death. Was it possible to credit so fearful a story? Was it possible to believe that the prisoner's motive for committing such a crime was to obtain possession of a few old dresses and some plate to raise money on—that for this she forgot her love and friendship for the murdered woman?

It might be that circumstantial evidence was sufficient in some cases—but in this case could the evidence brought forward be relied upon when it had failed to develop and explain the whole mystery of the dark cloud which hung over the tragedy enacted at Sandyford Place? He instanced a recent case where a man had been sentenced by the unanimous verdict of the jury to twenty-one years' penal servitude for rape. A month or two later it had emerged that he was absolutely innocent. If the case had been one of murder, that innocent man, by the time proof came, would have perished on the gallows.

The case for the prosecution was that the woman was proved to be poor but had raised the money she needed by pawning the plate. But then it was proved by the defence that she had paid off her rent *before* pawning the plate. He had been amazed when the Advocate-Depute had got himself out of this difficulty by suggesting that the dead woman had had money in her trunk. There was no proof whatsoever of this, nor had the prisoner been charged with the theft of money. Such a proposition should never have been put forward.

And then. . . .

'What my learned friend says is this, that the person who had stood over the body of a friend, mangling it with that weapon, having committed the bloody deed by the infliction of upwards of forty wounds, and having done that in a house where she knew that a person (old Mr Fleming) was living, and after a severe conflict between herself and the deceased—that instead of going away from the house as fast as she could get . . . she stayed apparently in that house until a little before nine o'clock in the morning, washing at the floor and washing the dead body. . . .' Was it a conceivable proposition?—that she should remain for what must have been hours, since she was said not to have got home till nine o'clock, washing out the traces of the crime from the kitchen, from the lobby, even from the bedroom. But this was the prosecution's case: they did not suggest that old Mr Fleming had been elsewhere than in his bed throughout.

And if she were going to stay so late—why not have spent her time in gathering together more plunder than the few pieces she was accused of having taken? For plunder was put forward as the only motive for the murder.

As to the facts upon which the prosecution relied—the Advocate-Depute had said candidly that the frankness of the prisoner as to her intention of visiting the deceased that night would not sustain the theory of premeditated murder. That she *had* visited her had in no way been proved. She had not been seen anywhere near the house—not nearer than the Gushet house, ten minutes walk away. A bottle was relied upon to prove her presence there—a common pint bottle with a little rum in it, found in a cupboard among a lot of other bottles; a similar bottle having been found missing from her home. Moreover, she was said to have returned home at nine o'clock in the morning—but this was on the unsupported evidence of one witness only; and it was possible that the prisoner had a key to the house which this witness knew nothing about. Then there were the footprints to which his friend Mr Gifford had referred in a rather poetical way. There were said to be three footprints—only two had been produced in court; and all that anyone could say was that they could have been made by the prisoner. Dr Macleod said so—but Dr Macleod was not infallible nor could his evidence receive the same weight when he was found to have omitted from his report any mention of the remarkable bruise which Dr Watson had observed upon the dead body. And in the absence of any clear proof that these footmarks were absolutely identical with the prisoner's, it was impossible to rely upon them to prove that she was in the house that night.

As to the plate—it had been in the house on the Friday morning (when John Fleming left for Dunoon), but the only proof that she had taken it lay in the fact that her story of how she came by it was contradicted by old Mr Fleming. There was nothing in her pawning the plate to prove that she got it from the house that night. She said she got it from Fleming and, 'even accused as she is, I would believe her word sooner than the word of Fleming.'

And then the dresses. There was no proof that they had been in the house up to the time of the murder; the prisoner had an explanation of their having come earlier into her possession. Mrs Campbell said the prisoner had come home that morning wearing the dead woman's cinnamon-coloured dress—but confronted with this dress later, it having meanwhile been dyed, she said that the trimming was different from that on the dress the prisoner wore that morning. Nor was there clear proof that the black box which had gone back and forth had been the one the prisoner purchased—and none at all that it had meanwhile contained these particular dresses. All the prosecution could do was to confront her with her own declaration—obtained from her when she was ignorant that the police already had these articles in their possession—and then accuse her of contradicting herself.

Then as to the rags picked up around Hamilton. These were

not proved to have been in the prisoner's custody at any time, and were not found in her custody. What proof was there that they had belonged to her? Identification meant not that they were likely to be but that they were in fact the prisoner's clothes. But her own lodger declined to identify them. Mrs Adams and Sarah offered to identify them—but Sarah Adams had before this given false witness; and her mother was a woman who, having quarrelled with the prisoner in that case, had then got her child examined as to the truth of her evidence. (This does seem very hard on Mrs Adams, who, in fact, appears to have spotted the plot only when Sarah was rewarded, thrashed her daughter soundly, which she would hardly have done had she been party to the arrangements, and sent her off to confess; and *then* quarrelled with her friend—for having bribed the child.)

And, said counsel, holding up to the jury the blood-stained rags of brown coburg, wincey and wool, could anyone tell with certainty that this had been a petticoat, a certain petticoat?—that this had been a certain dress? 'Hearing of this case, they think they can be no other than the prisoner's; hearing of this case, they proceed to their identification. Do you suppose that if these articles had been found in a place where the prisoner had never been, and which place she never was near, they could have identified these articles . . .?' As for the flannel petticoat, the rags of a common flannel petticoat with no particular marks on it, the prosecution pathetically relied upon one unsupported witness, who said it had belonged to the dead woman, Jess M'Pherson. Moreover, in the trunk and on the kerchief that were said to have contained all these blood-stained articles—not a trace of blood. And anyway—was that really the way a guilty person would have gone about getting rid of such compromising matter?—making no secret of her presence in Hamilton, going to Mrs Chassel's house, giving away the kerchief to the boy. . . .

Mr Rutherfurd Clark turned next—and with some relief perhaps, for here he was on surer ground—to the matter of old Mr Fleming. The case for the prosecution was that Mr Fleming was wholly unconnected with the murder, and they relied upon his evidence, a man who had actually at one time been in custody over the murder. He was said—on insufficient proof—to be eighty-seven; he had himself slipped up and said he was seventy-eight—at any rate he was in full possession of his faculties. Unlike the prisoner at the bar, he was not on good terms with the dead woman—she had complained to many friends about him.

He took the jury through the episode of the 'squeals in the night', through Mr Fleming's declarations regarding the front door—that he had found it unbarred on the inside. Of course it was of importance to Mr Fleming to show that the murderer might have got out of the house—and so he said that the door was unbarred. But the milk-boy, calling there before eight o'clock, gave evidence that he heard the chain taken off the door before it was opened to him. All other exits were, by Mr Fleming's own statement, locked from within.

Thenceforward Mr Fleming continued to live two nights and three days in that house: having heard the screams in the night, found the airing screen knocked over and blood spots on the linen, having found the bedroom door locked and the woman missing—he had yet lived there and never thought of harm having come to the servant, never thought of mentioning to anyone, even casually, that she had disappeared. The kitchen was splashed with blood; yet, able as he was to read the newspapers without spectacles, to observe the servants next door, he never noticed those stains. But of course—in the meantime someone had washed over the stains; even Mr Fleming must have acknowledged seeing them had they been as they originally were. Who, then, had washed the floors? And why? And when? Dr Fleming had found the lobby floor at seven o'clock quite moist. Other witnesses found at nine o'clock that it was dry. It had taken only two hours to finish drying out completely; could it possibly have been washed eighty or ninety hours before? The last time that the accused could be supposed to have been in the house had been the Saturday morning, three days ago.

James Fleming had known of the woman's death—it was proved by his having come to the door when the milk-boy called. 'These matters cannot be explained consistently with his innocence: and surely that would be in itself sufficient to show that there is a case of far graver suspicion attaching to him than to the unfortunate woman at the bar . . . ?'

And—since Mr Fleming was admittedly alone with the dead woman from six o'clock that night, while the prisoner could not have been there before about half-past ten—let them suppose for one moment that she did go to the house: what awful deed might have been committed by that time? And she came there alone—and found herself in the presence of that crime. . . . Even supposing that it was the case that she had in fact gone to the house, were they to assume that she was the guilty person, or was concerned in the frightful murder of a person for whom she entertained the greatest friendship?—and who at the same time was in disagreement with James Fleming.

All the Crown could show might be this—that the prisoner was with Mr Fleming in the house; and prosecuting counsel called upon the jury to select one of the two as being the guilty party. He asked them to select the prisoner at the bar as a woman who would destroy a friend in this savage manner. Was it not a more plausible theory that—accepting the suggestion that she did go to the house—she found the deed done and, being in terror at seeing it, took the things away after the deed was done, even though it would militate in favour of Mr Fleming and against herself. A weak woman, placed in such a position—what else could she do? And they must look to the washing of the wounds, which appeared to have been an act of kindness to the injured woman. 'If there were not two people there, these wounds, which were not immediately fatal, were washed; but if two were at the committal of this crime, is the person likely to commit the crime who would befriend the other? If these wounds were given before the fatal blow, I think it is a man's hand and not a woman's. At all events, you have this cloud of witnesses here to say that the present has been proved by conclusive evidence to have been one of the most foul and atrocious murders ever committed.'

The above quotation is typical of the slightly muddled and inconsequent style of Mr Clark's speech throughout. It is perhaps the speech of a very weary over-anxious man. Accompanied by voice and gesture and, one may assume, by the force of his own personal integrity and sincerity, it may have been more inspiring to listen to than it is to read; but it does read heavily and rather confusedly. It ended with a reference to the extraordinary circumstances in which the prisoner's declarations were obtained and a plea that the prisoner should not be 'convicted in respect of them', with a further reminder that the jury must be sure that every link in the chain of evidence be strong and certain; and finally with a reference to the two women seen by P.C. Campbell on the steps of No. 17 Sandyford Place on the Saturday night—the night after the murder. If that were true—and there was no reason to doubt it—then there were women about the house on the day after the murder was said to have been committed, and that might explain the footprints. . . .

And finally—finally, if there were those who felt that the blood of the poor dead woman cried aloud for vengeance, he hoped that the jury would leave that to Him who had claimed it as His own and, humbly acknowledging human law and human justice to be prone to error, would remember that it is better that a thousand guilty persons should escape than that one innocent person should perish.

Amidst loud applause from the audience, Mr Rutherfurd Clark sat down.

Lord Deas adjourned the Court till the following morning, the jury having decided that it was more than they cared to undertake to listen to yet a third address. They asked leave to take the plans with them to study overnight—they must have been gluttons for work; but the judge appears to have had a rooted objection to blueprints and turned down the suggestion. They could see the plans when they came to consider their verdict. If they took them now they would be unable to refrain from making up their minds in advance. How the plans could possibly have had any such effect one cannot conceive—but anyway he needn't have worried. The minds of the jury, like his own, had been pretty well made up before ever they came into Court.

CHAPTER SEVENTEEN

Saturday, September 20—the fourth and last day.

Before the Court assembled Jessie asked to see her advisers. She had all along wanted her statement used; now she insisted that, whatever the outcome, it should be given out in open court. She would have the choice—if things went against her—of making it herself or of having it read. Mr Rutherfurd Clark agreed to read it for her. He may still have had hopes that it would be unnecessary —he had not yet heard the second speech for the prosecution, as delivered from the judicial bench by Lord Death.

At half-past ten the Judge opened his charge to the jury.

The public reception of Lord Death's charge was largely unfavourable. It was 'stern and iron-cased'; according to Sir Archibald Alison, 'able but one-sided and unfeeling'; according to the *Law Magazine and Review*, vastly less judicial than Mr Gifford's address for the prosecution. The conduct of Lord Deas, said this highly responsible legal journal, had been almost universally censured. His charge 'lasted four hours; and from beginning to end of it there is not an observation favourable to the prisoner; not one fair consideration of doubt in her favour. . . . On the contrary, facts that in our humble opinion tell strongly in her favour are either quietly ignored or disposed of by reckless assertion or the most transparent sophistry. . . .' No advocate would dare be so reckless in argument, or rather in assertion. . . .

When he came into court on the Friday he carried the black cap openly in his hand and laid it on the desk before him, and this was, not surprisingly, taken to mean that he was prepared for the worst and quite ready to give the jury a broad hint to that effect. In England the black cap, a square of material about the size of a woman's handkerchief, is carried as part of the judge's ceremonial robes whatever type of case he may be trying. Only in murder cases has it any significance; it is unfolded and laid upon his wig while he pronounces the death sentence. In Scotland it is triangular, survivor of the tricorne hat of earlier days, and is not carried but kept in a box on the judge's bench, not visible to the court until sentence of death is to be pronounced, when the judge himself holds it a little above his head while he speaks the words. 'I never before saw the symbol of death paraded in sight of a pannel during the judge's charge,' writes a legal observer of the trial; and 'Philo Justitia' was 'horrified to see Lord Deas so ostentatiously bringing in the black cap on the Friday, as if delighting in expectation of putting it on. It was on the desk at his side on Saturday.'

Having established the fact of murder, the judge turned to the 'fact' of theft. 'These dresses were in the possession of the deceased up to the Friday——'

Mr Clark begged his lordship's pardon. There was no proof, no witness spoke to the fact of the dresses having been in the house up to Friday.

'We shall see what may be the evidence on this point,' said Lord Deas calmly; but they did not see any evidence at all. All they got was a reminder that the prisoner had declared that the dresses had been brought to her *on the Friday night*. His lordship was keen enough on the unreliability of her declarations except in such places as they might be turned to her destruction.

And now into the teeming pond of facts that might militate against her his lordship tossed a contribution entirely his own. All those things in pawn, including almost the whole of her husband's wardrobe—and the husband expected home at any moment!

James M'Lachlan's possessions were in pawn because he could not give his ailing wife enough money to keep them out of pawn; we have the assurance of Mrs Adams, who knew her well, that she lived as economically as she possibly could and spent nothing whatsoever on personal, or any other, extravagance (unless it might be a little in matters of dress, Mrs Adams had said; but even that not for a long time now). And they had been in pawn for some considerable time, for she had since been reduced to pledging all but one dress and even her cloak, without which she couldn't go out. But James M'Lachlan was in and out of his home every week, never absent for more than three or four days. He had left only the day before the murder was committed. Did Lord Deas mean to suggest that in the intervening twenty-four hours his wife had rushed out, pawned all he possessed, blown the proceeds on some nameless orgy of extravagance and now, lest he discover it, hastily redeemed his possessions at this horrifying price? Except that it is relatively unimportant, this piece of gratuitous innuendo is almost the most monstrous injustice in the whole unjust and wickedly one-sided affair.

(However, his lordship was not alone in his theory—'Justice' subsequently dashed into print to suggest that Mrs M'Lachlan had had to get money to conceal from her husband her mismanagement of their financial affairs and had gone to borrow from Jess M'Pherson for this purpose. Jess refusing, she killed her. If James M'Lachlan was not already aware of the state of things at home he must have been a very unobservant young man.)

There follows a long discourse—almost a third of the total—setting out the story as it had been brought out in the evidence, which is certainly remarkable for its clarity. Not for its charity, however; no smallest point against the prisoner goes unrecorded or, indeed, unemphasised. Nevertheless, a fair enough summary, which, strong and clear and coldly reasoned, must have been deadly in its impact, compared with the rather muffled confusion of last night's passionate plea for the defence.

But as soon as he moves away from the mere recital of facts, the judge's violent prejudice in favour of old Mr Fleming at the expense of the wretched woman at the bar becomes so apparent as to be scarcely credible. The prisoner's statements had been perfectly fairly obtained and the jury were entitled to take them into fullest consideration. As for the incident of the policeman having seen two women on the steps of the house on the evening after the murder—that could perfectly easily be explained away. He probably mistook the night he saw the women there, or else he mistook the door: 'you can account for it very easily by supposing that he mistook the door.' What was more, the policeman said that there was another man with him and that the other man's recollection corresponded with his own—but the other man had not been produced before the Court. This was tantamount to the judge's saying that the policeman's claim as to this other man was not such as could be substantiated—a suggestion that all his evidence might be equally unreliable. In fact P.C. Campbell had made no claim whatsoever as to this man; he had said simply that he went to speak to a man standing by the railings of Sandyford Place, and while he was there one of the women passed him and went away. Of course, if the women had indeed been seen, the conclusion must have been that Jess was still alive on the Saturday evening—and where would his lordship's case against the prisoner be *then*, poor thing? So the evidence of the policeman must be demolished without more ado. Just toss out this bit of the jigsaw—it doesn't fit in.

When it came to his protection of the old man, he outdid himself; and yet his defence is clear and reasoned and extraordinarily telling—except that it is based on facts deliberately angled to reflect only the light of innocence. The poor dear old gentleman is very deaf and doddery and just a bit eccentric anyway. He wakes at night, hears a noise, the noise ceases and he goes back to sleep and thinks no more about it; 'a natural enough thing.' In the morning he wakes at six and lies waiting for the maid to bring him his breakfast. It seems a long time—longer than in fact it is. He thinks it is nine o'clock when he gets up, but really, the judge suggests, it's eight. He goes down and knocks at the maid's door, gets no answer and, going to the front door, finds that it is unbolted. So he automatically rebolts it—and then forgets having done so, just as you and I might so easily forget doing a thing like that, members of the jury, mightn't we? Then when the milk-boy knocks, being already up, he goes to the door. Wouldn't that account for it all?—even for the boy believing that he remembers having heard the rattle of the chain coming off the door (which in his lordship's opinion he doesn't really remember at all). Looked at that way, how neatly and innocently, members of the jury, it all falls in, does it not? The time the old man got up wasn't nine at all, it was eight. 'And the time for the milk-boy to come was between eight and nine. He says [Mr Fleming says] he sometimes came even later.

Mr Clark: 'It was twenty minutes before eight when the milk-boy came. That was the statement of both the boy himself and his master.'

Lord Deas said they would see that when they came to the evidence, it didn't touch his present observation at all. But it touched it very nearly; and in fact, once again, they didn't see, for there was no evidence for them to come to—only the comment of the old man himself, rambling on about the irregular hours kept by the milkman—in direct contradiction to the very positive statements of the man and his boy, who both said they called that day at twenty to eight, and invariably called at twenty to eight.

But, anyway—why should Mr Fleming have denied opening the door to the milkman, members of the jury, if in fact he remembered doing so? What good could it do him? As to the boy saying he heard the chain taken down, well that would be only too easy to explain away, just as the judge himself had just explained it away. So why should he bother to deny it? The jury would ask themselves whether the whole thing wasn't just a mere confusion after all. . . .

And so back to the prisoner. And here there comes a most monstrous suggestion, a most irresponsible and provocative suggestion, not only unsubstantiated but actually negatived by the evidence. He drags up for the second time the poor bottle, smelling of rum, found at Sandyford Place—the ordinary bottle, like a hundred thousand bottles, found among a lot of other bottles in the kitchen cupboard there. A trifle, he admits, but all these trifles add to the likelihood of the prisoner having been at the house that night. And then: 'You will consider the circumstances as to this bottle of rum and the fact that Jessie M'Pherson, an admittedly sober, honest and steady woman, *had that night been induced to partake of rum.*'

It is a most wicked, unjust and false conclusion, based on no evidence whatsoever—suggesting as it does, deliberately premeditated murder, premeditated from the time of going out and buying the rum. Poor Jessie with her seven penn'orth of rum and her few poor little biscuits—shared first with her friend Mrs Fraser and the rest to be taken round to be shared with Jess. The very fact of the purchase was in fact entirely in her favour. It was bought openly with the declared intention of taking some to Sandyford Place; and this free admission of her intention of visiting her friend that night, was frankly acknowledged by the prosecution to negative any suspicion of premeditation. Yet the judge puts it forward as just that—evidence of premeditation; builds up from this false premise a story that the Crown never dreamed of suggesting—were far too scrupulous to suggest, had they even dared. The purchase of the rum, with this intention: the stupefying of the victim (there is no evidence whatsoever that Jess was unaccustomed to spirits); and then . . . 'It was a deed of darkness.' An excuse would be made, suggested his lordship, to stay the night, the unsuspecting friend of course easily acquiescing. Whether or not the murderess actually shared the bed with her, need not matter. She would wait till the victim was asleep and then, while she lay there trusting and defenceless, the first blow would be struck—the great cleaver raised and brought down with sickening ferocity across the sleeping, upturned face. One great blow across the forehead, two across the eyes, smashing into the bridge of the nose. But the injured woman rallies, drags herself somehow from the bed and escapes from the room and into the kitchen. There she is pursued, struggles, falls to the floor and, lying on the floor, is literally hacked to death. For a handful of silver, friend has savagely slaughtered friend.

Of course, conceded Lord Deas, it *might* not have happened like that; but it didn't really matter very much how it was done.

There follows more comment on Jessie's movements, Jessie's finances; the dresses. Then back he comes to Mr Fleming. At one time it seemed to his lordship that an attempt was about to be made to prove that this old man was a man of bad character. But they had in fact heard nothing against him (Lord Deas himself had seen to that) except that he 'looked too much after the servants', in his own house and next door. Naturally they resented it. That was all it amounted to.

Mr Clark: 'Then there was Mrs Smith's evidence. . . .' (The confidence Jess could not impart because of Mr Smith's presence.)

But the judge would have none of it. What the dead woman had intended to confide to her friend was probably that she was thinking of emigrating. (Why this should have been not fit for male ears, his lordship did not make apparent.) She may perhaps have added, he conceded, that the old man was so inquisitive that she couldn't live with him. The fact was that some of the maids had admirers coming about them, and the old gentleman might look a little too sharply after them; and it all boiled down to that.

And so on, through more and more of the evidence—invariably with the bias against the accused. As for counsel's warning about circumstantial evidence, as to his remainder of that case of rape where the man condemned was found to be innocent after all—well, if the judge knew anything about that case (and he evidently did) it had been not a very good one to quote in this instance. If the Crown decided there was a doubt about the evidence and remitted his sentence, it didn't follow necessarily that the man was innocent. And he turned the whole thing neatly round to pour a little more discredit upon P.C. Campbell and the low-set, stout woman with the red, fat face whom he claimed to have seen on the night after the murder. 'A man might state that he saw people come to a house at night when it was not that house at all; and say that he saw people come out of one house when he saw them come out of another.'

Back to Jessie again, and once more through the 'declarations', balancing fact against the poor, desperate fictions—coldly and clearly and always to the prisoner's disadvantage. Always with some measure of exaggeration of the facts against her, always with a toning down of what might be in her favour. The keys to the Broomielaw apartment, the dresses, the trunk, the visit to Hamilton. . . . 'As to the question whether the prisoner was a person of improvident habits, it is not one with which we have to deal, nor the question of what it was that the prisoner did with her husband's wages.' What the prisoner did with her husband's wages, as had been amply shown, was to spend them—all eighteen shillings per week of them—on rent, heat, lighting, and food, on clothes for herself and her husband and her child; on help with the work she couldn't possibly do herself and on doctors' bills. 'Whether the prisoner was a person of improvident habits. . . .' One might have thought he could have spared her this final little jab; here at least have given her the benefit of the doubt.

And so it was over. If as reasonable men they felt no doubt that she was guilty, it was their duty to themselves, to their consciences, to God and to their country to say so. But if, *notwithstanding all that evidence*, they thought there were reasonable grounds, etcetera, etcetera—then they also knew the course that they must follow. And he handed over his bouquet. The case 'has received from you as great attention as ever I saw paid by any jury. . . .' and packed them off to consider their verdict. It was twenty-five minutes past two.

Nineteen minutes later, they were back again.

Verdict unanimous.

GUILTY.

CHAPTER EIGHTEEN

'The deathly pallor of her countenance seemed to increase,' says the contemporary record, 'but the same strength of will she had heretofore displayed was again shown. Nervous sweat covered her face; and she now and again lifted up her hands from under the black shawl beneath which during the day she kept them folded together, and pressed them over her face, wiping away the sweat. She for an instant leaned forward and covered her face with a handkerchief as if crying, but sitting upright again, she folded her arms together under her shawl, drawing it close around her.'

The Clerk of the Court had written out the sentence and now handed it to the judge for signature. The Advocate Depute rose to his feet. 'My lord, I move for sentence.'

A rumour had run round the court while the jury were absent: an extraordinary statement was to be made, either by the prisoner or for her. And now Mr Dixon was seen to go over to the dock and speak earnestly to her, and Mr Rutherfurd Clark joined them. After a brief discussion she took a paper from his hand, stood up in the dock and put back her veil. Mr Rutherfurd Clark turned to the judge. 'My lord, I understand that the prisoner desires to make a statement before sentence is passed, whether by her own lips or to be read by someone for her.'

Lord Deas: 'She is at liberty to do so in any way she prefers.' And much good may it do her, he doubtless added to himself. He had heard prisoners' statements before.

Every eye in court was fixed upon her: the 'poor pale prisoner' standing there so slender and graceful in her straw bonnet and the lilac gown. She raised the paper as though to start reading. But her courage failed her. She gave it back to Mr Clark and raised her white face to the judge. 'My lord, I desire to have it read.' And she cried out, distinct and clear: 'I am as innocent as my child who is only three years of age at this date.'

Mr Rutherfurd Clark took the paper from her and, still standing there, one arm propped on the high ledge of the dock, into 'a thrilling silence', clearly and coolly, every word articulate, read out Mrs M'Lachlan's story of that night. . . . *

It had been just ten—the clock in the Broomielaw was striking —as, with Mrs Fraser and Tommy and the little girl, she set off down the stairs; carrying the basket with the biscuits and the rum. 'I meant to give Mrs Fraser a dram, and have a dram for Jessie, and enough to taste with them.'

At ten minutes past ten she parted from her friends at the Gushet house, and went on alone. She went to the front door and rang. Jess answered the bell. She said to come away down to the kitchen; but the old man was still up.

He was sitting in a big chair by the kitchen table. There were two plates and two glasses on the table, and bread and cheese. 'Oh, is that you, Jessie?' he said. 'How are you?' She gave him a greeting and sat down opposite him. After a little while he rose and went off upstairs.

She gave Jess her little offering and Jess poured out a glass of rum for each of them and put the empty bottle away in the cupboard. They were settling down comfortably when the old man reappeared, carrying a bottle with some whisky in it and a glass. He poured a little whisky into the glass and handed it to Jessie. She took a sip. 'Come on,' he said, 'drink it up!' But she couldn't 'drink it up' on top of the rum, and he picked up the glass and poured the whisky back into the bottle. 'What sort of way is that to treat a person?' said Jess, disgustedly. 'Why don't you offer it round?'

He looked doubtful. 'Well, ye ken, Jess, we've had twa three since the afternoon.' He wouldn't mind, he said, but his son had complained of the amount of drink they got through when he left them alone in the house together. Of course it was really young John who took it, said Grandpa, but Mr Fleming was accusing *him*. 'However, haud your ill tongue, and I'll gie ye half a mutchkin if ye'll go and fetch it.'

'Aye,' said Jess, 'I've a tongue that would frighten somebody if it were breaking loose on them.' The old man muttered something to himself, tipped the remaining whisky into a tumbler on

* Here for almost the only time, I desert the actual wording of the text; but everything is in substance exactly authentic, including of course what was said.

214

the table and handed the empty bottle to Jessie—a bottle with a long neck, it was, and a flat, round base. 'Go and get half a mutchkin.' He gave her a shilling and twopence. (A mutchkin was half a pint—Jessie herself had bought half that much rum for her sevenpence ha'penny.)

Jess gave her the key of the back garden door and she went off, her grey cloak hung round her shoulders, into the lane behind the house. A woman was standing at the corner of Elderslie Street and another woman joined her as Jessie turned out of the lane and crossed Elderslie Street going towards North Street, and the two stood gossiping. She was making for a spirit shop in North Street on the right-hand side as you come up from St Vincent Street, and not far from M'Gaw, the fleshers (there is a spirit shop still in much the position she indicates. There is no M'Gaw's, but it was something of a shock to the author to observe just opposite, a 'flesher's' under the name James Lachlin). But by the time she got there it was two or three minutes past eleven and the shop was shut. There was a light in an upper window and she knocked a couple of times; nobody came, so she gave it up and started back, going on up North Street, left along Sauchiehall Street and this time down Elderslie Street to the mouth of the lane, completing the square. The two women were still standing talking and she saw now that one was Mrs Walker, the grocer's wife. But they were on the other side of the road and she passed on without any greeting and turned into the lane. She had locked the garden door behind her and now she unlocked it again and went in, relocking it once more.

She had left the back door open—but now it was shut. She knocked at it but nobody came. She went round to the kitchen window—the gas was burning but there was no one in the kitchen. She went back to the door again and rapped at it sharply, using the key of the garden gate which she still held in her hand. At last the old man came. 'I shut it against them brutes of cats,' he said, and let her in, locking the door again behind her. She went into the kitchen and put the empty bottle on the table, and the unspent money. 'I couldn't get it,' she said. 'The place was shut.' And she asked: 'Where's Jess?' There was no use staying if the old man was going to be hanging about all the time. It was after eleven and she'd left her child alone. She might just as well go home.

215

He said nothing but turned and went out of the kitchen. She followed him and, standing there in the passage outside the bedroom door, she heard somebody moaning. He tried to stop her; but she pushed past him and, in the bedroom doorway, stood incredulously staring.

In the corner of the room opposite the door, Jess lay on the floor, supported on one elbow, her head drooping, her hair, hanging down over her face, saturated with blood. All round her, the bare boards of the floor were splotched with blood.

Jessie flew across the room and, tearing off her bonnet and shawl, knelt down by her friend. She was lying there, clad only in her petticoat and a dressing-gown, and she seemed in a stupor. When Jessie lifted her head she saw that there were three great wounds across her face, one across the forehead, two across the eyes and nose. She cried to the old man, sick with horror: 'What have you done to her?'

'I didn't mean to,' he mumbled. 'It was an accident.'

She knelt by the injured woman, supporting the head and shoulders. 'Bring some water. Lukewarm water.' Holding poor Jess in her arms she implored, 'Jessie, Jessie—what happened?'

Jess moaned and muttered but it was all unintelligible. Perhaps, she thought, he's been trying to force himself on her and in the struggle she fell and cut herself. The old man came back with the water but it was too hot. 'Get some cold,' she said. 'And bring a handkerchief.' He went off again and got them and stood by while she tenderly bathed away the blood. 'How could you do such a thing to her?' she cried, seeing now for the first time the extent of the terrible wounds. 'I don't know,' he said. 'I don't know.' He seemed anxious and distressed.

'We must have a doctor,' said Jessie, at last. 'I'll stay with her; you go and get one.' But he demurred. He didn't think Jess was as bad as all that. She'd be better soon, let them get her fixed up a bit and then he would go. He went out of the room and left her kneeling, holding Jess in her arms, and in a little while Jess opened her eyes. 'Jess, what happened, what happened?' But Jess only looked back at her, dazed and uncomprehending and though after a little while she seemed to begin to understand what was said to her, could give no coherent answer. They stayed so for a long time, Jessie just holding her friend in her arms, trying to staunch the bleeding, not troubling her with any more questions.

But the old man did not return and after a while Jess seemed more rational and she said: 'You ought to have a doctor. I must go and get a doctor.'

Jess understood that. She muttered, 'No,' and insisted, 'Stay here with me.'

'Yes, yes,' said Jessie, reassuringly. 'I'll stay.' She raised her to a sitting position, still kneeling on the floor beside her, still holding the wet cloth to the wounds. The old man came back again.

He was carrying a large tin basin with water and soap and a cloth and he went down on his hands and knees and began to mop up the blood all about them, wringing the cloth out into the basin. But in getting up he slipped and fell on his elbow and the blood and water slopped over Jessie's feet as she knelt there. Her skirt and petticoats were soaked and her boots and stockings so wet that she had to take them off. She sent him to fetch another handkerchief and with it bandaged the forehead, and got Jess to her feet and helped her over to a chair beside the bed.

Jess was terribly weak. She murmured that she wanted to lie down and together they got her on to the bed just as she was and pulled up the covers over her. There was a crocheted night-cap hanging on the looking glass and Jessie fetched it and put it over the handkerchief-bandage to keep it in place. The wounds across the nose were still bleeding and while Mr Fleming went on cleaning up the room she sat by the bed still trying to staunch them. Jess lay still with her eyes closed. She seemed very weak and getting weaker. 'We *must* get a doctor,' said Jessie.

The old man came over and stood by the bed looking down at the wounded face. But no, he said, there was nothing to be alarmed about. It would be time enough in the morning—he'd go for a doctor then, himself.

She would have insisted but Jess opened her eyes and again whispered, 'No.' Torn with indecision, she sat on beside her and after a little while Jess fell asleep—so perhaps, after all, there was no immediate danger. Mr Fleming left the room again and she heard him moving about, upstairs and down. She went out to the kitchen a couple of times, once for fresh water, once to put her wet shoes and stockings by the fire to dry. On the second occasion she found him in there, making a pot of tea.

Jess woke, and now she seemed a little stronger and her mind was clear. Jessie sat on beside her and as the hours passed and the dawn grew near, with the old man coming in now and then to look at the sick woman appraisingly and go away again—in murmurs and snatches, with long pauses of exhaustion, there emerged the story of that night.

The old man was afraid, whispered Jess. It was because she had made that remark about having a tongue that would frighten 'somebody' if it were let loose. The fact was that three or four weeks ago a gentleman, a brewer, had come to stay and on the Friday afternoon, the family having left for Dunoon as usual, it fell to Grandpa to see him off at the station. He didn't get back till eleven and then he was 'gie 'en tipsy'. Jess helped him off with his coat and went away downstairs to her bed; but an hour later he came down to the basement and tried to get into her bed and 'use liberties with her'. She turned him out of her room in a fury and next morning she said she would tell his son about him, as soon as he got back from Dunoon. He begged her not to— not even to say that he had been drunk; if he hadn't been, this would never have happened. She'd had no intention of telling Mr Fleming really, she'd have been too much ashamed, but she thought she would make the old man pay for his sins; and when, in his terror he offered her money to keep quiet, she thought she might as well let him pay in that way too: she was set upon going to Australia now, and this would help to finance the expedition. They had been continually at war ever since, and already today they had had words about it. When Jessie left the house to go for the mutchkin of whisky, he had turned upon her—Jess—for hinting that there was something she could tell. She 'gave him some word' and flounced out of the kitchen. Her stays were uncomfortable and she went into her bedroom and got out of her dress and put on a polka, and began to unlace them. He stood in the passage outside, shouting abuse at her and she, with her hands behind her unlacing her corsets, gave back as good as she got and, when she was ready to take them off, went over and shut the door in his face. She had slipped off the corsets and was standing tying her petticoats, when the door burst open and he rushed at her, struck her three times across the face and felled her to the ground.

Jessie was appalled by this story. 'What will you do now?'

'Am I badly cut?' asked Jess.

'Yes, badly, very badly.'

'Then I'll have to see a doctor; and I'll have to account to the doctor for the injuries. . . .'

The old man came back into the room. 'How could you have done such a thing?' Jessie said to him. 'How could you strike a girl like this?—and after the way you've behaved to her already.'

He gave her no direct answer—it was done he said, and couldna' be helped now, but he was sorry and of course he would 'make everything right for Jess', and he would make up for it to Jess, as she very well knew. 'And for you, Jessie,' he said, 'if you'll haud your tongue and say nothing about it, never mention what you've seen—I'll not forget it to you, either.'

It was after two o'clock in the morning, she was worn out with the shock of what had happened, with anxiety and strain. She did not know what to reply, what Jess would want, what she ought to do. 'I wish I had never got mixed up in it,' she said. She felt she could not leave Jess, and yet—'What am I to do? I can't stay here all night, my baby's all alone at home with no one to look after him. . . .'

'Mrs Campbell will look after him,' said Jess. 'Stay with me till the doctor comes.' But when the doctor did come, she added, she'd have to explain to him; and when Mr Fleming got back from Dunoon, 'I'm afraid I'll just have to tell him who did it—and why.'

'No, no, Jess, ye'll no need to do that,' cried the old man, anxiously. 'And you, Jessie, there's no need to tell, say nothing about it, tell nobody and I'll put all to rights. . . .'

'Who should I tell?' she said. 'It's no business of mine.'

'You won't tell?'

'No,' said Jessie. 'I've got no occasion to tell—why should I? You and Jess can take your own way—it's no business of mine.'

'You promise?'

It cost her nothing to promise: as she had said, who should she tell?—it was all no concern of hers. But he would not be satisfied, he went off upstairs and came back with the great family Bible, in its black cover, and there, in Jess M'Pherson's presence, made her swear. 'Swear by the Almighty God that you'll never tell anyone man, woman or child what you've seen or heard this night between me and Jess. And I'll never forget it,' he also swore, 'to either of you. I'll make Jess comfortable for the rest of her life.'

It meant nothing to her to tell or keep silent; and if there were to be some little alleviation to be got out of it in her ever-pressing money troubles, she doubtless thought—well, all the better. She put her hand on the Bible and swore the oath. He calmed down again; and sat down beside the bed and remained there, quietly.

At about three o'clock, Jess told him to go away. He said he was all right where he was. 'She told me she wanted to rise and make water and she got up in bed.' So Jessie sent the old man off and helped Jess out of bed. She was very stiff and cold and said couldn't she go by the fire? Jessie wrapped a blanket round her and called to the old man and together they helped her through to the kitchen—though she seemed pretty strong by now, she could have managed on her own—and she sat down on a small piece of carpet by the fire with the blanket hugged round her. Jessie sent the old man back to the bedroom for a pillow and bed-clothes and made a sort of bed for her on the floor, and she dozed off again. But she woke and said she was now too hot, so they moved her, without raising her, away from the fire a little and turned her so that she lay with her feet towards the hearth and her head between the table and the corner cupboard, towards the sink, and there she lay, restlessly dozing. Mr Fleming went off again, upstairs and downstairs and once or twice into Jess's room.

Another hour passed. Jess grew more restless and at last woke and now she said she felt very ill. Jessie fetched water for her but she grew rapidly worse and at last admitted that she thought she ought to have a doctor. The old man was upstairs. Jessie pulled on her stockings and boots and went into the bedroom where she had thrown down her cloak and bonnet when she rushed to help Jess. The skirts of her dress were still damp and draggled with the spilt water and blood and she took down Jess's everyday brown merino from its hook and put it on over her own dress and got on the cloak and bonnet. As she hurried out again she met Mr Fleming coming down the stairs. 'Jessie's worse,' she said. 'I think she's very ill, I'd better get the doctor right away.'

He said he didn't know—to wait a minute and he'd see for himself how Jess was. But she'd wait no longer. She realised at last that he had no intention of calling a doctor if he could help it, he was afraid of what Jess would tell. But there was no more time to be lost. She knew of one doctor in the neighbourhood—she would go and get hold of him, without any more delay. She hurried off upstairs.

The front door was locked and the key was not in it.

She went down to the kitchen again. He was standing bending over Jess, his hands on his knees, looking down at her. She went forward to ask him for the key and now she saw that Jess was already far worse than when she had left her only a few minutes ago—and for the first time it came to her that she might die. She was still alive, for though she seemed to be unconscious she was moving; but unless help came very soon it might well be too late. She asked for the key.

He would not let her go, he would arrange it all in his own time, he said. She did not stay to argue but went off upstairs again—it was dawn by now and growing light, perhaps some of the neighbours would be stirring. She threw open the shutters in the ground floor parlour looking over the back gardens, and flung up the window. But there was no one. She was hurrying through to the dining-room to try the front of the house when, at the head of the basement stairs, she suddenly stopped. A moment later she was running down them as fast as she could go.

She saw the upraised cleaver, dripping blood, and the poor blood-streaming, mutilated head, tumbled off the pillow to the stone of the kitchen floor; and even as she stood in a paralysis of horror, again and again the terrible weapon crashed down.

She gave one wild scream and ran forward into the kitchen; but the old man turned and looked at her and at that look she took to her heels and started to run back up the stairs again. He came after her and halfway up the stairs her terror-stricken heart betrayed her and she stood, violently palpitating, spread-eagled against the wall, powerless to move another step; and began to scream for help.

He came to the foot of the stairs. 'Come down,' he called. 'I'm not going to meddle with you.' But she saw the blood-dripping cleaver still in his hand and could only stand trembling and weeping, pressed against the wall, imploring, 'Oh, let me away, let me go; for the love of God let me away.'

'Come down,' he insisted. 'I'll do you no harm.'

'She's dead,' sobbed Jessie. 'She's killed. Oh, what shall I do?' And she prayed again, 'Let me away, let me away.'

He came up the stairs and caught her by the cloak. 'I kent frae the first she cou'dna' live; and if any doctor had come in I would ha' had to have answered for her death, for she'd ha' told.' But she only sobbed and cried, 'Oh, what shall I do?—out of my house all night, and Jessie killed!'

'Aye,' he said. 'If you tell what you know, you'll be taken for her death as well as I. But there's no need to be feart. Come down; it need never be found out.'

Cowed and terrified, she crept back down the stairs. It was true —out of her house all night, and now here lay the murdered body of her friend. She looked at it and shuddered. He must have seen the look, for he said eagerly: 'You see—my life's in your power; and so is your life in my power.' If she informed upon him, he said, he would deny the whole thing and charge *her* with the murder. But the fact was, it was as much as both their lives were worth that either should ever say a word about it. Let them both keep it secret, and it could never be found out who had done it. 'Help me now,' he said. 'We must get her out of here and wash up the blood from the floor. . . .'

'I couldn't,' she said. 'I couldn't. Not if I were never to move from here again. . . .' And she besought him, 'Let me go away, let me go.'

But he ignored her. He tore away the sheet and blankets and tossed them on to the kitchen table and took hold of the poor, terrible body by the shoulders and dragged it out through the passage and into the bedroom, and came back and took the sheet off the table and began to clean up the floor with it. But in disturbing the heap of bedclothes he revealed the bloody cleaver which he must have put down on the table; and at sight of it, her terrors redoubled and she began again to implore him to let her go. She would never reveal a word of it, never, never; even if she were charged with the murder as well as he, she would never say a word. Only, for God's sake let her go!

'We must pretend there was a burglary,' he said. 'I'll leave the pantry window open and tell them I found the house robbed in the morning.' And he went back into the dead woman's room and came back with an armful of dresses. 'Take these away. We can say her box was robbed.'

'Take them away? What could I do with them?'

'Buy a box somewhere, pack them up and take a train to some out-of-the-way place and get rid of them. Or send to box to some railway station or other, to lie till called for. Then it can never be found out what happened to the things.'

She looked at poor Jess's treasured 'best clothes' and, her own terror a little abated, gave way to a purer grief. 'How could you do such a thing?'

'I couldna' help ma'sel',' he said. 'Ye ken verra weel that I liked Jess fine; but I kent frae the first she couldna' live.'

'But what could ever tempt you in the first place—to strike the poor girl like that?'

'Ay, weel,' he said, 'ye ken, Jessie, she had a most provoking tongue. She'd been casting things up at me and I was mad at her. When she was at me I seemed to have nae powers of speaking, and I just struck out at her in a passion.' He had been on the brink of doing it a week ago, he said, and had only just stopped himself.

The hours passed. Dawn broke, a new morning was born, 'a lovely morning, still and calm.' She sat sick, shivering, appalled with care, in the blood-splashed kitchen while the old man 'dichted up' the floor and took the cloth out to the lobby and rubbed over the bloody trail where he had dragged the body through. He came back for the blankets and sheets and returned with some things and stuffed them on to the fire—she thought they were clothes belonging to Jess. He had taken off his coat and was working in his shirt sleeves, but even the shirt was saturated with blood and he took it off and put that on the fire also, and filled a tin basin with water and washed himself, and put on a clean shirt from the airing screen. Then he went off upstairs and changed his trousers and waistcoat and came back again and fetched more coal from the outside shed and made up the fire. Six o'clock, seven. . . .

And then a bell rang.

It must have turned cold their hearts, the sound of that bell shrilling through the deathly silence of the house. But he pulled himself together. 'Go and answer it.'

She utterly refused. 'No, I'll not go to the door—go you.' So he went up, still in his shirt sleeves. When he came down again, he had on a coat. It was the milk-boy, he said; but he had taken no jug up with him and returned with no milk. The open dining-room door, however, had perhaps given him a new idea; for he went off again and came back with a collection of silver. She had better take this too. It would lend colour to the idea of a burglary. 'Take it to Lundie's and pawn it in some false name—Mary

M'Donald or M'Kay or something like that, and give a false address, give No. 5 St Vincent Street, then no one can ever trace where it came from.' But he thought better of it. After all, perhaps it would be unwise to pawn it. 'Put it in with the other things and get rid of it.'

'Get rid of it?' she said dully.

He had told her already. She could buy a tin box at any ironmongers, it needn't cost her more than five shillings—and he fished out his purse and gave her twenty-seven shillings. Pack the things in the box and take the box to somewhere where she wasn't known. Was she known in Edinburgh? No?—then take them to Edinburgh, and go where there was some water and drop the box in. And once again he swore her to secrecy—promise never to breathe one syllable of what has happened here tonight! For if you do, he reminded her, it will be your life as well as mine.

She swore; not a word, she would never breathe a word of it.

'I'll look after you,' he said. 'I'll set you up in a shop, Jessie, you shall never want again. . . .'

It was after eight o'clock and the world was astir. She had better get home. She lifted the big bundle of clothes and silver and hid it beneath the grey cloak and together they crept down to the end of the garden and he unlocked the door into the lane and let her through. It closed behind her and she heard the key turn in the lock again. With her burden of terror, she was all alone.

She went along the lane, westward, and home by a roundabout route by way of Kelvingrove Street, and turned at last into Broomielaw Street. But the people were coming out on their way home from night work and she dodged up Washington Street to avoid them and down James Watt Street and slipped in at the back door of the 'close' and up the stair and rang at her own front door. Mrs Campbell let her in.

Over the blood-stained, bedraggled skirts, she still wore the cinnamon dress.

Throughout the court there was no sound, no movement as, in his clear, cool, unemotional voice, Mr Clark read the concluding lines of the statement. 'I never had any quarrel with Jess. On every occasion we were most affectionate and friendly. I was not pressed for money. I paid my rent on Saturday, July 4, before I pawned the plate. I paid £4.'

CHAPTER NINETEEN

This then was the statement that Mrs M'Lachlan had made to Mr Wilson—the statement Mr Dixon had carried round with him, stuffed into his pocket—the statement that had lifted those legal hearts to a sudden enthusiasm of interest and hope. As has been said, we may accept it at this distance, as exactly what it purported to be: 'all her own work' and made at a time when neither she nor her advisers knew more than the broadest outline of the case against her.

Sound and movement returned to the stunned and silent Court. The jury, hitherto so cocksure, now looked ill at ease, some shaken, some unconvinced, but all utterly taken aback. A policeman, unnerved, broke into tears. The prisoner who had sat weeping during much of the reading, especially where Jess M'Pherson was mentioned, pulled herself together and—her strength of will was amazing—returned to her former outward calm.

There were at this stage two courses open to the judge. He might defer sentence until the statement could be examined and investigated; or he might question her on it then and there.

If we place ourselves for a moment (he himself spent only a moment on it) in the position of Lord Deas, faced with this most extraordinary *volte face,* we shall see that there were three aspects of the statement open to examination. First the character of the prisoner and the circumstances of its making. Second the external evidence. Third, the internal evidence, the mute witness of the murdered body and the scene of the crime.

As to the first, two points do seem very greatly in favour of the truth of the statement. One is that the prisoner had till the moment of Mr Fleming's release from custody evinced a calm conviction that of course he would 'clear her'. (When asked by her fellow prisoners if she could really be 'in' for the murder, she replied innocently, 'Oh, no, Mr Fleming's in for that.') But why, if she were guilty, should she suppose for one moment that he would defend her? Either he was an innocent witness to her guilt or he knew nothing whatsoever about it. He swore that the latter was true: why then, or why in either case, should she expect him to protect her from justice? Why her utter astonishment, her subsequent despair, when the old man was released? Was she so cunning, let alone such an actress, that she could evolve such a plan of behaviour in advance and so carry it through as to deceive prison officers, cell mates and lawyers alike? And then, having spoken never a word against him, reiterating only that he would explain everything and make a' right—the moment she knows for certain that he has gone off and left her to carry her burden alone, she begins to speak: she feels free—free to accuse; feels absolved, she would claim, from that oath taken on the Bible, an oath which this religiously-minded Scotswoman would doubtless hold sacredly binding; might well be also superstitiously binding; and she launches into this long, circumstantial, connected story.

And the second point is that it *is* a long, circumstantial and connected story. She had proved herself in her three earlier statements and indeed throughout the days that followed the murder, to be an extremely bad liar—contradictory, unconvincing, easily startled into recklessness. Now she comes forth with this sustained narrative, *impossible of contradiction at any save one unimportant point* and covering every detail in the long, long tally of the indictment against her—and before she can possibly have known what any of them were.

And secondly, where there were outside witnesses their evidence is nowhere in conflict with her story. In some cases indeed, it supplies supporting proof which seems absolutely unassailable; but this was not forthcoming until after the trial, when extra evidence was taken in investigation of the statement; and though most of it was covered in our earlier chapters, sitting here as we do for the moment in his lordship's place, we are as yet unaware of it. We must judge upon the facts that when Jessie says she went out at eleven for a mutchkin of whisky, she is supported by the two gossiping women who saw her go out and return; when she says that the old man answered the door to the milk-boy's ring—that the door was locked—that he took 'nae milk'—and, gratuitous detail, that though he went up in his shirt sleeves he returned wearing a coat—she is in each instance supported by M'Quarrie. And though they are small points, unimportant and not at all conclusive, the fact that the three sisters saw lights burning in the dining-room in the early hours of the morning, does lend colour to her story of having heard the old man moving about the house. If (as is our judicial opinion) the murder was committed at four in the morning, it would not have been necessary for her to light the gas in her search for the silver; it was quite light by then. Nor, surely, would she have dared to light it at any time—with the old man asleep on the same floor. And even the mysterious gentleman who did or did not admit to having seen old Fleming on the steps of the house that night, adds his crumb of support: if only to her implication that Mr Fleming went up at some time in the early hours and removed the key from the door so that she shouldn't go out and call a doctor. He need not have gone outside for that, certainly, but being there, it is by no means impossible that he poked out his head to see if anyone was stirring who might have heard poor Jess screaming. It would be a foolish but a very natural thing to do.

As for the internal evidence, this does explain to an extraordinary degree many things which remained unaccounted for by the prosecution. The two sets of wounds, the second set all on one side of the head, inflicted while the victim was lying down. All three doctors agreed that it was at least possible for the wounds across the face to have been inflicted while the woman was standing. One thought it unlikely but Dr Hamilton roundly declared that it was 'an absurdity' to question it. He had studied a great number of murders during his work in South Africa and he knew what he was talking about; he did not actually add 'if others didn't'. The fact that there was blood on two different weapons, the hammer and the cleaver. The fact that the face of the injured woman appeared at some stage to have been bathed (there was rather confused evidence later about the neck also having been washed, and the doctor thought this had happened after the second lot of injuries had been inflicted, that is to say, after death. This seems so inexplicable and unlikely that it is easier to suppose the doctor mistaken. The other doctors did not concur. In any case, it does nothing to discredit Jessie's story). The fact that the bed had at some stage been slept in, that the pillows and bedclothes had been pulled off and later thrown back again on to the bed. The fact that the pillows were blood-stained, but not nearly so much as if the second attack had been made while the head was lying on them: Jessie says that when she saw the old man attacking her, Jess was lying with her head no longer on the pillows but on the kitchen floor. The fact that one sheet, damp and much blood-stained, was rolled up and thrown under a wash-stand—she says the old man mopped up the kitchen floor with it. The fact that part of the bedroom floor had been washed—a detail inexplicable except in the light of her story, for though the kitchen and the lobby might have been cleaned up to post-pone discovery, this would not apply to the bedroom where behind the locked door the body was openly lying. The fact that she says the old man spilt soap and water on her skirts and shoes—and her skirt was found to show patches of bleaching from some such chemical as soda, and marks of her naked foot were found in the bedroom and (though not proven hers) in the kitchen.

In the kitchen are the famous 'marks of a severe struggle', number three in the list of Conclusions drawn up by Doctors Fleming and Macleod (of which list Lord Deas said that there were matters in it—and he later specified this evidence of a struggle—not proper to a medical report; in which remark, just for once we must heartily agree with him). Their 'conclusion' does certainly, as was earlier observed, seem based on very meagre evidence—'confused footprints, the marks of twisting heels, of the ball of a foot', some of the footprints being of bare feet. (No bits of wood seem to have been produced to measure these.) There was also the mark of a bloody hand on the sink, as though someone had clutched at the sink in falling. It was later put to the doctors that these marks were not inconsistent with Jessie's story of how she and the old man had assisted the injured woman into the kitchen and later, without raising her from the ground, moved her to a place further from the fire; that lying there she had been attacked, and the corpse had been sub-sequently dragged away. One doctor held out but the others acknowledged that the marks were equally consistent with either theory. A third was put forward in a letter published in the papers by a lady signing herself 'Another Housewife'. It reaches a double-edged conclusion. When a woman washes a floor, the writer says, she gets down on her hands and knees to it. A man just stoops down or squats and the turning heel marks on the kitchen flagstones might well be those not of any 'struggle' but of a man trying to wash the floor. In contradiction to this quite interesting suggestion, one must recall Jessie's own evidence that in the bedroom at any rate, Mr Fleming 'went down on his hands and knees' and began to mop up the blood, wringing the cloth out into a basin.

Quite an interesting point was made by a woman writing to the papers over the signature 'A Housewife'—doubtless the precursor of 'Another Housewife' who wrote about the washing of the floors. This woman reminded readers that it was common usage to keep the kitchen fire in at night with a 'gathering coal', a large lump of coal placed in the centre of the grate—all it needs is to be broken up next morning, and it was indeed the custom in the Fleming household, for the servant next door could often hear the coal being broken. But, she points out, both the old man and Jessie speak of the fire in the kitchen being 'mended' between seven and eight in the morning. If Jessie were the murderer, there would be no reason to keep the fire stoked up: the only need might be so that incriminating garments might be burned there, but Jessie did not burn her bloody clothes but took them all home. Only in the light of her story, is this fact, that the fire was kept stoked up in the kitchen, explicable—that the old man was in and out all night, at one time making tea: that Jess lay there for some time between the two attacks, to try to get warm, and that subsequently he destroyed his blood-stained clothes there.

And so to the hours which followed the second, and fatal attack. Here there does seem a possible discrepancy in Jessie's story, and if it was a mistake it was a strange one to have made. But it was made also by the two doctors who, with all the advantage of long and dispassionate examination of the position of the murdered body, could still announce it as their final 'conclusion' that 'the body was drawn by the head with the face downwards, along the lobby from the kitchen to the bedroom.' For Jessie's statement says, in the vernacular, 'He took the body by the oxters and drew it ben into the laundry'—'he took the body by the shoulders and dragged it through into Jess's room.'

But the corpse was found in the bedroom lying between the bed and the centre table—a passage about two-feet wide—the head towards the door; the clothes being pulled up over the top part leaving the lower part bare, the face lying inside the sort of sack made by the pulled-up skirts. If it had been dragged into the room head first, the feet *must* have been left nearest the door. It would be impossible to turn the body in the narrow space between bed and table; and anyway, why on earth do so? The rucking-up of the clothes also suggests very strongly that the body was pulled through by the feet. This method would be much easier than lifting the dead weight of the head and shoulders and then tugging the body along, moving backwards; and the terrible condition of the head, with mangled flesh and blood-clotted hair, would make it an almost impossibly ghastly task, besides adding to the risks by covering the murderer with blood. Why the doctors came to so extraordinary a conclusion it is difficult to imagine. Dr Macleod based it upon the dirt on the front of the legs, the ruffling of the skin of the knees and the fact that the streaks of blood on the face were not disturbed as they would have been if the woman had been dragged with her face along the floor. He did not see her, however, till after the enveloping skirts had been removed, which might surely have protected her face to a very great extent.

Dr Watson who also saw the body *in situ* thought it had been dragged through by someone who had stood between the legs, got hold of them by the ankles and, facing forward, pulled the body along like a cart, the face protected by the clothes.

Why then should Jessie say that old Fleming had 'taken the body by the oxters'? Could this be the one slip in a carefully fabricated story?

A realistic explanation would be that in fact at first he did do so. The body lay, according to her story which is supported by the fact that that part of the kitchen floor was washed—between the table and the corner of the kitchen cupboard, the head towards the door. It could not be turned in that space any more easily than it could have been in the bedroom. He would take it by the shoulders and start dragging it back towards the door and then, finding this method too exhausting, turn it in the larger space between the cupboard and the sink—very possibly clutching with a bloody hand at the sink, as he did so—and then take hold of it by the legs. (This would also account for the 'ruffling of the skin' and soiling of the knees and shins noted by Dr Macleod.) Whether Jessie thought it not necessary to describe all this in detail, or whether in her horror and distress she hid her face and refused to see what was going on, needn't really matter. The point is that it does seem possible to reconcile her statement with the truth when she says simply that he 'took her by the oxters'.

There are marks of blood in the kitchen, in the lobby, on the stairs. They prove nothing but they are in no way inconsistent with the statement. Her skirts were blood-stained after the first attack on Jess and she further says that she ran forward into the kitchen when she saw the second attack; the marks may equally have been made by her, by the old man, or, in some cases, by the dragging of the body with its trailing, blood-stained garments. And there is the blood-stained piece of carpet thrown down on top of the body as it lay in the bedroom; she says that Jess lay by the kitchen fire with just such a piece of carpet under her.

All these details are, of course, not inconsistent with Jessie having committed the murder herself—they are all things she would have known and may simply have twisted to fit her own story. Their interest lies chiefly in the fact that they do in such minuteness and continuity fit her story—that in it every point brought forward by the prosecution is accounted for, and long before she could know what these points were to be. Was she capable—a woman who could have uttered those three other muddled, inconsistent, self-incriminating and wholly unsatisfactory statements—of setting up all these circumstances in advance like pins in a lace-making cushion, and weaving a fabrication that would leave literally nothing unaccounted for. The statement, says Mr Roughead, 'fitted the proven facts so perfectly as to render its fabrication incredible. If it was false, then in Mrs M'Lachlan we have lost a fictionist more marvellous than Defoe; one so adroit as to foresee and account for facts and circumstances which it is humanly impossible she can have known she would be called upon to meet. And this masterpiece of mendacity, this feat of fraudulence, this dexterity in deceit was achieved by the illiterate authoress of those clumsy and idiotic declarations, concocted in her early efforts to escape from the meshes of the net wherein she had been so cunningly entangled—which, as Euclid would say, is absurd.'

But if all else is no more than 'not inconsistent' there still remains the fact that the floors had been washed.

Jessie says it was the old man who 'dichted up' the kitchen floor and the lobby. What other explanation, indeed, can there be?

For why on earth should Jessie herself, had she been guilty, have washed those floors? What possible consideration could have induced her to remain in that house, with the old man in the room just above the kitchen, and get down on her hands and knees and scrub the bloodstains away?

She has just battered a woman to death—a 'wiry' woman, taller and much stronger than herself, a woman capable of putting a policeman on the floor in a friendly trial of strength; and the woman has put up a long struggle, for in this case the evidence of the twisting footmarks is probably true, and her screams have been loud enough to be heard in the house next door and, according to his later statement, by the old man upstairs. Is it conceivable that she will not grab up her few poor ghastly, ill-gotten gains and get out of that house as fast as she can go?

She knows the house well, she has been an inmate of the house, she knows where keys are kept: there are two exits, she can easily get away. Why should she stay? To scrub up the floors. But why? The old man might do so to delay discovery, to make it credible that he saw nothing amiss: but what good could delay do to Jessie? And anyway, what delay would she accomplish? She could hardly foresee the remarkable forbearance of the old gentleman in regard to the missing woman—he who so perseveringly enquired into the affairs of the servants, and above all of Jess. So why? Why lug the body, so dreadfully heavy in the inertia of death, out of the kitchen through the lobby and into the bedroom? Why wash the bedroom floor? The body is lying there for the first to see who enters the room. Why scrub away a few bloodstains? And if so, why leave her own naked, bloody footmarks?— clearly visible even later when the blood had dried and lost colour, far more so when newly made. (That the old man overlooked them is of course entirely explained by her story—they were made *after* he washed the floor in the bedroom, it was as he finished doing so that he spilt the water over her boots and obliged her to remove boots and stockings and go barefoot.) And then, the heavy task of scrubbing the stone floors of kitchen and lobby. Why? Why undertake such a thing now, at the end of this long night of tension and horror and exhaustion—the first attack, the (unexplained and otherwise inexplicable) lapse of time before the second attack, the final death struggle and murder. Her heart was weak, she had been warned that undue exertion might kill her. Would she not be afraid that at best her heart might give way and leave her palpitating and helpless to move—as indeed she says it did—at the scene of the crime?

Of course it is true that Jessie did in fact remain at the scene of the crime. Why she should have done so she does not explain. She may have felt too ill and exhausted to face the long walk home. They may have thought it best to wait till the streets were more busy so that she would not be remarked, so early in the morning, abroad with her bundle. The likeliest reason, perhaps, is that she dared not disturb Mrs Campbell at this hour and so impress it upon her memory that she had been out all night. If she rang the bell later, Mrs Campbell would assume that she had already gone out that morning and was now coming in again. Mrs Campbell does, in fact, seem to have done so, for she made no comment when she let Jessie in at nine—though we may well believe that she later had second thoughts. Alternatively, she had lived at the Broomielaw only a few weeks, she may have supposed a night's absence to be part of her landlady's routine and 'no business of hers'.

This reason, certainly, would equally apply if Jessie were the murderer. But would she in that case ever have remained in the house? Would she not rather have gone out and wandered about the streets till the time came when she could safely ring the bell at home? That she didn't do so is clear from her knowledge of the old man's answering the milk-boy's ring. And by the same token, if she was there, wouldn't he have seen her? —he was by his own admission up and dressed by twenty-to-eight, and had been downstairs to the basement looking for Jess. (This, of course, would be why he at first insisted that he hadn't got up till nine?—by that time she would have left the house.) On the other hand, once again—it is true that there was a bloody mark inside the cupboard in the lobby which could have been made by a person hiding in there. Yet, how revealing—though Mr Clark, hampered by his line of defence could not remark upon it—is the old man's famous reply under cross-examination, 'We kent it was all ower wi' Jessie'—elsewhere given as 'We knew Jessie was dead and could not go to the door.' In both cases 'we'.

But—even if she did remain, even if the old man did see her: if she alone were guilty—why wash the floors?

And even if she did wash them—how account for their being still damp three days later?

Only Jessie's statement can explain the newly-washed floors. The old man could not live with them as they were and still pretend that he had not suspected that harm might have come to Jess. Like Lady Macbeth he went on and on trying—but he couldn't get rid of the blood. He must have gone on trying almost to the hour when discovery was at hand.

These were the considerations before Lord Deas at the end of the prisoner's statement.

Two official enquiries held later, revealed nothing contradictory to her story—though of course the judge at this stage could know nothing of that. In some cases, true, medical opinion clashed but these cancel one another out; in the opinion of the great Lord Lister, then Professor Lister, the medical features were in remarkable accordance with the statement; he wrote to this effect to the still violently pro-Fleming *Herald*—the editor must have been delighted! A bevy of ex-servants gave evidence of the extreme propriety of old Mr Fleming's conduct towards them, though one or two had seen him come home 'tipsy'—always when the master of the house was away. But Elizabeth Halliday told how as much as two years ago Jess had complained to her that the old man was 'a nasty body' or 'a dirty body'; she had understood Jess to mean that he had made improper attempts on her virtue (if you could call it virtue; there is always poor Jess's son in Australia, and that other 'misfortune'.) And several people knew that Mr Fleming would have liked to marry Jess, and was quite serious about it, though to her the idea was only by turns amusing or disgusting. From the moment she came to work there, he had haunted the kitchen and he was for ever talking about her and praising her. She had told her friend Mrs Smith that she was well enough when the family was at home, it was when she was left alone with him that her misery began.

Miss Janet Dunsmore, however, did not come forward to speak to Mr Fleming's virtue—perhaps, to be fair, she couldn't, since the newspapers reported that she had died some years previously. But Mr Gilchrist, an elder of the Anderston United Presbyterian Church, supported by the testimony of the rest of his session, felt obliged to relate how in the year 1852 Mr Fleming, already by his own account close to being an octogenarian, had confided in a very distressed state of mind that he had had a child by a girl who was a domestic servant: to wit, the above Miss Dunsmore—whether or not she actually worked in the Fleming household is not known. Later, said Mr Gilchrist, he and a fellow elder had the old gentleman up before them, whereupon he confessed his guilt and seemed, to Mr Gilchrist at any rate, so painfully conscious of the sin he had committed that he could hardly speak. So great was his repentance that he was let off with a caution and had only to suffer his name being put down (incorrectly) in the records. It must have been the wonder, not to say admiration—tinged with envy?—of all the reverend elders who beheld it there.

And a Mrs Samuel Grey was found to inform the anti-Fleming press that at the time of the birth of her own child, a girl baby was brought to her by a doctor who told her that the father was Mr James Fleming. She had brought up the child as her own, Mr Fleming appearing punctually once every two months to pay for its keep, at first at the rate of £1 a month, then 10*s* a month, then up to 12*s* again. She confidently expected him in a fortnight or so, when the next instalment fell due. Elizabeth, she said, who was now going to school, was not over-fond of her aged P., much preferring—naturally—Mr and Mrs Grey.

Thus encouraged, an inhabitant of Kilsyth likewise gave tongue. Among the lovely scenery of the village, he announced, via the press, was set a cottage tenanted by a respectable gentleman of Glasgow, Mr John Fleming. In the year 1854, two years that is to say after the confession to the elders of his kirk, old Mr Fleming was left alone in the cottage by the family and straightaway invited a kindred spirit to share his solitude. Not that solitude was quite the word, for two girls were smuggled in who were known to be 'promenaders along Trongate and Argyle Street' and the girls were seen (and recognised?) by a ploughman as they scrambled in through a window.

There was much scandal and a deputation of villagers waited upon Mr Fleming. The old gentleman became all of a sudden verra deef though he was not known to have been deaf before, but when he could be got to hear, he said that aye, a window had been found open and thieves had been in and robbed him. (Could this incident—if true—later have given Mr Fleming the idea—if guilty—of the allegedly open pantry window at Sandyford Place and the pretence of robbery?)

These last witnesses did not show up at the official enquiries, but Mrs M'Kinnon, a foster-sister of Jess M'Pherson, put in an indignant appearance to say that if old Mr Fleming had said in court that when he heard the screams he had thought she might be spending the night with Jess, then that was a very strange remark indeed. There was a woman she ca'd her sister, he had said, and it bood to be her. There was only one woman in the world, declared Mrs M'Kinnon, that Jess called her sister, and that was herself. But she had never in her life spent a night at Sandyford Place and there was no reason on earth for Mr Fleming to suppose she was there. She repeated the same thing in several forms, and seems mysteriously to have considered herself insulted by the bare suggestion. Perhaps she wondered, as we ourselves can't help wondering, what on earth he supposed they were up to, anyway.

And then there emerged a very interesting piece of confirmation; for Alexander Blair, a brewer, came forward to say that on the Friday three weeks before the murder, he had indeed had a few drinks with old Mr Fleming and when he had seen Mr Fleming into a cab and paid the driver to take him home, Mr Fleming had been 'not tipsy, but hearty; in good spirits'. He must have worsened very rapidly for the cab driver found him on arrival, sitting forward with his head hanging down, very drowsy; and decided that he was under the influence of liquor. He had to be assisted up the steps where he was handed over to a middle-aged female 'of rather dark aspect'—though whether this referred to Jess M'Pherson's complexion or to her reception of erring Grandpa is not apparent. The cabby was by this time 'satisfied that he had got drink'.

Both gentlemen thought it would be soon after six that Mr Fleming arrived home on this occasion; so Jessie is wrong if she says it was eleven. At risk of over-partiality one must concede that it would not necessarily be a very damaging error. Jess had told her the story under circumstances of extreme stress, and may easily have been misunderstood. If the old man went straight to bed, as she says, he may have slept several hours before waking up and going down to the basement; and not just an hour.

An interesting scrap of testimony was added during the course of the enquiries by the sixteen-year-old girl, Mary Black, who said she had gone to Sandyford Place on the morning after the murder, and scrubbed part of the ground floor hall. Mary was much discredited by the *Daily Herald* and several discrepancies do appear in her evidence; but they are not such as to effect Jessie's story—Mary is accused for example of having named a false address as her place of employment. She was further alleged by the *Herald* to have given out a whole tarradiddle of nonsense: that on her way to Sandyford Place she had met Mrs M'Lachlan, carrying a large bundle, that Mr Fleming had had blood on his shirt sleeves, that he had led her down to the basement where she had seen another woman, a stout woman with 'the bloody mark of a hand on her cheek'; that this woman had shown her a bundle with blood dripping from it, informed her that one of the servants had just been delivered of a child and offered her a pound to get rid of the bundle. The *Herald* rightly poured ridicule on it all; but did not pause to consider whether Mary had really said it. In the existing state of rumour and conjecture it would be quite enough for the girl to let slip that she had visited the house, for all the rest to be added by others. She certainly suggested nothing of the sort when officially questioned. The *Herald* gets quite ecstatic over her having testified that Mr Fleming had fetched a pail from a water closet on the ground floor, when in fact there wasn't one there, but Mary simply reminded the enquiry that she hadn't said a water closet, she'd said a closet, meaning a cupboard; and a ground floor cupboard does appear in the isometrical plan.

Her official story does certainly seem faintly suspect and yet there is no real reason to disbelieve it. True, she did not tell it till after the trial, but she had told her mother and a neighbour (she couldn't name the neighbour) soon after the murder was discovered and it was her mother who had told her to say nothing lest she get into a hobble. When she did at last repeat it, it was in confidence to her friend Bella Beveridge; and it was the faithless Beveridge who told a policeman, in consequence of which Mary was hunted out and made to come forward. There is no evidence, therefore, of publicity seeking on her part and the mother seems to have been anxious to avoid it. Nevertheless, such are the oddities to her evidence that it probably would not be wise to give it more than a fifty per cent credence.

She says that she got to the house somewhere about a quarter to nine. Questioned (presumably with reference to the rumoured statement) she answers that she doesn't think she met any woman on the way carrying a bundle; but that anyway she didn't know Mrs M'Lachlan and wouldn't have recognised her. (In fact, Jessie would have been well away by that time. It was a twenty-minutes walk direct to the Broomielaw and, by a very *in*direct route, she got there at nine.)

The old man took down the chain from the front door, says Mary, and admitted her. We know from the milk-boy that it had been replaced after Mr Fleming said they wanted nae milk. He now replaced it again.

One may suppose that Mr Fleming would be taken unawares by this sudden appearance on the doorstep of a girl declaring that she has an appointment to come and work there. Having been surprised into letting her in, he would cast about for some job she could do which need not take her down to the basement. As to the sooty patch at the top of the basement stairs which she says she was set to scrub, Mary gave evidence three times before the two enquiries which followed the trial. The first two times she says that the floor was marked as though people had been trampling over it with soot on their feet and that she saw no signs of blood. The last time she has evidently volunteered information, bringing her mother (who was usually 'in a decline') to support her story, which that lady did, adding that Mary was a very smart girl, which phrase she used not as to her appearance but in the American sense. Mary now says that her mother had that day reminded her that when she first told the story at home she said that she did see blood—the bloody mark of a footprint. She has 'never had a bit mind of it till my mother told me today', but now she remembers it distinctly and that she thought at the time that the soot had been rubbed over the waxcloth to conceal the mark. (She adds that she 'couldn't be sure it was a woman's footprint', but these reported statements are often misleading. She was probably answering a question, whether it could or could not have been a woman's footprint, and what she said really amounts to 'I don't know.' The footprint appeared to be leading into old Mr Fleming's bedroom and, innocent or guilty, there would be no object in Jessie's going there.)

But whether or not Mary did see any footprint is of no great importance, except in testing her veracity; and though it seems possible that this is a piece of embroidery, she will have become something of a heroine after two appearances at the enquiry, and a little wishful recollecting of a sensational nature need not, perhaps, shake our faith in her earlier statements. Moreover, it is all supported by her mother. If Jessie's statement is true, it is by no means unlikely that there were in fact sooty footmarks, or coal-dusty footmarks (though Mary says she recognised the smell of soot), at the top of the stairs. The old man was making up the fire, says Jessie, and burning things, and he went out to the shed and got in more coal. She herself went up after the first attack to try to go out and fetch a doctor, having pulled on the boots over which blood and water had been spilt—so there may have been a footmark after all—and which had been drying in the kitchen hearth; and she says the old man was up and down stairs all night, specifically to fetch the silver and open the door to the milk-boy. As far as Mr Fleming is concerned, there needn't have been anything incriminating about the soot marks. They simply furnished him with a job to give the girl to do which would not necessitate her going down to the basement.

And in this, if Mary's story is true, lies most of its interest; and how tremendously interesting it is! It bears out Elizabeth Brownlie's statement about borrowing the spade—she, too, was headed off from seeing into the kitchen. The basement was in no condition on that Saturday morning to be inspected by observant young women; and—especially in view of his claim to have noticed nothing unusual there—if the old man went out of his way to prevent these girls from seeing into it, it is a most significant point in favour of Jessie's story.

And here is yet another person—a girl actually arriving, commissioned to do work for Jess—to whom he fails to mention that the maid has disappeared.

And once more the low-set, stout young woman raises her fat red face, and P.C. Campbell takes time off from the chastening of the bothersome prostitutes to come and repeat with embellishments his story of having seen her with the woman in the white mutch and long white ties over her shoulders, at the door of No. 17 the night after the murder. He remembers the date by the fact that he posted a letter to his father that evening, and he produces his landlady to say that she saw him writing it. His friend Allan M'Lean, blacksmith, was with him that night and will say how he waited, leaning against the railings of Sandyford Place, while he, P.C. Campbell, went up and examined the door of No. 18. But alas! M'Lean, though he agrees that he met Campbell that Saturday night, says nothing of the kind. He is certain Campbell couldn't have posted the letter in the Sandyford Toll as he says he did: he wouldn't have had time. And he doesn't remember leaning against any railings and doesn't remember Campbell going up to No. 18, and doesn't remember seeing a woman with a fat red face, or indeed any woman; in fact he doesn't remember having been in Sandyford Place at all—none of which is astonishing, for he has been in the ale-house since soon after five, and P.C. Campbell's vision didn't take place till between half-past eight and nine. . . .

And finally there comes one electrifying piece of evidence—the evidence of Miss M'Intyre, who, homeward hastening on the night of the murder, passed the two gossiping women and heard them remark on the woman in the grey cloak just turning into the lane that ran behind the houses in Sandyford Place.

This witness, a lady of 'very retiring disposition', did not appear at the trial. She had to be persuaded by the minister of her church to come forward at all and offer her story at the official enquiry. Had she told it earlier, she could hardly have been ignored; it is very hard to see how the evidence can be otherwise than conclusive.

Miss M'Intyre was a needlewoman employed for the moment by a lady in Sandyford Place and temporarily sleeping there. Her story bears out the statement in an astonishing degree.

At eleven o'clock, says Jessie, or about that time, she went out for the mutchkin of whisky, and her story is confirmed by Mrs Walker, who saw her turn out of the lane into Elderslie Street, and by both Mrs Walker and Miss Dykes, who saw her return, this time coming down Elderslie Street from Sauchiehall Street. (The odious Mrs Walker volunteers the gratuitous piece of information that Robert Robin's shop in Elderslie Street was—she believes—still open: the implication being that, if she had really wanted spirits, Jessie needn't have been put off by the fact that the North Street shop was closed. One can't see what difference it makes—it is not suggested that she was out for any other reason than to buy whisky. All that matters is that she did go out, and Mrs Walker herself confirms that.) She furthermore fixes the time pretty exactly. Her husband, for whom she was on the look out, arrived from the top of Elderslie Street, coming down it towards her.[1] 'That's an odd direction to be coming from,' said his lady at once. But he had only walked back that way with a friend, and 'It's no' so late,' said he defensively, taking out his watch. It was just a quarter past eleven. It was four or five minutes since the woman in the grey cloak had turned into Sandyford Lane.

At that moment Miss M'Intyre was going up Elderslie Street, so close to the two gossipers that she heard them comment on the woman going into the lane and wonder what she was doing there at that time of night, and whether it had any connection with a man who had just passed by her and glanced into her face. Afraid lest they set about her own reputation next, Miss M'Intyre hurried on, but as she turned the corner into Sandyford Place—which must have been about the same moment Jessie came to the garden door of No. 17, leading in from the lane—she was held up by a little group of people who were standing there discussing some strange sounds coming from 'that house where the light is'.

Miss M'Intyre went on. The house in question had lights in the windows of the front basement room, and from this room came 'the moans of a person in very great distress'. She was later quite certain that the house the moaning came from was No. 17.

The evidence of Miss M'Intyre is surely to be relied upon? The all-observant Mrs Walker saw her in Elderslie Street at the time she says she was there; and when on the Monday evening she learned of the murder—no one then knowing how long ago it had happened—she said to several witnesses, 'If it had been on the Friday, I'd have thought that was what I heard.' She described the whole incident and seemed to be 'put about' by what she had heard.

Two other witnesses support her story, though not officially— there was a pretty widespread rash of modesty in coming forward among those who really could have helped Jessie, perhaps be- cause of the pretty widespread rush of those who had in fact nothing to tell. A young man, a very respectable young man, who lived just across Elderslie Street from the mouth of Sandyford Lane, was arriving home at exactly ten past eleven that night when, as he was closing his door, he heard two screams. He told his mother about it and said that he supposed they must come

[1] See plan, page 31.

from the waste ground, haunt of the bothersome prostitutes (no one seems to have thought it mattered if *they* screamed, poor things), but that it sounded much more muffled like, as though it came from inside one of the houses. And a servant, out with a gentleman friend, heard moans as she passed No. 17 Sandyford Place some time after midnight, and a woman's voice cried, 'Oh dear—oh dear!' 'One of the servants is catching it in that house,' remarked the gentleman humorously. She told her mistress next day but, despite that lady's anxious insistence at the time of the trial and the subsequent enquiries, was too much afraid of the notoriety to come forward. It may well be that the injured woman cried out at this time—perhaps when she was making the effort to struggle to the bed: Jessie says she sat for a long time on the floor with her before they got her to bed. It seems terrible that these two did not come forward in support of Miss M'Intyre; a patch-work of their three stories might well have turned the tide at the trial. For Jessie's story and Miss M'Intyre's dovetail with one another. Jessie says that on her return from the expedition to buy whisky she stood in the basement lobby and heard the sound of moans coming from the bedroom. This exactly coincides with the time Miss M'Intyre also heard them; indeed, it fits in quite per-fectly—if moans could be heard from the street, so probably could any loud conversation also. Jessie says she went first into the kitchen and put the unspent money on the table. This would allow time for Miss M'Intyre to pause and stand listening. If she had stayed a minute longer she might well have heard Jessie cry out 'What have you done to her?'

We may surely accept it as a fact, therefore, that shortly after eleven on the night of the murder Jess was heard moaning.

And at four o'clock in the morning there is the sound of screaming. Whichever was guilty, both Jessie and Mr Fleming separately agree that there were screams at four in the morning. Mr Fleming, if he were guilty, would admit this much, in case others had heard the 'squealing' and think it strange that he, in his room just above the kitchen, should have slept right through it; he would surely never make it up if there hadn't in fact been any 'squealing'. Jessie, actually, doesn't specifically mention scream-ing; she says that when she was up on the ground floor trying to get out to go for the doctor she heard 'a noise' from the kitchen; but if Jess did scream, of course that is what the noise was. It doesn't matter very much; the point is that an attack was certainly made at four in the morning.

Mr Stewart next door also heard someone screaming—though he heard only one scream. His evidence is rather odd, for he says it was then 'very dark, as dark as when I went to bed.' It can't have been very dark when he went to bed, for that was just before eleven, and at that time Mrs Walker and Miss Dykes could see well enough to be able to describe the clothes of a woman who passed on the opposite side of the street. His impression was that it was not very late, not after one o'clock. He had said to his wife when he heard about the murder and began to put two and two together that, whatever Mr Fleming might say about hearing screams at four in the morning, they would find that the murder had been committed nearer midnight. He was confused about the whole thing, he acknowledged. He might have been asleep a quarter of an hour or two hours.

Our guess is that it was a quarter of an hour. However dark it may or may not have been, it was 'as dark as when he went to bed.' That is probably just exactly what it was. He went to bed round about eleven and he fell asleep at once, so quickly that he had not even time to settle down but was still half sitting up against the headboard. And just as quickly he was woken up again—by a single scream.

In other words, what Mr Stewart heard, he heard at a few minutes after eleven. And what he heard was the first attack on Jess.

For at this time it seems reasonable to accept that there were indeed two separate attacks. At eleven Jess is moaning. At four in the morning she is still alive, for she is heard screaming.

Or, if there were not two attacks, then the single attack can only have been made at or before eleven o'clock—because soon after eleven Jess is heard moaning.

And the whole long, complicated business resolves itself at last into a single question: could Jessie have attacked Jess M'Pherson at somewhere round eleven o'clock on that Friday night?

Not after her return from trying to buy the mutchkin. She and Miss M'Intyre would have had about the same distance to walk, she along the lane to the gate of the No. 17 back garden, Miss M'Intyre parallel with her along Sandyford Place to the front of the house. Miss M'Intyre was hurrying, Jessie was 'skliffling along'.

Even had she been running, even had she been able to get through the garden gate and up to the house, and rush in and strike Jess down then and there—she still could not have raced Miss M'Intyre to the corner; and when Miss M'Intyre got to the corner, already there were people there discussing the moaning.

She could not, therefore, have made the attack after she came back.

Before she left, then?

The judge's contention was that Jessie waited till her victim was asleep before attacking. She arrived not earlier than twenty past ten, and it makes the time limit rather narrow—to allay suspicion by the customary greetings, to dispense the rum (with which to stupefy the victim), to make some excuse for remaining in the house itself, to induce Jess to go to bed (clad in a vest, a chemise and a dressing-gown, by the way!), and to allow time for her to fall into a drunken slumber—all within forty minutes. Moreover, if as the judge suggested, Jessie had arranged to sleep the night, and was therefore presumably sharing her friend's bed, it seems odd that her *outer* garments should have become blood-stained. Did she, taking a leaf from Mrs Campbell's book, go to bed fully dressed—boots and all? Or did she get up and dress before she attacked? There are cases, notably the *Wallace* case, where the assailant is supposed to have stripped before the crime so as to avoid incriminating blood-stains on his clothes. Here we have an allegedly cunning murderess doing just the reverse.

But of course this was admittedly only the judge's theory. She might have attacked Jess in much the same way as she says the old man attacked her (why she should afterwards have got her to bed and bathed the wounds is beside the point for the moment). In whatever circumstances—did she attack Jess before she left the house?

The old man is in a room at the top of the stairs, having by his own account gone to bed only an hour ago; and his room looks out over the back garden and the gate into the lane. She attacks Jess and fells her to the ground—hardly a noiseless proceeding, for, apart from anything else, Jess was a big woman and would fall heavily on the wooden floor. If our theory about Mr Stewart is correct, Jess screams loudly enough to be heard next door. In any event, she lies, gravely injured but still alive to tell the tale, in a lighted room, its windows looking out to a sufficiently populous street where, if she makes any sound, it will be easily audible. (To anyone inside the railings that divide that part of Sandyford Place from Sauchiehall Street the interior of much of the bedroom is plainly visible.)

Is it conceivable that Jessie should leave her there and hurry round the corner to a liquor shop; should go and return by way of the long, bare garden just under Mr Fleming's window, on a light summer's evening with a good many people still about?— we know that the Stewart household next door, for example, were only just going to bed. If she needed spirits to bolster her flagging energy—well, she had lived in the house, she would know of Mr John Fleming's decanters in the ground-floor parlour. But it is nonsense of course; no imaginable need could have been great enough or urgent enough to have driven her to quit the house— with her dreadful task only half finished and the old man in his room upstairs.

Jess M'Pherson was attacked before Jessie went out for the mutchkin—or while she was out for it—or after she came back. But it couldn't have been after Jessie came back; and if it had been earlier, she would never have gone. There is only one alternative. It was done while she was out, and her statement is true.

What it has taken all these pages to consider, Lord Deas digested in a flash. After the breathless hush in which the reading of the statement had been heard, a murmur of excitement broke out. It was immediately interrupted by the judge.

'Jessie M'Lachlan.' She stood there calm and still, hopefully expectant, looking up at him through her veil. 'According to the evidence led before us, the position in which you now stand is this . . .' And, coldly and clearly, he went through it once again. Respectable family—one time servant in the Fleming household— good husband, who freely gave her the use of his wages, thirty shillings a week (whittled down to eighteen, as we know, but the judge did not remark that). What she did with the money he could not imagine—she had only herself and her child to keep (and her husband for half the week, but that wasn't mentioned either. His lordship's salary, by the way, would be something over £3,500 a year. Jessie's money works out at under £50). She was not in good health, true, but had her habits and conduct been what they ought, she should not have had much difficulty in maintaining herself and the child on that account—especially as she often got presents of money from her brother. But whatever she did with it, at the time of the murder she was very much in want of more and was in debt to Jess M'Pherson, her most intimate friend, a friend always kind and affectionate towards her, who trusted her, whose last thought it would be that her life might be in danger at Jessie's hands. In that state of matters she went to the house on that Friday, and she would have no difficulty in producing some plausible excuse for sleeping with her friend all night. 'It is now stated upon your own confession that you did remain there all night. In the course of that night, probably when she was asleep, you did attack her with that cleaver we saw here, or some other deadly instrument, and did disable her; and though she apparently recovered to some extent from the first blow, you did repeat the blows till you made on her body all the numerous wounds spoken to by the medical witnesses, the result of which was her death. Whether you did that in bed or in the kitchen—whether partly in the one or partly in the other—whether, after you had disabled her in bed when she was asleep, she had so far recovered as to struggle into the kitchen and there you continued your bloody work and dragged her body back to that room after she was disabled in the kitchen—all these particulars we do not know. But we know this, if we go by the evidence that has been adduced, that upon that night you did most barbarously and most cruelly murder that unsuspecting woman, who believed you up to that hour to be the best friend she had in the world. . . .'

She had had the privilege of as attentive and intelligent a jury as his lordship had ever seen in the box, her case had been investigated with all possible care and presented by the ablest imaginable counsel, and at the end of it all she had been found guilty by a unanimous verdict 'with which I entirely concur'. She had chosen to put in a defence to the effect that a gentleman whose character up to this time had been *quite unstained* was the murderer, and now had repeated that statement with all the details to which they had just listened——

For the second time in all those long, long days, Jessie spoke. 'Well, my lord——'

But she was hushed immediately, and immediately was silent.

'I sit here,' said Lord Deas, 'primarily to do my duty in the trial and conviction of those who are guilty.' But he sat there also to protect the innocent; and it was his imperative duty to say now that there was not upon his mind a shadow of suspicion that the old gentleman had anything whatever to do with the murder. If anything were wanting to show the danger to the lives and liberties of the people of Scotland, if the statements of prisoners were listened to who were capable of committing such crimes as Jessie had committed—of giving such statements the least credibility, then he thought the example they had just heard would be quite sufficient to satisfy them of that danger. He had been counsel on both sides in such cases, it had been his misfortune to sit upon trial in many such cases, and 'I am bound to say that I never knew an instance in which the statements made by prisoners after conviction were anything else than in their substance falsehoods. Your statement does not convey to my mind the slightest impression—it conveys to my mind the impression of a tissue of as wicked falsehoods as any to which I have ever listened.' Indeed, if anything were a-wanting to satisfy the public mind of Mr Fleming's innocence, the judge thought that this most incredible statement was just the thing to do it. Be that as it may, he must go upon the evidence and the verdict. . . . And so . . .

The prison wardress gave her a sharp tap on the back. She stood. Lord Death picked up the black triangle of cloth and held it above his head.

And so to the sentence.

'That you be removed from the bar to the prison of Glasgow, therein to be detained and fed upon bread and water only, until the eleventh day of October next, and upon that day, between the hours of eight and ten o'clock of the forenoon, to be taken from the said prison to the common place of execution in the burgh of Glasgow and there by the hands of the common executioner to be hanged upon the gibbet till you be dead; and ordains your body to be thereafter buried within the precincts of the said prison; and ordains your moveable goods and gear to be escheat and inbrought for Her Majesty's use.

'Which is pronounced for doom.'

He added, as the custom is: 'And may God Almighty have mercy on your soul.'

You could hardly hear her voice, but she whispered out into the terrible silence of the stunned court: 'Mercy! Aye, He'll hae mercy, for I'm innocent.'

CHAPTER TWENTY

The public outcry was loud and long and largely in favour of the condemned woman, only the *Glasgow Herald* wholeheartedly triumphing. Crowds milled round the newspaper offices, as the days and weeks went by it was reported that several people had become insane through brooding over the wrongs of Mrs M'Lachlan, and that doctors were treating cases of extreme nervous irritability from the same cause. The steps of the house in Sandyford Place were being whittled down by the chisels of the morbid collecting souvenirs. The first consideration to come under fire from the Flemingite faction was the authenticity of the now famous statement, and Jessie's agents were obliged to publish a long letter setting out the exact conditions under which it had been made—Mr Wilson got into a bit of a tangle about exactly what she had said to him in that first interview, which must have made him wish that he had written it down at the time as she had suggested. In every street little knots of people were to be seen in eager discussion, every lamp-post had someone under it, holding up the latest edition to the light, not able to wait till he got home to read it. Old Fleming and Jessie were saints or sinners according to the bias of the speaker, the judge and jury were deified or execrated in special articles, leaders and innumerable letters in the papers. 'Vindex', 'Sigma', 'One who Balances Probabilities' and dozens more seized up their pens; 'Candidus', 'Microscope', 'A Sympathising Sister', wrote off in reply. 'A Lady who Admires Disinterested Truth Wherever it is to be Found' sent a pound for Mrs M'Lachlan, small factories and businesses got up little subscriptions, a few pounds here, a few shillings there. 'A Poor Servant Girl' from a small hamlet in the remote country sent a shilling out of her wages of fifty shillings a year, 'for Jessy M'Lachlan, who has the sympathy of allmost the whole community here.' 'A Working Man' wrote that any poor person could be accused of murder; if you had a hundred and eighty pounds in the bank you had nothing to fear. 'An Inquirer' wondered if steps had been taken to ascertain whether Jess M'Pherson had been pregnant; there was a good letter asking why old Fleming, who had been famous for his curiosity and inquisitiveness, should suddenly have become exactly the reverse when the servant 'disappeared', and another very good one remarking upon the judge's assertion that he had never known the statement of a convicted prisoner to be true: what had this to do, the letter most pertinently asked, with the case of Jessie M'Lachlan?—the laws of chance hardly entered into the matter; if the judge had heard a hundred false statements it did not make the hundred and first any less or more likely to be false or true. A lady archly styling herself 'Mis-rule' was tremendously ironical. The judge was a stupid old man, of course, trial by jury antiquated and out of date, and the only way of ascertaining truth was to hoot at a man and call him names, etcetera, etcetera. 'Precaution' wrote 'A Hint about Servants'—let this case be a lesson to the gentry now that they had had a glimpse of what went on below-stairs. Not all servants, she conceded, were untrustworthy, but masters and mistresses should be untiring in checking over their property and locking doors and windows at night, especially those in the basements—no respectable servant could take exception: the more honest, the more they would welcome it. Did not this case show what perils might arise from the continued existence of 'previous servants whose own abodes formed receptacles for plunder'. Above all, no member of the household who remained alone in the house with a servant could be really safe. To this 'A Domestic Servant' replied with a touching and dignified, indeed a magnificent, letter. She quoted the reply of a mother to her child, who had asked the difference between itself and a servant, 'My dear, you know the difference between china and earthenware.' That was the way the domestic servant was looked upon: no more than a machine to do the drudgery. Even the poor prisoner in jail had rules whereby he might now and again see those he loved, but servants were forbidden to have their friends to visit them, must live in solitude except on their rare days off. A servant might be honest or dishonest, true: so might anyone. (She did not dwell on the disparity in temptation.) As to the danger to the gentry of remaining in the house alone with a servant, let her assure 'Precaution' that here the boot was indeed upon the other foot. 'Oblivio' wrote 'a word anent forgetfulness,' and a humble joiner contributed a very tem-

perate and delicate letter saying what in fact could well be true—
that no woman, or no woman of Jessie's temperament, would
have left poor dead Jess lying there stripped to the waist; her instinct would have been to pull down the clothes and cover her
nakedness.

The old gentleman, meanwhile, was reported to be cosily residing at Inellan, a favourite watering place but perhaps rather
comfortably deserted at this season—we are now in late September—reading the reports with the greatest interest and apparently
highly satisfied with his own part in it all. The Reverend Aikman
had called round and had another of his chats: perhaps he thought
the old gentleman might append his name to the growing roll of
those petitioning for a reconsideration of the verdict—that really
would have been something. If he did, however, he was disappointed. Mr Fleming only shook his head over 'the depravity of
the human heart', though rather in reference, apparently, to the
things Jessie had suggested against himself than as to the crime
of which she now stood convicted. (His organ, the *Herald*, had
drawn pointed attention to the recent case of one, Mary Tinney,
who had tried to lay the blame for a murder to which she later
confessed upon her own mother.) Informed of the probability of a
great number of signatures for the petition, he told Mr Aikman
that he wished and earnestly prayed that the Lord would gie Jessie
time that a' might be cleared up, or that she might be led to make
a confession to clear him.

The petition was, in fact, enormously subscribed to. It had been
resolved upon at a crowded meeting held on the Friday after the
trial ended and a memorial was sent to the Home Secretary, Sir
George Grey, begging him to delay execution until further enquiry should be made. Jessie's agents also sent a memorial, setting
out legal grounds for a respite of sentence, and eventually a stay
of execution was granted until November 1—with a warning to
'the convict' that this was only for purposes of further investigation, and if that investigation did not bear out her statement there
was no hope for her. So Jessie was sure of an additional couple of
weeks at least before she was hanged in Jail Square.

Meanwhile a private enquiry had begun on the instructions of
the Lord Advocate for Scotland, presided over by Sir Archibald
Alison, Sheriff of Lanarkshire—Sir Archibald, a lawyer of wide
experience and the deepest integrity, was to prove one of Mrs

M'Lachlan's stoutest champions. 'I had become convinced,' he writes in his autobiography, 'of the woman's innocence.' But there was a general expression of opinion that an investigation by none but officials already connected with the case wouldn't satisfy the public mind, and an outsider was called in, Mr George Young, Sheriff of Haddington. His powers as Commissioner were rather limited; he couldn't compel anyone to attend nor did his witnesses testify under oath—but anyone who chose to might volunteer and he did examine a large amount of evidence from sixty-nine witnesses (there were seventy-six at the trial), his reports being forwarded to the Home Secretary. The proceedings were held behind closed doors, no one else being present but the ubiquitous Jno. Gemmel, Procurator-Fiscal, and Mrs M'Lachlan's solicitor, Mr Dixon. The organisation of the whole thing was in the hands of Jno. Gemmel—a somewhat Gilbertian state of affairs, Mr Roughead suggests, since the official instigator of the recent prosecution seemed hardly the ideal person to be now enquiring into his own conduct.

The evidence elicited under these circumstances has been embodied elsewhere in different parts of this book. As has been said before, it did nothing to discredit the condemned woman's story; in many instances it bore it out to a remarkable degree, and it threw up one fact of quite startling significance—the testimony of Miss M'Intyre that at soon after eleven that night Jess M'Pherson was heard moaning. (No one then or since seems to have given much consideration to this point or to have taken the time factor into consideration; yet there it sits, solid fact and, to the author at least, conclusive. Either Jess was attacked and left, still alive and noisily moaning, while her assailant popped round the corner for a drop of something, or she was attacked while Jessie was innocently out. You pays your money and you takes your choice.)

But, alas!—having taken it you are thrown straightway back into confusion.

With so much agitation going on, the enquiry under Mr Young not yet started and the postponed execution date less than three weeks away, Mr Dixon got permission to interview his client in the condemned cell. There were persistent rumours that old Mr Fleming had been seen—by the mysterious gentleman who did or did not tell Mr Ritchie, who in turn did or did not tell Mr Sheridan Knowles—at the front door of No. 17 in the early hours of the morning of the murder. Mr Dixon wished to confirm with Jessie that this might have been possible; it would naturally go a long way in support of her story.

He found her, he subsequently related, in a highly overwrought condition, inclined to hysteria, divided between easy laughter and easy tears. She seemed to want to talk about anything but her statement. However, that was what he was there for. He pressed her to answer: did she think the rumour could be true?

To this Jessie replied that she was quite sure it wasn't true; and what was more, she added, they needn't trouble themselves hunting round to confirm it, because it couldn't be true.

Mr Dixon was naturally somewhat taken aback. Had she any reason for saying that it couldn't be true?

She evaded the question, she went off again into irrelevances—she didn't think much of the portraits in the pamphlet account of the trial. (They are certainly very unflattering.) He brought her back to the subject, however, and persisted. 'Well, then, where was the old man at this time?'

She didn't say anything for a moment; and then she looked into his face and said: 'I may just as weel tell ye—the auld man wasna' there at a'.'

'Wasn't *there*?' said Mr Dixon. 'What do you mean?'

What she meant, said Jessie, was that she hadn't seen Mr Fleming at all that night.

Poor Mr Dixon! 'Do you mean to tell me that he wasn't there, that he wasn't sitting in the armchair when you went down to the kitchen——?'

'I didna' go "down" to the kitchen at a',' said Jessie. 'I didna' go by the front door.'

'Not by the front door? Then how did you go in?'

'I went by the back way.' And, she added, she hadn't been upstairs at all that night.

But . . . 'Do you meant to say it wasn't the old man who sent you out for the whisky?'

'I was not out for whisky at a'.'

'But you were seen. Miss Dykes and Mrs Walker saw you. What were you doing out?'

'I hadna' been in,' said Jessie. 'I was just arriving.'

'You left Mrs Fraser at the Gushet house at ten past ten. What were you doing after that?'

She wasn't doing anything, said Jessie. She'd gone straight to Sandyford Place.

'But it's only a ten minutes walk from the Gushet House. It was after eleven when Mrs Walker saw you.'

'I went straight there,' insisted Jessie.

That was just nonsense. Doubtful, incredulous, he began to test her. One thing at least he knew for certain—impossible to doubt the evidence of the milk-boy, Donald M'Quarrie, and George Paton, his master. 'Mrs M'Lachlan—who opened the door to the milk-boy?'

'I opened it to him myself,' said Jessie.

'You opened it yourself? Then where was Mr Fleming?'

'I didna' see Mr Fleming at a'. He'd be awa' in his bed.'

'But then . . . do you tell me that it was you who committed this murder?'

'I dinna ken,' said Jessie. 'I ken naething about the murder.'

'But if the old man didn't do it—then it must have been you?'

So she told him her story—positively the last story of Jessie M'Lachlan as to the events of that terrible night. She and Jess had been drinking. There was a good deal of drink going, and finally Jess became drunk and lay vomiting on the kitchen floor. So she, Jessie, herself somewhat the worse for wear, cleaned Jess up a bit and washed over the floor, and brought some bedclothes through and covered Jess with them as she lay on the floor by the fire. But Jess was only sick again and she had to wash the blankets too. By the time Jess recovered, what with nausea at her unlovely tasks and the drink she had taken, she herself was retching. So Jess, who was a great one for laudanum whenever she had anything wrong, made her take a large dose. The effect of laudanum was always 'to take her in her head and make her delirious'—her husband and her sister would confirm that. Once when the doctor had given her a sleeping draught, instead of composing her, it made her start out of bed and go rushing round the room, and they had to hold her down. The laudanum that night had had the same effect, and from the time she took it she had no recollection of anything, of any quarrel, of any struggle—only a confused memory of Jess crying out, 'Jessie, Jessie, what are you doing?' And then she was creeping about on her hands and knees in the

253

dark, but where she was or what she was doing she didn't know. And then nothing. She awoke in the morning and found Jess dead.

'And you never saw the old man at all?'

Not at all. She repeated it over and over again. She hadn't seen the old man at all that night.

'And it was you who opened the door to the milk-boy?'

'Yes.'

'And if the milk-boy says, and his master says, and they both swear that it was Mr Fleming who opened the door——?'

'I know they say that,' said Jessie. 'But I opened the door.'

And then?

And then she supposed she just hung about the house, too sick and dazed with the laudanum and drink to have the sense to escape. It was almost nine when she finally pulled herself together and went. She went by the back door.

He did not know what to do. All Scotland and all England were in an uproar over this woman's conviction, execution had been postponed, an official enquiry was pending. He said at last: 'Well, I don't know what to make of it all. But one thing I do know. It puts me in an awkward position, Mrs M'Lachlan. I'm not sure that I can go on acting for you.'

'Not act for me?'

'How can I—after what you've told me?'

'But you don't really believe it?' said Jessie. 'Of course, there's not a word of truth in it—the whole thing's just nonsense.'

'Then why did you say it?'

'I just wanted to see how you'd look,' said Jessie. Mr Dixon's narrative doesn't tell us whether when she said it she was laughing or crying.

But that was a bit too easy. She told him something and, when he threatened to desert her, then she contradicted it. 'I shall have to think it over,' he said.

'But you won't tell anyone?' she begged him anxiously. Of course it was all nonsense, all lies—the statement she had given him to read out in court was the truth.

'I am your lawyer,' he said. 'I'm bound to secrecy. Of course I shan't tell anyone.' And for her part, as long as her fate was in suspense, she had better be very careful herself and not go repeating to anyone, not to her visitors or to anyone else, what she had just said to him. She had better not enter into the subject at all. . . .

She went on entreating him—don't tell anyone, not anyone, not even Mr Wilson or Mr Strachan. . . .

Mr Dixon did not tell his associates, but he did feel the need to consult somebody, and he finally took into his confidence two non-legal friends—it seems a very odd choice—and asked their advice as to the propriety of his continuing to act for Mrs M'Lachlan; and made up his mind at last that he couldn't at this stage desert her—he was known to have had a private interview with her and it would look too pointed.

Only, as it happened, on the way home from the prison, full of thoughts upon this extraordinary interview, Mr Dixon ran into two detectives whom he knew to speak to, Audley Thomson and William Smith, popularly known as 'Black Will'. They all three stopped and had a cosy little chat.

The Home Secretary didn't take his choice either way—he sat on the fence in the middle. Mr Waddington, Chief Under Secretary in the Criminal Department of the Home Office, received a long memorial from Sir Archibald Alison, who had originated the initial enquiry after the trial, and who as Sheriff of Lanarkshire had been concerned with the case throughout. Sir Archibald's submissions, Mr Waddington reported, were unanswerable. (As we know, Sir Archibald was now himself convinced of the prisoner's innocence.) 'The prisoner was an accidental and constrained witness of the murder but not an actor in it. She can never be hanged.' (It was being said in Edinburgh that 'it would take a regiment of soldiers to hang Mrs M'Lachlan') But, 'having concealed and adopted it' advised Mr Waddington, she would have to be punished.

Lord Grey accordingly wrote off to the Lord Provost of Glasgow. The Lord Provost had requested the Post Office to forward immediately any official letter addressed to himself and, all honour to him, the moment he received the letter, though it was after eleven at night, he hurried round to the jail. There was a glorious mix-up when he hammered at the locked gates—dogs barked, voices demanded to know who he was, and only when that information finally filtered through were the doors hastily thrown open to the great man. Everyone was in bed, but the Governor hastily got up again, and as the clock struck the midnight hour he was conducted down the endless corridors, through the innumerable locked doors, to the condemned cell. He had arranged for a message to be sent off at once to James M'Lachlan. He enquired of the prison wardresses how the prisoner had been. She had been very much distressed after the trial, but now she seemed more composed again. He went into the cell and there read the letter to her. It was November 6—five months since the murder, five weeks since the trial had ended; five days before Jessie was due to die. She said: 'Will there be naething done on Saturday, then?'

Not on Saturday or ever. That was all over. She was 'respited until further significance of Her Majesty's pleasure.'

Her Majesty's pleasure was made known to her nine days later. A conditional pardon—the condition being that she be kept in penal servitude for the term of her natural life. Such was the Home Secretary's conception of a suitable punishment for an accidental witness to a crime who had subsequently, having taken an oath on the Bible and being threatened with her life, kept silence. Penal servitude for life.

How sad, how bitter, how hopeless, is the cry that comes down to us from that interview over the long, slow lapse of a hundred years! 'And I'm tae be kept in jail a' my days?'

For so it was to be.

No one, of course, was made happy by this decision, Mr James Fleming least of all. The old gentleman had had a rough time of it lately. He had been hooted and hissed as he left the court after giving his evidence, pelted with mud and stones, and might even have been set upon had he not been hustled away in a cab; and for a long time no elderly gentleman was safe in the streets of Glasgow if he had a bald head and a stoop. Mr Fleming himself had sought sanctuary at his son's summer house on the coast, all to no avail, for his fame had long gone before him and there were hostile demonstrations even in quiet little Dunoon. On one occasion, it was reported in the press, he was recognised when he went to the barber to be shaved and was actually stoned; and the poor barber had to throw all his tackle into the sea—no one wanted to share so much as a shaving brush with old Mr Fleming.

The reprieve was received with screams of rage by the Flemingite press. 'The unreasoning public have been taught that,

if they only cry loud enough, they can snatch a convicted murderess out of the hands of the High Court Justiciary and of the
British Executive.' And the judge had been denounced, cried the
Herald, as a hard-hearted, bloodthirsty wretch, an ogre thirsting
for blood, execrated 'as though by the enraged associates of convicted felons'; and the jury stigmatised as idiots and savages,
cursed in the streets and spat upon in omnibuses. So, poor old
jury, they seem to have paid dearly for those bouquets from the
bench—the most attentive and intelligent the judge had ever seen
in any box. (Mr Roughead points out that the very few signs of
any particular intelligence or attention manifested by them had in
fact been by no means appreciated by Lord Deas; i.e. when they
called attention to his dear Mr Fleming's little slip in stating his
age as seventy-eight, when they asked to see the plans, and when,
on one occasion, a misguided member preferred the accuracy of
Mr Rutherfurd Clark's notes to the Judge's. His lordship's reaction to this last had been such as to cause the offending juror to
'sit back with a very red face.') Perhaps now they wished that after
all they had taken a little longer than fifteen minutes to consider
the evidence and argument of four very long days, with a woman's
life and an old man's reputation at stake. Their method of arriving
at their conclusion was proudly described by the *Herald*. Upon
arrival in their room, their foreman had retired to a corner and
invited the rest to file up and whisper their conclusions to him, one
by one. When the last murmur died away he had only to announce
that their verdict was so far unanimous, add his own, and lead
them all trooping back into court without wasting any more time
on futile discussion.

And now, with the prisoner reprieved, it would be worse than
ever for 'the maligned old man'. His lawyers wrote off to the Home
Secretary—would he, in view of his decision, state that it was not
intended to imply that in his judgement Mr Fleming was otherwise
than innocent of the murder. The Home Secretary, unfortunately,
didn't feel able to do this. He 'must decline to express any opinion
on the point'. The lawyers wrote again. It really wasn't fair. It had
been said that Mrs M'Lachlan's sentence would not be commuted unless the enquiry following the trial substantiated the
truth of her statement: the public were drawing the inference that
it had done so. And Mr Fleming hadn't been represented at that
enquiry. The reply to this was that the enquiry was in respect of

the prisoner and not of Mr Fleming, and that, though no witness could be compelled to come, anyone who wished to *could* have. If Mr Fleming's advisers had wanted to send witnesses, why hadn't they done so? As to their request for a further enquiry still, in the interest of Mr Fleming—you couldn't institute an enquiry upon someone who was not charged with any offence, and Mr Fleming not only wasn't charged with any offence in this matter but, having been a witness at the trial, couldn't be. There is a general air about the letter of 'so now pipe down'. Mr Fleming's lawyers did not quite pipe down, but wrote once more to complain that the enquiry had 'brought suspicion upon the hitherto unblemished character of Mr Fleming, in a manner most injurious to himself and his family', and renewing their demand for publication of the evidence taken at the enquiry—which as he knew had been held *in camera*—and the appointment of a Royal Commission to look into it all. The Home Secretary wrote back and told them to read his letter again, and that for the moment was the end of that.

On November 10, Mrs M'Lachlan had been removed to Perth Penitentiary to begin her commuted life sentence. She had so far been considerately treated in prison. On account of her health some rules were relaxed; she was not for long confined to the bread-and-water diet of the convicted felon—they had to keep her strength up, of course, for the execution. At the close of her trial, the prison authorities reported, her extraordinary fortitude had given way; she had to be kept in bed, and lay there 'all courage lost'. (She told her sister that during the trial she couldn't weep in court, but that in the quiet of her cell she cried all night.) A 'dull, moping state succeeded her resolute bearing', and seems to have lasted throughout the long weeks while the petition for her reprieve was under consideration. She was bombarded with tracts, pamphlets and letters from the public which, after scrutiny, were shown to her; and much bothered by the solicitations of clergymen offering ghostly counsel, and of 'charitably-minded ladies' wishing to express their sympathy in person—we may with like charity believe them innocent of sensation seeking at the expense of their miserable sister. However, she refused them all and suffered only the attentions of the Reverend Mr Doran—a gentleman who was later reported to have believed throughout in her guilt and depravity. Her close relatives were allowed to visit her

to take their harrowing farewells. She had persuaded James
M'Lachlan to let her own family have the care of the little boy—
perhaps James had already decided to emigrate (leaving Jessie all
alone, engulfed in Perth Prison) and he could hardly be burdened
with a three-year-old child. James brought the boy once to see her,
and then her sister, who was taking him back to their brother in
Inverness, brought him for the last heart-breaking good-byes; the
poor mother was terribly overcome. Her father came also and saw
her. To them all she reiterated her innocence. They told her that
the people all believed her statement, and she said, 'Well they may,
for it's true.'

No one says what became of her poor little dog.

A description headed 'Female Life in Prison', by a woman
officer, appeared at about this time in the London *Times*. It shows
something of the type of woman Jessie was now to be thrown
amongst—she who, whether we believe her innocent or guilty,
was not in the ordinary sense a 'criminal', certainly was far removed by her background and temperament from such a company. The female convict, says the writer, is more depraved than
the male, a class desperately wicked, deceitful, crafty, lewd and
malicious. Punishment may bring them to death's door but im-
proves them not at all. They are satanically proud of their crimes
—mostly theft with violence—and vain and mischievous beyond
belief. The most terrible punishment of all to them is the fact that
on admission to prison their hair is cut off: brutally insensible to
other privations, yet faced with this invariable rule they without
exception struggle against it—weep, pray, fight, implore on their
knees, are overcome by shivering fits. A prisoner re-admitted will
often plead that in the meantime she has married, and 'it's my
husband's hair now, you can't cut it off.' One prisoner in the
writer's experience became 'delirious', broke away from her cap-
tors and ran screaming down the deserted corridors. 'The cry of
"Dinna cut my hair!" still rings in my ears.'

They were fantastically destructive. Bed-linen was so in-
evitably torn apart that eventually it was decided to use string for
the sewing; but it was still destroyed. The most common punishment was that prisoners should 'go to the Dark'—bare, unlit cells
where they remained for long periods in solitary confinement.
They would be dragged off, undaunted, and revenge themselves

by ceaselessly stamping, thumping and screaming so as to disturb the warders. 'The cry wells up from the ceiling like the defiant song of the caged tigress.'

Among these caged tigresses, Jessie M'Lachlan was to spend 'a' my days.'

She was taken to Perth by train, her head and face muffled in a shawl, but despite all precautions the truth had leaked out and there was a little rush of people to see her hustled into the railway carriage. It was to be fifteen years before she saw Glasgow again.

But still the controversy continued to rage. If she was guilty—why wasn't she hanged? If she was innocent, why was she sent to penal servitude for life? The Home Secretary's decision that, though she was now believed to have been an accidental witness after the crime and to have kept silence under coercion, she must nevertheless be severely punished, satisfied no one. On Friday, June 26, when she had been already seven months in prison, Mr Stirling of Kier, member for Perthshire, raised a question in the House of Commons. As a result the evidence given in secret at the enquiries following her trial was made public. In the debate following this move, Mr Stirling spoke at length on the injustice to Mr Fleming of the course pursued by the Government; Mr Dunlop, the member for Greenock, claimed that there had been a miscarriage of justice and Mr Fleming should have been in the dock. There was argument as to the law in Scotland by which a person could or could not be put on his trial who had given evidence in a case in which he was supposed to have been an accomplice, as old Fleming had done.

The Lord Advocate summed up. The Secretary of State had not said that the prisoner was innocent or that Fleming was guilty; he simply said that in the doubt and mystery which attended this case it was 'better not to break into the house of life' but to commute the sentence to the next highest punishment and leave it to time to unravel a mystery which all his care and patience had not enabled him to unveil.

Meanwhile Convict No. 389/21 ate out her heart in jail.

And meanwhile, also, a Dr Buchanan decided that the time had come when he was entitled at last to contribute *his* mite to the letters in the papers. While the woman's fate was in the balance, he wrote, he had held his peace, but he really couldn't allow this suggestion of overwhelming medical charges to go unrefuted. It showed him in a dreadful light which was entirely unwarranted. He had attended Mrs M'Lachlan as—so her husband himself had informed him—her sole medical adviser. At the time of her confinement he had sent in a total bill of £1 12*s*, and this was all his medical attention had ever cost her. As to her heart, she had never complained to him about it, there had never been mention of palpitations or of any other cardiac sympton; to his personal and certain knowledge she had been in bed after her baby was born for three weeks, and not four months as was stated in court. He quite certainly had 'never said that if she did not take care of herself she might drop dead.'

Oh dear!

Mr Stirling was not the only person concerned with possible injustice to Mr Fleming. Mr Dixon, the great Champion, brooded over that last interview with his client—'I may as weel tell ye that the auld man wasna there at a'.' Really, how dreadful if that had after all been true! After all, the reprieve had now been granted, she was serving a life sentence, nothing worse could befall her, she had nothing to lose. . . . Of course, he had promised that he would never tell anyone; of course she had said it to him under the seal of professional secrecy. . . . But all the same. . . .

Mr Dixon sat down and wrote a note to Mr Fleming's solicitors. He must have been far more impressed by the incident than, at this distance, it is possible for us to be. He had recognised at the time that she was hysterical, alternately laughing and crying; she had now been three months in custody following the appalling shock that the murder—however and by whomsoever committed —must have been to her. She had endured the four very long, bewildering, frightening days of the trial, her evident confidence falling lower and lower each day; had since then existed—this woman alleged to be extremely delicate, with a faulty heart condition—in a condemned cell, on a diet, for some time at least, of bread and water, waiting to die. The threat of public execution still hung over her, not three weeks away; she had been expressly warned that if the enquiry being conducted under Mr Young didn't bear out her statement, she would be hanged. Under these circumstances Mr Dixon comes and begins to question her all over again. She tries to get out of it, she refuses to answer, she giggles, she weeps, she talks of other things; and when he persists she bursts out into what surely is an hysterical farrago of nonsense, divided between laughter and tears.

For the story was like her first three stories—and in complete contrast with the famous fourth statement read after the verdict—in many places at least, palpably false. She couldn't have taken an hour to walk from the Gushet house straight to Sandyford Place (she insists she walked straight there, and if she didn't then what was she doing?). She says she went in by the garden entrance but she would have no key and there was no means of attracting attention—the gate in the wall is a considerable distance from the house; when she went for the whisky she took a key with her. Nor would she have been coming *down* Elderslie Street to get to the gate—as she was when Mrs Walker and Miss Dykes saw her. She would come that way from the spirits shop, because it was at the top of North Street, she would turn left into Sauchiehall Street and left again into Elderslie Street and so make a round, or square, walk of it—but not if she were simply coming up by way of North Street to the back gate of Sandyford Place. She gives no account of the stealing of the clothes and silver—and how can she have come by the silver if she 'never went upstairs at a' '? (Mr Dixon confided elsewhere as will be seen that 'the silver was too bulky for her to carry', that was why she took as little as she did; but this is not mentioned in the account of the interview which he himself carefully edited. He further suggested that she had hidden in the cupboard in the basement lobby when the old man came down in the morning and remained concealed from him there; but this again is not in his account of their interview.)

And she says she washed the kitchen floor—(she does not account for the washing of the bedroom floor)—'not because of bloodstains at all' but because Jess had been sick there; but there was no sign of vomit and the floors had been cleansed *after* blood had been shed there. There was no sign of vomit on the bedclothes, nor does she account for the naked footprints or a hundred other details all covered by the statement read in court. Of course a great deal is blanketed by her claim to have known nothing of what she was doing for most of the night; but Mr Dixon had checked with James M'Lachlan and her sister and both denied that laudanum had any untoward effect on her whatever, or that there had ever been an incident when they had to restrain her from rushing about the room. Finally, of course, she in no way accounts for the old man's astonishing complacency in the matter of his missing favourite or for the fact that the floors had been washed long after she can have washed them; or, above all, for the fact that while she says she opened the door to the milk-boy, he and his master and—eventually—old Mr Fleming himself, all swear that *he* did. Yet as Mr Roughead says, among all the doubtful and elusive elements of the case, this one fact at least was established beyond dispute.

False self-accusation is of course no uncommon phenomenon, especially under conditions of stress such as Mrs M'Lachlan had endured for so long a time. Mr Roughead suggests that she was a liar of the neurasthenic type 'and it may be doubtful whether at any time she told the whole truth'. Why he should say this of the statement read in court—unless of course we regard it as altogether untrue—it is rather hard to see; indeed it seems to contradict his later opinion quoted on page 231. For if the statement was substantially true, where lay any necessity for lies? Of course if she was a psychopathic liar, no reason would be necessary: we all know of otherwise normal people who just simply and literally prefer to tell untruths. But even so, where in the statement are detectable lies? Everywhere that proof was possible, the proof bore out its truth. In one particular only does there seem solid room for doubt, and that rather in an omission than an actual lie—an omission based on no neurasthenic vagaries but on sound common sense. Before ever Jessie pawned the silver on the Saturday following the murder, she paid off four pounds of her rent, she gave Mrs Rainny a 'paper note', she bought the box and perhaps, a bonnet. Yet she is known to have been quite penniless herself the evening before; and James M'Lachlan gave evidence at the enquiry that he had no money put by.

She made no attempt at any rational explanation of where the money came from. Two alternatives are possible. Jess M'Pherson had been paid her half-yearly wages, £7, shortly before her death. She was to have bought 'a filled plaid' with part of the money, but it rained and she didn't go out to the shops. Some money was found in her room, but we don't know how much; and it was positively suggested by the prosecution at the trial that Jessie took money as well as the dresses and silver. The suggestion was improperly brought forward since no evidence had been offered upon this point—yet it remains a possibility. On the other hand, it does seem likely that if in her extremity she had brought herself to take any money, she would have taken it all. The more likely alternative—suppose any of it to be true—is that Mr Fleming gave her something in advance on condition of her keeping her mouth shut. He had promised she should never want. She says he first suggested her pawning the silver and then changed his mind. May he not then have turned out his pockets and given her all he could raise 'to be going on with' including the twenty-seven shillings which she admits he gave her towards the cost of the tin box and her proposed junketings with it? It can't have been more than four or five pounds, for, despite his advice, she is still found on the Saturday morning resorting to the very dangerous expedient of pawning the silver. It is noteworthy that though he went into the office on the Saturday morning he didn't pay in his takings till first thing on Monday. It does seem quite possible that he scraped around and added this sum—two pounds odd—to what he had on him, and handed it all over to Jessie; raising the money somewhere in the meantime, to be paid in on the Monday. If either conjecture be true—if she stole her dead friend's money, or received money further than the twenty-seven shillings 'expenses' on condition of her silence—then it would need no quirks of the psyche to suggest she keep quiet about it.

However, Mr Dixon took the statement sufficiently seriously to inform the Fleming faction—now about nine months later—of its existence. Then, at last, the counsel of legal advisers was resorted to. He and Mr Fleming's lawyers together put the matter before certain members of the Law Faculty and it was finally ruled by the Dean, unanimously supported by his colleagues, that without his client's consent, Mr Dixon could not make the 'confession' public. Mr Dixon, who seems all of a sudden to have become very tender of old Mr Fleming's reputation, hurried round to the prison to press Jessie to give him her sanction.

The Governor, the prison doctor and the matron were present at the interview. She was led to the Governor's office and once more—and for the last time—faced her one-time friend and champion.

He began by explaining to her that nothing she could now say could have any effect upon her sentence. And nothing in the case could ever again put her in danger of execution.

She said, no: she quite understood that.

All right. Now, did she recall a conversation she had had with him long ago—almost a year ago—about having taken some laudanum?

She had never said a word to him about laudanum in her life, said Jessie.

Well, about her having had laudanum administered to her?

She had never mentioned laudanum to him in her life.

But when he had seen her—that last time, after the trial——

She had seen him once only after the trial and that for a very short time. She had never mentioned laudanum to him in her life. And she was as innocent of the murder of Jess as *he* was, Mr Dixon himself.

'In that case—Mr Fleming is guilty?'

'He did the act,' said Jessie.

'So you now say. But, you know, his friends believe him innocent.'

'How can his friends know anything about it?' said Jessie. 'They weren't there.' And she—who now had no friends, for even Mr Dixon had apparently deserted her—burst out that it was a terrible thing that she should be kept here, while her delicate child——

'Your child is all right, he's with your relations, he'll be taken good care of. But the Flemings are ruined, every one of them; they're going to have to leave the country.'

It was hard on those who were innocent, no doubt; but she would not move an inch from her resolution. She also was innocent—the old man was guilty.

'This case has actually twice been debated in Parliament.'

It meant nothing to Jessie. She was innocent; the old man was guilty. She absolutely refused to have the confession made public. She absolutely denied ever having made it.

Mr Dixon gave up and went away.

All this while, the *Glasgow Herald* had never given up its championship of old James Fleming; and for some time had been throwing out hints that they had knowledge of a confession by Mrs M'Lachlan. In the third week of June, nearly a year after the murder, they wrote to Mr Dixon and told him of a statement made to them by the two detectives, Audley Thomson and

William Smith. These two men had been concerned with the original investigation; it was they who had tried the keys of Jessie's front door, had discovered the bottle smelling of rum and had received from Mrs Adams the sleeve of the brown coburg dress and the blood-stained wires of the crinoline; it was to Thomson that James M'Lachlan had sent the black japanned box. They announced that a few days after the temporary respite of the execution—which would, indeed, coincide with the date of Mr Dixon's fantastic interview with Jessie—he met them in West Street; and told them that Mrs M'Lachlan had confessed to him that she had 'done the deed herself, without the aid or knowledge of Mr Fleming.'

Immediately upon publication of this letter, Mr Dixon replied. The story was absolutely false, he had never stated to the detectives that the prisoner had made such a confession as they specified, or in fact that she had made any confession of guilt whatsoever. 'In their whole concoction' there was only one item that was true—namely that Jessie had said to him that when she left the house there was a man mixing lime in the lane and she was afraid of his seeing her. Otherwise the whole thing was untrue.

But the fuse was lit and now, more than a year after that 'deed of darkness', the last firework of poor Jessie's story soared up into the night of the long mystery and blazed for a little moment—and fizzled out. On July 6, the *Mail* published a statement by Audley Thomson and 'Black Will' of exactly what Mr Dixon was alleged to have said to them. Running into them in West Street he had said, 'Well, you see we've beaten you and got her off'—this referred, of course, to the reprieve. They had replied, 'Yes, but you yourself know that she shouldn't have got off—no one had anything to do with it but herself, and Mr Fleming is innocent.' Mr Dixon said, 'That's my own opinion—that the old man is innocent, for she's a damnable woman, she was ranging up and down that house all night for what answered her. When he came downstairs she hid in the cupboard in the basement lobby. It was she who answered the door to the milk-boy, and then she went off by the garden way; she left the back door open, and threw away the key.' They asked him why she hadn't taken more valuable plate and he said it was too bulky to carry. The only thing she had been afraid of was that a man mixing lime in the lane might have seen her leave; he, Mr Dixon had sought out this man, and he had indeed been there but he did not remember seeing her. The detectives had quite clearly understood Mr Dixon to have been quoting what Mrs M'Lachlan herself had told him. All this they most solemnly swore to and both appended their names.

The firework might be only a rather short-lived little squib, but it pretty severely burned Mr Dixon in the handling of it. Faced with this letter, he was obliged to retreat: who was going to believe that two well-known and established policemen had concocted a pure fabrication? In his extremity, he turned to the *Herald* which now held out welcoming arms to the former black sheep. On July 8, they published a new letter from him. In justice to the detectives, he wrote, who were being branded as liars, he hastened to say that it was perfectly true that he had met them as stated and had talked with them. It was only that they had misunderstood him. What happened was that they asked him what he really thought of the case. He replied that in his private opinion Mr Fleming was innocent and added the other 'somewhat emphatic expressions' of his opinion of the woman. He did mention the business of the man mixing lime, but the rest was all purely hypothetical, he was interested to see what these two clever detectives would make of his theories and put a suppositious case to them. As to his saying in the earlier letter that their statement was false, this was the version of Messrs Smith and Wright, Mr Fleming's solicitors; all he had meant was that it wasn't correct that what he had told the detectives was by Mrs M'Lachlan's confession. He extended his apologies to them.

And so anxious was Mr Dixon that Jessie's last statement to him should not be incorrectly reported that he now issued it as edited by himself. There is nothing of her having hidden in the cupboard in the basement (we cannot but recall that there were bloody marks on the inside of the door which looked to one doctor as though they were the marks of hands, though he later said they might have been made by a bloody cloth, or of her having left the back door open—in fact the old man had given evidence that in the morning he found it locked as usual). But there is also nothing of the man mixing lime—and this both Dixon and the detectives say he did in fact mention. So the whole thing is very odd, to say the least of it; but then so was the whole of Mr Dixon's behaviour. Jessie seems to have been possessed of some peculiar magic of infecting with strangeness everyone and everything that at this time came within her aura.

So now the whole story was out; how she had confessed that the old man had not been there at a' that night, how she and Jess had been drunk, how Jess had given her laudanum and she had woken from a coma to find Jess dead. . . . Mr Dixon, her own agent, publicly testified to it all.

But it was, as has been said, a dampish squib; the world was growing weary of Jessie M'Lachlan and her woes. The newspapers gave the statement little credit, their insight into feminine psychology being, perhaps, somewhat deeper than young Mr Dixon's. The confession was 'worthless'; a statement obtained from a woman in the last stages of mystery and hysteria, 'labouring under an uterine disease which frequently leads to temporary insanity' by 'an agent by some misery pressure turned informer'. Mr Dixon indeed, came under heavy fire. The English journals thought he might consider himself fortunate in finding himself on that side of the border where he was not answerable for breach of professional confidence and liable to be disbarred, the *Morning Journal* called it an unparalleled breach of honour, 'blackening a little more the already dark enough fame of his poor and miserable client'. Only the *Herald,* who once had rendered themselves liable to libel action in their execration of him, now rose up in defence of Mr Dixon's moral courage in bringing this new light upon the innocence of 'this venerable old man', and burst into ink in what was to be their last great leader on the subject of Mrs M'Lachlan. It is a splendid affair, more than two columns in length and heavy with journalistic irony. When 'this convicted murderer' declares her innocence, she is sane; but when in a rare burst of honesty she declares her guilt, why then she is mad, she doesn't know what she is saying. You could believe a liar, concluded the *Herald,* when and only when he admitted something that criminated himself; and they for their part were quite ready in this instance to believe 'the heroine of the cleaver'. And Mr Dixon, who while he fought for his client had been the worst of men, now that he had betrayed the confidence placed in him while he was still acting as her agent, and in conflict with the ruling of the Dean of the Law Faculty and the expressed opinion of literally every member thereof, found himself clutched to the Heraldic bosom. He became their trusted correspondent and indeed is suspected of having written the laudatory article himself.

And so it might all have ended; but the poor firework lying guttering in the mire, gave one more dying fizzle. Messrs Smith and Wright, indefatigable in their fight for the Fleming family's good name, nagged away at the prison authorities until they finally consented to the publication of the Governor's account of Mr Dixon's last and final meeting with Convict 389/21. What good it could be expected to do to the Fleming cause, it is difficult to see. It related only Jessie's total denial of any such confession as Mr Dixon had described, her total denial that she had ever so much as mentioned laudanum to him, her total repudiation of any suggestion that she should clear Mr Fleming in the eyes of the world by confessing to her own guilt; for she was innocent. And the prison Governor added a note of his own.

On the morning after this interview, said the Governor, the prisoner requested to see him. She asked him what Mr Dixon's object had been in seeking this interview with her.

The Governor knew that it had been to seek a word from her that would exculpate old Mr Fleming. He temporised, however. He said he hadn't quite been able to make that out himself.

'Well,' she said, 'I do now remember saying something about laudanum to him. But what I said was that I knew no more about the murder than if he'd placed a glass of laudanum on the table fore'anent me'—in other words, than if she had been drugged.

So the 'deed of darkness' remained dark and now will remain dark for ever. One ray of light there might have been but that was extinguished at its very first glimmer. A Miss Hislop, Scripture Reader in Jessie's prison, several times visited No. 389/21, consoling the convict as was her wont, with the reflection that she was a lost sinner in the sight of God. On one occasion, she reported, this apparently unaccountably failed to comfort Jessie; for she remarked that her case was a very sad one. Such presumption burst the bounds of Miss Hislop's pious tolerance. Since Jessie had brought up the matter of her crime, she said, she would state her own mind on the subject. 'I believe you to be the guilty person and to me you seem to have acted as a guilty person throughout. You have been guilty of a deed for which you ought to have been hanged, as God has never repealed His law that blood should answer for blood; but by a very mysterious providence your life has been spared. . . .' Miss Hislop reports that Jessie looked at her and said, 'Well, Miss Hislop, I am obliged to you for your honesty'; but Jessie, if she did say so, must surely have added *sotto voce*, 'if for nothing else'. She was silent for a while and then, says Miss Hislop, she burst out: 'I had as little thought of it an hour before I left my own house, as you have at this moment.'

Says Miss Hislop. Differently framed, the sentence could simply mean, 'How could I dream when I left home so unsuspectingly, that such a thing was going to happen?' As reported, it sounds very much like an admission and so of course Miss Hislop took it. 'I had never supposed it to be a premeditated crime; but one sin led to another till the deed was committed.'

Jessie might have retorted as she had about Mr Fleming's friends, 'How can *you* know—you weren't there?' But she was silent. We can see her sitting there at the scrubbed wooden table in her drear prison dress with her poor, weary head in her work-worn hands. She said at last: 'I feel sometimes as though I could go through these prison walls. I often think my mind will give way.' And she began again to talk about the crime. Mr Fleming had asked her to go out for some spirits. . . .

What might have come out then? But Miss Hislop, high-flown with spiritual pride, was set only upon getting back to her lecture. 'It's no use going over it all again, nothing you can say will alter my opinion.'

'But Mr Fleming was not a good man,' protested Jessie.

Miss Hislop would not hear. Nothing Jessie could say, she reiterated, would alter her opinion.

It was the last chance to have heard anything that might have altered ours.

The London *Daily Telegraph* was not at the mercy of Miss Hislop's interruptions and thundered reverberatingly. 'Even in a Scotch gaol we can scarce believe that Scripture-readers are allowed to act as private inquisitors, and to report their investigations to the authorities of the gaol . . . Really, this is too bad! Let gaolers, lawyers and policemen try, if they like, to extort some statements to her own detriment from the lips of the unhappy woman who has fallen to their tender mercies; but for heaven's sake, let us have no more Scripture-readers acting as amateur detectives. Our law does not admit of moral torture . . . Surely there are some other ways by which the partisans of Mr

Fleming may establish his innocence, if that be possible, than by torturing this poor creature into some garbled admission in his favour. Let them show, as they have never done before, what his character was—what his relations were with his family, his servants, and the murdered woman—and they will do more to clear his repute than by recording every doubtful expression twisted none knows how, from a woman half-crazed with misery.'

Let us hope that Miss Hislop read that; though, armoured in conscious virtue, it may be doubted that she would be vulnerable to such arrows from more merciful hearts. Mr Dixon, too, may have quailed a little—that shining champion whose banner now trailed in the journalistic mud. At any rate it does seem that from then on the prisoner was left in peace—such peace as, innocent or guilty, her sad heart could find behind those prison walls. 'And I'm tae be kept in jail a' my days?' So it was to be.

James M'Lachlan had emigrated after her reprieve, leaving the little boy with Jessie's brother in Inverness. Her sister, Ann M'Intosh[1], had gone with him. She had written at the end of November after Jessie's penal servitude began, to the *Morning Journal,* begging for financial help, a letter written from the Edinburgh Female Institution. She had put down £1 she said, towards her passage to New Zealand, but she now found she had bills to meet for lodgings and so forth, and she had no money, she was friendless, she couldn't get work (because of the notoriety of the trial?) and she couldn't raise money to fit herself out for her new life. The *Journal* made enquiries and evidently found it all genuine, for they sent her £3 for which she wrote back a charming letter of gratitude. But when the *Glasgow Herald* tried to raise a subscription, she would have none of it. 'I want no subscriptions gathered for me by you and I advise you for your own sake not to put my name in your *Herald* again.' Poor little threat!—but at least the *Herald* had to publish the letter (with a sneering comment which did not obliterate the snub.) In December she and James M'Lachlan sailed away. Another sister, Mrs Jack, meanwhile had gone out of her mind under the distress of Jessie's situation and the taunts of the neighbours and had been conveyed to a lunatic asylum—so the poor little boy found his family

[1] It was for a certificate for this sister that Jessie had intended visiting Mr. M'Gregor on the evening of July 4th.—which may well have suggested the further visit to Sandyford Place and so precipitated the whole terrible affair.

sadly whittled down. It is good to know that grown to man-hood he stood by his mother to the end.

In 1892 a dying woman created a small sensation by declaring with her last gasp that she had been guilty of the murder. Her niece reported what had happened and it proved that the woman had been an inmate of the Perth Penitentiary for 'three terms' with Jessie. Nothing came of it all; but the niece told enquirers that her aunt had told her that Jessie always maintained her innocence. She said that she had suffered but, 'You will maybe find out all about it when I'm gone' and that it would all come right at the Judgement Day.

But as the years went by there were fewer and fewer left who might have assisted in finding out all about it. Out of all those legal lights who had been concerned with her case, not one sur-vived her (in the light of Dr Buchanan's letter, it does make one think a bit!). Mr Strachan, three years later had absconded, been outlawed and struck off the Rolls. In 1879 Mr Wilson had died. In 1882, aged only forty-nine, Mr Dixon also had died—in the odour of sanctity, however, for it was said of him that no stronger or more incisive intellect existed in all Scotland and that his place among lawyers there was almost unique: so the mystery of his conduct in the matter of Jessie M'Lachlan remains a mystery. And in the fullness of time Sir Archibald Alison was gathered to his fathers, faithful to Jessie to the last; so that by the time she had served ten years of her sentence none remained of her champions but counsel for the defence. In the year of her release died both the prosecuting counsel—Mr Gifford and Lord Deas; and in the year of her own death, Rutherfurd Clark. Both he and Adam Gifford, distinguished lawyers, had in due course been raised to the Bench.

And old Fleming was gone and stood at last before that Bar where he had assured all and sundry he was so ready to appear. To the last he had attended the church at Anderston and now he lies buried there—a bleak, black graveyard, 200 years old, with rank grass growing up between the tumbled tombstones, the rotting houses surrounding it now coming down to be re-placed by new—those high, thin tenement houses, each with its narrow, dirty 'close' and the marks still of the old original out-side wooden stair. The gravestones are black with the blue-black weathering of Glasgow soot and fog, the names for the most part undecipherable. Soon, perhaps, even these will be removed, pushed aside so that gardens or a playground may flourish above those forgotten, ancient bones. Till then he lies undisturbed, guarding his secret still. To the end of his life he lived under the 'black shadow of her accusation'. Hoots and cat-calls followed him wherever he moved, he was jostled, mobbed, jeered at, threatened with death a hundred times. But he bore it all with outward equanimity, continued to linger, unescorted and apparently deliberately, drawing the hostile crowds about him as though he rather gloried in his notoriety. His family doubtless accepted it with less resignation. A great peace must have fallen all round when old Mr Fleming was at last laid to rest in that churchyard at Anderston.

And so the years fall, veil upon veil, hiding her away from our sight: the frail, broken, friendless creature, 'half crazed with misery', walking through the weary, endless days, withdrawn and silent, except in invariable declaration of her innocence when her innocence was challenged; associating not at all with the common felons of the prison, even in the chapel sitting apart from them, curtained off, by the mercy of her jailers, from their curiosity. A 'model prisoner', her conduct 'exemplary'. And in the autumn of 1877—suddenly the veils of fifteen years were lifted: and she was free.

Fifteen years in prison had earned her thirty pounds. With this she must creep forth into the bright light of a changed and alien world and begin life anew. She was forty-four.

She went straight to Greenock—a cousin living there offered her asylum. Some reports say that James was there with the boy—now eighteen years old. She had avoided Glasgow, and in little Greenock doubtless hoped for obscurity and peace, but the *Greenock Advertiser* soon hounded her out and the publication of a so-called interview for the last time roused the Glasgow press to fireworks. 'We can conceive of nothing more cruel than this transfixion of the unfortunate woman upon the spear of notoriety. A disgraceful attempt has been made to achieve popularity and profit, by harassing an unfortunate woman and hawking the result about for a ha'penny.' So Jessie was left alone. Some time later she emigrated to America—under what circumstances it is hard to discover. Some say that her husband and the boy were already there and she joined them, some that she went alone after James M'Lachlan's death—he died suddenly, two years after her release—and that the son followed her; it seems far more likely that he at least went with her. At any rate, in the new world she married again, and settled there for the rest of her days. In 1899 her son wrote from Port Huron, Michigan, to the cousin in Greenock: 'Dear Cousin, I am very sorry to let you know that my poor mother is dead. She died of pleurisy of the heart on New Year's morning, at 10.20 o'clock.'

What secrets did it hold?—that fickle, flickering heart of hers that, having surmounted so much stress and strain, so much of anguish, did finally let her down. Or was it empty of secrets, all the truth told? We shall never know now. The judge at her trial believed her guilty and carried with him fifteen jurymen in a city where opinion was on the whole on her side. Her own husband, reputedly devoted, failed to stand by her; and as soon as her sentence began emigrated to Australia. Had he really believed her wrongfully convicted, one would have thought that a sailor might have contented himself with long voyages, from which he could from time to time return and not leave her quite alone. Her ghostly counsellor, the Reverend Doran, is reported— though only reported—to have believed in her guilt; and it really is rather shattering to find her closest adviser throughout, declaring to the world his conviction that she was in fact 'a damnable woman who all that night was ranging the house for what answered her'. Moreover, true or false, there is something a little alarming in the cleverness of her last story to him, the one about the laudanum—obviously false in some parts, failing in others to cover the facts, it does all the same in its central 'plot' answer many questions if Jessie were really the murderer; and its details ('I was creeping about in the dark on my hands and knees, not knowing where I was or what I was doing') are as convincingly vivid as any in the famous statement; nor have the marks of blood in the lobby outside the kitchen been explained away—those marks high up inside the door as though someone with blood on his hands had been hiding there.

And finally, that letter from Dr Buchanan! We may doubt that James M'Lachlan spoke the truth when—possibly to spare the doctor's feelings—he told him that Jessie saw no other practitioner, but there is the undoubted fact that it was he who attended her on the birth of her child: and if at such a time no mention was made of the famous heart trouble . . . ? Ah, well— we shall never know now.

A bonny clear summer's night in Glasgow, just a hundred years ago—and a harmless, good-natured woman done violently to death.

Did the senile admirer strike her down for fear of what she might tell? Did the loving friend turn to ferocious murder for what she possessed?

Old Fleming—or Jessie M'Lachlan?

Heaven knows who.

INDEX